Town in the Empire:
Government, Politics, and Society
in Seventeenth-Century Popayán

Latin American Monographs, No. 45
Institute of Latin American Studies
The University of Texas at Austin

Town in the Empire
Government, Politics, and Society in Seventeenth-Century Popayán

Peter Marzahl

Institute of Latin American Studies
The University of Texas at Austin

International Standard Book Number 0-292-78028-1 (cloth)
0-292-78029-X (paper)
Library of Congress Catalog Card Number 77-620062

The Latin American Monographs Series is distributed
for the Institute of Latin American Studies by:
  University of Texas Press
  P. O. Box 7819
  Austin, Texas 78712

For Dietrich Gerhard

Contents

Maps

Tables

Preface

Popayán is a provincial town in southern Colombia, with some pretensions to importance because of its history. In this century Cali, its
neighbor to the north, has overtaken Popayán; it is today the undisputed center of southern Colombia. Given the town's relative insignificance, one might ask, Why study the colonial antecedents of such
a place? For a Popayanejo or a Colombian there is an easy answer: it
is a part of their own history that needs to be reconstructed patiently,
with attention to events, individuals, and places, and also to groups,
economic structures, and social movements. The elements of such a
history are being assembled today, for the writing of history is becoming
a professional enterprise in Colombia. But this history has an interest
independent of the perspectives of locality or nation. It is here, perhaps,
where this book can make its contribution.

When I started this work, I had in mind a detailed study of the functioning of one town council. My idea was to study the imperial machinery of government at the point where it most closely intersected
with the interests of Spanish settlers in America. Such a study, I
thought, might allow a realistic appraisal of how imperial government
operated; it also might show how towns as nuclei of Spanish settlement
functioned in a new environment. But the town council, by itself, has
turned out to be an unsuitable vehicle for dealing with these questions.
My earlier ideas as to how to proceed are still visible in this work, but
on the whole I have followed an eclectic approach, using evidence where
I could find it. At a later stage of my work the marvelous catalogue of
the Archivo Central del Cauca—a veritable calendar at times—has
helped me quite a bit, but it opens its riches only to the cognoscenti.
The method, then, has to take account of the sources, as is only natural.
It begins with the assumption that a town's life forms a coherent whole
that one can unravel like a piece of cloth if one begins in the right
place. The starting point one chooses is important since it will, to a
degree, determine a work's organization and also its argument, as is
inevitable. Another point of departure will open up a different per-

spective, not necessarily opposed, and perhaps complementary. The sources for the history of any particular town can be quite varied. Under favorable circumstances, they may allow the reasonable reconstruction of a town's politics, of its social and economic structure, and even of prevailing mentalities. I am only too aware that this book falls short of such a reconstruction, but I hope that it will constitute a contribution toward such a goal.

But what is the purpose of such a reconstruction? A regional study such as this should answer the question of how Spaniards managed to establish overseas settlements in a peninsular image without, in fact, remaining subservient to Spanish ways. Only in this fashion, by perceiving the relations between continuity and adaptation to circumstance, can we explain the particular cohesion of Spanish expansion in the New World, taking account of the immense space and the small number of settlers. The relation between continuity and adaptation varied over time and place. In this particular study I have chosen the seventeenth century because it represents a relatively unexplored hiatus between the period of conquest—characterized by a continuing identification with the peninsula, so we assume—and the later eighteenth century, when metropolitan pressures and American interests entered an assertive stage. Also, so I thought, a town at the margin of empire would offer better evidence for an investigation of this sort than a colonial center in New Spain or Peru. As we see from recent studies, the same social and political forces were at work everywhere in Spanish America. Only their configuration varied. Once we have studied enough cases, we may be able to establish a typology of settlement that is more than a collection of formal attributes. More important, perhaps, Spanish America can then be seen as a series of loosely articulated urban networks that bore some correspondence to the imperial framework but were not congruent with it.

This, then, is the particular purpose of this study: to establish the particular configuration of one region, at one point in time, in its essential elements. If it achieves this for seventeenth-century Popayán, in the context of the "kingdoms" of Quito and New Granada, it will have accomplished its goal.

Acknowledgments

In the course of this work I have incurred some debts. I want to acknowledge the help and support of the late John L. Phelan, who served as my supervisor at the University of Wisconsin; of my friend James Lang of Vanderbilt University, whose common sense improved much of what I have to say; of my former colleagues Charles F. Delzell and J. León Helguera, also of Vanderbilt University, who made suggestions. Also, this work depended on the cooperation of the directors and staff of the Archivo Central del Cauca (Popayán), the Archivo Nacional del Ecuador (Quito), the Colegio de San Gabriel in Quito, the Archivo Nacional de Colombia (Bogotá), and the Archivo General de Indias (Seville). A particular debt of gratitude is owed to the late don José María Arboleda Llorente, whose patient work over forty years in establishing the sources for the history of Popayán has made this work possible. In Quito, Padre José María Vargas, O.P., made the Vacas Galindo collection in the Dominican monastery available to me. Javier Piedrahita Echeverri, Pbro., sent me his study of the diocese of Antioquia. Financial support has come at various stages from the Center for Latin American Studies at Vanderbilt University under its director, William H. Nicholls. My debt to Dietrich Gerhard for help and inspiration is expressed in the dedication. My wife knows the burdens that the completion of this study has entailed.

Introduction

This book is about a colonial town in Spanish America. Towns were the fundamental units of Spanish settlement in America. During the Christian reconquest of the Iberian peninsula, the town corporations (concejos) had already played an analogous role. But there the crown had granted jurisdiction and other privileges not only to towns but also to lords of vassals, knightly orders, and ecclesiastical institutions. In the New World, by contrast, the towns remained the only jurisdictional units in their own right, although they were joined by a new set of institutions that represented royal authority. The viceroys embodied this royal authority directly, and the audiencias exercised royal jurisdiction. As innovations appropriate to imperial expansion, these two institutions have attracted attention. Their role in the functioning of the empire has been studied extensively. Vis-à-vis the bureaucratic authority represented by these institutions—in the sense of delegated functions—the Spanish settlers sustained their own claims to political authority in the town corporations (cabildos). How did the towns actually function in America? Did they serve the settlers or the interests of the crown? Did they represent a popular or even democratic element? Actually, these questions are put too narrowly. Towns were something more than jurisdictional or political entities. It is with this in mind that I propose to study one of them.

The towns of America have had many chroniclers but few historians. Our view of towns has remained either miscellaneous or schematic. An emphasis on recurring features is not false, but it neglects the dynamic role of towns in settlement, politics, and the transmission of culture. Towns were points of cultural clash or fusion, where traditions merged or were kept apart. They were also the place where the business of making a living joined larger considerations represented by crown and Church. And, ultimately, towns were centers of crystallization that created a loosely articulated framework of regions that in its ensemble made up the empire.[1]

Cities in America stood for a Mediterranean and Iberian tradition that had to take root in a new setting. From a European perspective, the constancy or mutation of tradition constitutes the most interesting aspect of European settlement in America. From an American perspective, two phenomena are of particular interest: the effect of the new environment on the newcomers, and the survival of the natives and of their ways. Towns were centers of political domination and cultural diffusion; the incidence and the speed of these processes varied from region to region.[2] The physiognomy of Spanish America does not result from a simple superimposition of European (and African) features upon a native substratum; another component is the pace of social and economic "development," punctuated by regression or stagnation. These differences in pace—rather than geographical determinants—are a main cause of regional differentiation in Spanish America.[3] Regions, therefore, have to be investigated in their own terms, as well as in relation to the empire as a whole.

The differentiation built into Spanish expansion was restrained by institutional factors and by social and economic forces. Some of these remain today: social hierarchy, cultural elitism, legal and religious formalism, export-import economies. They give Spanish America an appearance of peculiar homogeneity, the inheritance of an earlier condition when equality, popular sovereignty, and nation-building were unknown. To criticize colonial rule and imperial performance in these terms would be anachronistic. Yet the Spanish empire was not created in a fit of absentmindedness. The arrangements that bound metropolis and settlements together in durable fashion reflected a complex of ideas about the king's right to rule, the place of justice in the realm, the importance of the natives' conversion, and the fitness of material contributions. Here it is not my purpose to investigate these ideas in themselves. Rather I want to gauge their actual effects, by studying government in a limited and manageable setting.

Each empire has to solve the problem of making imperium effective at both the center and the periphery. The inevitable tension between these two poles of empire can be resolved in a variety of ways. The resolution of conflict can be incorporated into the formal structure of empire or it can be left to informal accommodation. If matters are sufficiently formalized, institutions may appear to be above the push and shove of politics. In the Spanish empire, a variety of procedures of an ostensibly judicial, fiscal, or administrative nature were in fact highly political in purpose. The most famous of these procedures was formalized noncompliance with imperial legislation and superior decrees.[4] Residencia and visita as formal judicial and administrative inquests also had a political function, as did composición, a fiscal device designed to legalize irregularities. If it is clear, then, that politics was present at all levels, how did it operate, who were the actors, whom did it serve?

The debate about politics in the Indies is an old one. Usually it is conducted in terms of how government operated and how it affected both the settlers of European descent and the natives. This debate has been colored by two assumptions that reinforced each other. One of these projected the ideas of early nationalism into the colonial past and judged "colonial" rule by them. In the context of another argument, the Spanish empire has been assimilated to the regimes of Europe in the Age of Absolutism. In this case the interpretation of Spanish rule has simply followed the canons established with regard to absolutism.[5] In practical terms, the two interpretations have yielded the same results, since they were derived from the same source: a rejection of the past that put obstacles in a free man's way, and the embrace of a future without the oppression of the past—in short, the creed of Liberalism. In recent years, these interpretations have lost some of their cohesion and simplicity.[6] What is thought of as liberal reform is now seen as beginning under absolutism; enlightenment was available to Creoles; paternalism may have been a good thing for the Indians. Despite these changes of view, the older assumptions still inform much current thinking.

Doubts about the older interpretations of government and politics in colonial Spanish America can be summarized under three headings. One point of view sees imperial government as absolute in intent but ineffective in execution. In general terms, this seems undeniable, although to carry the admission beyond a certain point would seem to deny the premise. A second opinion, in effect a refinement of the first one, argues that the bureaucracy of the empire tended to be absorbed by the Creole oligarchy and hence identified with Creole interests. According to this view, Creoles were recruited to all levels of administration and often held controlling positions in government. Also, many Spanish-born officials had ties of kinship and business arrangements with Creoles, despite regulations forbidding them. Carried to an extreme, this means that the empire became a facade masking an alliance between the Creoles and the bureaucrats they had co-opted that operated with impunity.[7] A third position denies that imperial government—at least under the Hapsburgs—was absolute either in intent or in fact. As proof, its advocates adduce the many procedures available to those affected by judicial or administrative decisions that permitted them to appeal and often to defy rulings contrary to their interests.[8] A variant of this position stresses that the professional bureaucracy, in particular at the level of the audiencias, possessed an esprit de corps based on its legal formation, a professional ethos of sorts that allowed them to counter any arbitrary decisions a monarch or viceroy might make. This could even make the bureaucracy the true power in the empire, based on its role as mediator and power broker.[9]

The next step is to move away from an emphasis on laws, government, and personnel at the imperial level and to scrutinize instead the politics of town and region, without, however, losing sight of the larger framework. Such a procedure implies the existence of distinct spheres of politics: one at the level of the bureaucracy running the empire, another at the level of the towns that in effect constituted the empire. Bureaucratic politics and town politics were not the same, despite the many ways they intersected. To use an analogy close at hand, they corresponded respectively to the politics of advancement in a profession and to those practiced in a university. Building blocks and stepping stones might be the same, but the operations as a whole are different. This book concentrates on the sphere of the town and investigates government and politics as they relate to the Spanish settlers and their descendants.

Towns in the Indies were formal institutions, not mere settlements, and as such they were designed to serve political purposes. A famous incident in the annals of conquest illustrates how that could be done. Hernán Cortés, eager to throw off the authority of the governor of Cuba, his formal superior, prevailed upon the members of his expedition to incorporate themselves as a municipality with an authority of its own, an authority promptly delegated to Cortés.[10] Formal authority in a town was vested in the regidores, who, in conjunction with the alcaldes ordinarios as magistrates, formed the cabildo and governed the town. The cabildo thus offers the most convenient point of departure for investigating local government and politics. Yet this procedure has major drawbacks, since cabildos had little power in their own right and in many towns were not the only repository of government. Hence, to the extent that politics has to do with the acquisition of power and its transformation into authority, the exploration of politics has to go beyond the cabildo to include all institutions of government; it also has to include an investigation of the basis of local power. Although power gravitates toward authority, the two need not be synonymous. The social structure of towns in Spanish America, though it followed a predictable pattern from the beginning, was not set in a mold that determined the allocation of power and authority in an unchanging fashion. Rather it was affected by events, whether these were of the crown's making, the result of population or business cycles, or due to generational changes. It also varied from region to region, in line with differing opportunities.[11] Although the conduct of politics might be formalized, its content had to respond to people and their interests and the circumstances in which they lived and acted. Hence the whole town becomes the object of the investigation, although its goal is more limited: to understand government and politics in a particular setting.

Three aspects of the town's history will be the main concern of this study. First, what were the fortunes of Spanish settlement in a region where the environment limited the settlers' ability to maintain town life in the Spanish manner? What kind of settlement resulted from these conditions? Second, what was the shape of settler society? How well did the first settlers, and the Creoles as their descendants, grasp local opportunities and adapt them to their advantage? The use of the word *society* in regard to the settlers is problematic, if we take this to mean that they formed a social order independent of crown and state.[12] Actually the "republic of Spaniards" was anything but well defined in territorial or social terms.[13] Cohesion and continuity owed something to the settlers' efforts, but crown and Church provided an essential framework without which they could not have maintained a separate and elevated status. A sense of social identity derived from descent and from family association, but it needed to be confirmed and buttressed by position under state and Church.[14]

The settlers lived under two kinds of government: their own, exercised by the cabildo, and the crown's, present in the governor. The Church was also an institution with governmental functions. It was closer to the inhabitants and more important to them than cabildo or crown. The third question raised in this study concerns the relationship between this "government" and the settlers. The answer, in theory, is clear. An apparatus of crown government, distinct from the groups of settlers, was imposed on the network of towns that formed little republics of conquistadors. The crown also invaded the sphere of the towns proper by considering office as part of its regalia, giving it away, and ultimately selling it to the highest bidder. The claims of the conquistadors and their descendants were not completely disregarded, but their consideration became a matter of choice and discretion with the passage of time. Yet the crown's tendency to acquire control over local affairs was not sustained, and intervention became a sporadic business rather than one of constant application.[15] Local power thus remained in the hands of the settlers or returned to them. What was the extent of this power? Did the Creoles manage to translate it into political and legal authority? A corollary question relates to the effect

of the Creoles' power on ·the structure of empire. Was colonial government a compromise between imperial sovereignty and settler interests?[16] How clearly would such a compromise be visible in local
affairs? Was it acknowledged, or were the Creoles content to subvert
imperial control without dismantling it?

The answers to these questions will vary to an extent from region
to region. This book will argue that the fortunes of settlement in
Popayán depended in a specific fashion on gold mining, which imposed
a fickle rhythm of its own. The shape of settler society remained firm,
despite considerable turnover in the top stratum.[17] The opportunities
for merchants to rise to the top were perhaps greater than in other
regions of Spanish America. These merchants, arriving as immigrants
from Spain, provided capital and entrepreneurial impetus in each
generation. Yet they did not become a status group of their own.
Rather they joined the Creoles, whose standing was vouchsafed by
ancestral merits, if not titles of nobility. Social authority was thus
linked to entrepreneurial talent in peculiar fashion. The clamp holding them together was kinship operating through the family and
through larger kin groupings. It was this "family system," manifest in
the family clan (parentela), that influenced—if it did not shape—
politics.[18] Political authority vested in the crown's agents and in the
cabildo was confronted by family loyalties that could extend over a
whole region. What were the resources of crown and Church in this
situation, that is, to what extent was government removed from control
by the locally powerful? It is not surprising to see that officeholders
were drawn into local affairs and became a part of them.[19] There was
no bureaucratic apparatus to support them nor a professional ethos to
sustain them, let alone an income sufficiently in line with expectations.
They were not civil servants in any modern sense. Office was not understood in functional terms but seen as a dignity and as property, ex-
pressing social rank and providing an income.[20] The cabildo was not
an administrative agency. No institutional insulation separated the
agents of empire from the town. Their chance for success lay in making
contact with the local networks of families and their leaders. These
contacts were easily established, despite the crown's efforts to impede
this kind of contamination.[21]

The book's emphasis on local affairs does not mean that the metropolis is ignored. Spain promulgated laws, set policies, and made
appointments. Even if not always effective, the crown remained in
charge, and the colonies remained objects. But such a statement raises
a difficulty. The town of Popayán was not a self-contained universe and
the settlers were not its masters. Yet, to an extent, they were, and it

is precisely this book's purpose to determine that extent. At the time no clear delimitation between imperial subject and colonial object existed. In this sense the Indies were not colonies in the modern meaning of the word. To achieve such a delimitation was the purpose of eighteenth-century imperial reform in Spanish America. The other difficulty relates to the fact that "colonial" history by definition involves a dialectical relationship in which subject and object are not fixed but rather interact. It is the purpose of this book to study such a moving object: a colonial town. Once we have a fix on this moving object, we can return to the metropolis, its perceptions and policies, and study them in relation to colonial reality.

The predominance of the center over the periphery is often assumed in discussions of European and Spanish expansion overseas. Control was exercised either directly by the state or indirectly through the operation of economic institutions and mechanisms that, for the first time, created a global economy centered in Europe.[22] But even if one grants that this expansion was characterized by greater coherence of the parts than was, for instance, the Arab or Mongol expansion, it was certainly neither smooth nor continuous in its progression. The movements for American independence are a conspicuous example. The decline of Spain's transatlantic power in the seventeenth century, matched by Spain's own decline, is another major break, not followed, in this case, by political separation.

The causes of Spain's decline are disputed. Lately the discussion has shifted from Spain to the New World, to a consideration of population changes and the fortunes of mining.[23] As important as these phenomena are, they cannot be considered in isolation. They bear a relation not only to developments in Spain but, even more, to the continuing growth of transatlantic societies based on networks of Spanish settlements.[24] While remaining tied to an Indian base, in many cases, and to the Spanish lifeline, these societies grew in territory, wealth, and social density; ultimately they became less dependent on the metropolis. Their economic organization changed as import substitution proceeded apace and Spaniards expanded their entrepreneurial and managerial range. The hacienda as a unit of rural production and the obraje as a manufacturing enterprise may be seen in this light—as economic and social institutions of the Spanish Indies that emerged at a certain point in their development.[25]

No substitution process operated in politics, at least not visibly. One explanation lies with the precocious development of the Castilian state and the ease with which it had established initial control. In the long run its institutions proved less suited to maintaining control. Yet the unity of the empire was not affected by the loss of Castilian control and the rise of (relative) economic independence. A balance between centrifugal and centripetal forces emerged. One way to discern its elements is to view it from the periphery, with a provincial perspective.

106   Offices and Officeholders

through marriage among the conquerors, their descendants, and successive waves of immigrants, was the most important avenue of consolidating that society. Yet vertical ties—to the land, its native inhabitants, and its resources—also played a role. Where they proved unstable, as in Popayán, the formation of a cohesive upper stratum could be delayed or interrupted for generations. Once it had been achieved on the basis of the extended family, the society's forum proved to be the family reunion rather than the council chamber.

ERRATUM

On page xxiv, the Introduction ends with the fourth line, after the phrase "with a provincial perspective." The lines below have been inadvertently added and should be ignored.

Town in the Empire:
Government, Politics, and Society
in Seventeenth-Century Popayán

1. Province and Town

Chains of mountains framed the core of the province. This core consisted of four longitudinal valleys: the tropical trough of the Cauca valley, the temperate intermontane plateau of Popayán, the hot and arid Patía valley, and the cool mountain region of Pasto. Altitude determined climate and defined ecological and agricultural zones. Cattle grazing developed everywhere. Wheat and potato cultivation, sheepherding, mule breeding, and dairy production were concentrated at higher altitudes. Corn, sugar cane, and cabuya (a type of sisal) flourished at lower altitudes. The two mountain chains held gold, often deposited in alluvial stream beds in the hot zone.

Formidable barriers separated the province from the continental centers of empire. The nearly impenetrable coastal cordillera barred the way to the Pacific Ocean. To the south, the mountain maze of the Pasto knot throws up range after range to make connections laborious in the extreme. The highlands of Antioquia to the north created similar obstacles. Communications were thus largely from the east, either through the Quindío pass or over the páramo (treeless zone) of Guanacas.

The events of the conquest, despite a certain random appearance, foreshadowed the later development of the region, if they did not determine it. As a unit of empire, Popayán had been the outcome of Sebastián de Belalcázar's efforts to fashion an independent fiefdom during the conquest.[1] Belalcázar was a lieutenant of Pizarro and Almagro during the conquest of Peru. He failed in his attempt to establish control over Quito and also in his quest for El Dorado when he encountered Gonzalo Jiménez de Quesada and Nicolás Federman already in Bogotá, in what became the New Kingdom of Granada. His consolation prize was Popayán, which was detached from Peru and made into a separate province over which he was appointed governor, with the title of *adelantado*.

The uncertainty of control and the fragility of arrangements are seen in a number of contests after Belalcázar returned from Spain, where he had obtained confirmation of his claims. One of his rivals was

Pascual de Andagoya, whose base of operations was Panama. Andagoya was easily beaten out of the field. His claim to fame now rests on his having been the first European to use the word *Peru*. Jorge de Robledo, once a trusted lieutenant of Belalcázar, was more difficult to deal with, since he relied on a hard-bitten contingent of Spaniards who had come from Cartagena, outpost of Spain's Caribbean frontier. He was eventually executed by Belalcázar. These rival attempts foreshadowed the later creation of Antioquia and the Chocó as provinces independent of Popayán. They also encouraged the founding of a profusion of towns.[2]

The establishment of towns marked the progress of the conquest. Within five years of their arrival the Spaniards had founded eight of them in the province: Pasto, Popayán (the capital), Timaná, Cali, Cartago, Anserma, Arma, and Antioquia. In the next generation additional settlements were established. Some served as way stations (Almaguer, Buga) and others as advance posts (Toro, Chapanchica, Trujillo) or defensive positions (Caloto). Buenaventura, close to Cali on the other side of the mountains, served as a port on the Pacific.[3] The extensive and rapid founding of towns contrasted with Spanish practice elsewhere, for instance Peru, where there were few formal Spanish settlements in relation to the territory to be controlled. The situation in Popayán responded to the inclinations of the conquerors, who were not held in check by a unified command. Robledo, for instance, founded Antioquia and Cartago to assert control and reward his followers. Another cause for the proliferation of towns was the region's character as a frontier with a multiplicity of native groups to be controlled. Indirect and informal means of control were insufficient, and formal ones, such as towns, had to take their place. This perhaps explains the paradox of Spanish "urbanization" in an area that had not known towns previously. Despite this dispersion the Spanish presence in Popayán remained limited to the intermontane regions of the Cauca and Patía drainage, where the native population, divided into numerous warring chiefdoms, was subdued within a decade of the initial arrival of Spaniards. Pockets of intense resistance remained, however, sometimes close to Spanish settlements, more often at the fringe of the area.[4]

A repetitious pattern of Spanish intrusion, Indian resistance, and Spanish counterattack characterized the fringes of the province into the seventeenth century. Outposts such as Timaná, San Vicente de Páez, or La Nueva Segovia de Caloto were destroyed several times. The Pijao Indians, who lived between the Quindío pass to the north and the Nevado de Huila to the south, offered the most pronounced resistance. It took three generations of warfare to subdue and practically exterminate them. Today the area is again one of dissidence where bandits abound and guerrillas mount raids and easily disappear again.[5] The lure of gold spurred Spanish intrusion into the Pacific lowlands. It remained nevertheless sporadic into the seventeenth century. Spanish expansion to the north was reversed when the town of Toro was moved east of the coastal cordillera late in the sixteenth century. Only in the 1660s was the Chocó again opened to Spanish penetration. An Indian revolt in the 1680s set back occupation for a decade, but from then on the area stayed under settler control. Even then, however, there were no formally incorporated Spanish towns in the area. Farther south, all attempts to establish a foothold in the gold-rich region of Barbacoas foundered until the 1630s, when a campaign mounted from Pasto wiped out Indian resistance and the town of Santa María del Puerto (Barbacoas) was founded.[6]

Indian labor and the requirements of production, trade, and transport determined the initial location of Spanish settlements. Anserma's and Cartago's importance during the sixteenth century rested on the gold of the vicinity and a sizeable Indian population to mine it. Cartago was also the stopover at the foot of the Quindío pass. A subsidiary treasury (caja real) confirmed its position for a while, but, as population fell and trade moved elsewhere, the town fell on bad times and the treasury disappeared.[7] Cali's fate was similar, although not as drastic as Cartago's. The town's prosperity rested on its role as an inland port, receiving goods transported via Panama and Buenaventura. It was the official seat of the treasury officials, the site of the smelter, and the governors' de facto residence until the 1620s.[8] Other centers of importance were Popayán, residence of the bishop, and Pasto, whose economic mainstay was the manufacture of cheap woolens. Some settlements never prospered. Almaguer, Yscancé, and Agreda in the central cordillera languished because they were "without trade and communication," as Fray Gerónimo de Escobar wrote around 1580. Almaguer, wrote a judge in 1616, had twenty-nine encomenderos who shared one thousand tribute payers among themselves; there were also twenty-eight other inhabitants; neither the church nor any of the houses had a tile roof (then an index of prosperity); the two Franciscan friars there subsisted on alms alone; the town's mines, once rich, had long been exhausted.[9] Settlements such as this—and who could call them towns except in a narrow legal sense?—were condemned to lead a marginal existence from their very beginning.

The early pattern of Spanish settlement was profoundly modified in the course of the seventeenth century. The town of Popayán rose to undisputed regional predominance, replacing the earlier centers of the

Source: *Pascual de Andagoya: Ein Mensch erlebt die Conquista* by Hermann Trimborn
(Hamburg: Cram, De Gruyter & Co., 1954)

province. Shifts in the area's population, the emergence of new centers of production both inside and outside the province, and the establishment of new trade patterns and routes were among the main reasons for this transformation.

Within three generations of the conquest the native population of the province declined to a small fraction of its former size. In Cartago it fell from 25,000 tribute payers in 1540 to a low of 62 tribute payers in 1628.[10] Such districts as Cali or Cartago that combined demands for native mine workers and for carriers over difficult pass routes were especially hard hit, while Pasto and Popayán were less affected. The increasing importance of imported African slave labor (never completely absent), especially in mining, contributed to the process that turned most of the province's Spanish settlements into mere shells of towns. Owners of slave gangs were free to choose their residence and to employ their property where they saw fit (a freedom that the encomenderos, in theory, had not possessed). The Arboledas, for example, a family of mine operators in Anserma and later in Popayán, shifted their slave gangs from Anserma to Caloto to Barbacoas and back to Caloto in the course of one generation.[11]

By the middle of the seventeenth century the focal areas of mining had shifted from the northern part of the province to its southern sector. When later in the century mining moved northward again, to the Chocó, the region's framework of towns remained fixed. By then the town of Popayán possessed sufficient political influence and economic power so that mine operators from there took a prominent part in the development of the new mining zone, even without having had much to do with the early exploration.[12]

The region's trading pattern also changed in significant fashion. In the early period of settlement the region imported its manufactures from Spain, via Panama and Buenaventura. By the seventeenth century Buenaventura practically ceased to operate. Reports of the time are full of complaints about its demise and the inability to do anything about it. Its demise is blamed on Indian attacks, the decreasing number of Indians who served as carriers, and Cali's inability to maintain a fort with four soldiers.[13] The main reason for the port's ruin (and it had never amounted to much) was the reorientation of trade that set in before the end of the sixteenth century. Also, in the 1620s the Campo Salazars of Popayán pioneered a toll road over the Guanacas pass that connected Honda and the upper Magdalena valley directly with Popayán, bypassing Cali and Cartago.[14]

Changes in trade and trade routes were caused by the shifting location of gold production, the rise of Cartagena as the port of entry for

European goods, and the emergence of the highlands of Quito as a major textile-producing area. It was of little import that freight from Cartagena now took three months, while it took fifteen days from Panama.[15] Cartagena had considerable advantages over the Isthmus of Panama. It was the most important slave market for South America. More important yet was the security of its location, which made it a safe entrepôt. The merchants of the province carried on their trade between two poles, Cartagena and Quito. The economic importance of Quito was based on the export of its cheap textiles, exchanged for the silver of Peru and the gold of Popayán. The trade link between Popayán and Quito was strengthened by the export of cattle. By the end of the seventeenth century, even herds from the upper Magdalena moved to Quito.[16]

In sum, the changes sketched here left only Popayán, Pasto, and, to an extent, Cali as towns of any importance in the province. As Governor Lorenzo de Villaquirán wrote in 1635, the inhabitants of most other towns were in fact scattered over the countryside with their herds or on their farms and came to town only once a year in order to elect alcaldes. Fifty years later Governor Gerónimo de Berrío wrote substantially the same thing. He described the towns as a collection of a few huts, with a miserable church, inhabited by citizens unable to sustain the cost of orderly administration. One should add that no peninsular prejudice entered into this statement, since de Berrío was from Bogotá.[17] Cartago offered a particularly telling example of a town in decline. By the end of the century scarcely twenty of the town's houses were inhabited, and then only during Holy Week. An alcalde's injunction stated the old ideal when he warned the citizens to shore up the town, stating that the king had granted them land and properties for living in a civilized fashion "and not for living in their fields among their herds, of which he does not intitulate himself king." But neither warnings nor threats that they would lose their land availed.[18] The common negative assessment at the time hides the fact that this process of dispersion was as much a part of adjustment to conditions as was the urban concentration described earlier.

From the time the province was established, the town of Popayán had been its nominal capital. It was also the bishop's residence after 1551. In 1538 it had received the title of city (ciudad). Yet not until it became the province's central marketplace and entrepôt did Popayán become its true capital. In 1628 the governor moved his residence from Cali to Popayán; by 1643 the treasury officials had followed suit. These moves amounted to official recognition of the primary facts of production, location, and entrepreneurial activity.

Popayán was the capital of a far from unified province. The governor represented the unity of an area divided between numerous jurisdictions: civil, ecclesiastical, fiscal, and military. Of these the split between the appeals jurisdictions of the audiencias of Quito and Bogotá was the most important. It bears some relating in detail.

In 1614 the audiencia of Quito dispatched a commissioner to Cali, with orders to arrest Governor Francisco Sarmiento de Sotomayor and conduct him to Quito. The governor evaded capture by simply removing himself to Toro, a town where Bogotá and not Quito held jurisdiction. The commissioner—in order to fulfill at least part of his duty—then proceeded to investigate the treasury in Cali. After inspecting the accounts, he imposed stiff fines on the treasury officials there. He was prevented from finishing even this limited task when the Tribunal of Accounts of Santa Fé de Bogotá, under whose jurisdiction the treasury at Cali fell, ordered him in no uncertain terms to desist.[19] A decade later, when all the papers and accounts were removed from the treasury at Cali and incorporated with those of a general inspection (visita) of the audiencia of Quito, the tribunal again had cause to complain.[20] These incidents provide only a hint of the maze of jurisdictions that characterized the province. In the sphere of justice, matters were still relatively clear-cut. The territorial line dividing the two audiencias fell between the towns of Buga and Cartago. Besides its judicial and supervisory functions, the audiencia's authority included promulgating ordinances, approving appointments and local elections, and sending judges on tours of inspection.[21] In fiscal matters the province was wholly subject to the jurisdiction of the tribunal at Santa Fé, but even in this sphere complications arose, since the treasury at Quito (subject to the tribunal at Lima) often collected the mining tax on gold and other dues originating in the province.[22] In the sphere of governance and war, the president of the audiencia of Santa Fé held a residual authority exemplified by his right to make interim appointments to the governorship of Popayán. The appointment of an interim governor by the audiencia of Quito in 1628 shows that even this authority was in dispute.[23]

Similar complications characterized the ecclesiastical sphere. Although the diocese of Popayán comprised Antioquia, Timaná, and La Plata, which were not part of the province, Pasto, which did belong to it, formed part of the diocese of Quito. In jurisdictional terms the diocese belonged to the archbishopric of Santa Fé de Bogotá. In a dispute involving appeals to both secular and ecclesiastical courts, matters might hang in balance between Quito and Santa Fé.[24]

Despite its fragmentation, the province did exhibit a certain unity. But this can scarcely be attributed to the institutions of government.

Such unity as existed came from an economy dominated by gold mining and from the social and familial ties that united groups and individuals throughout the region. To this must be added the hegemony the miners and merchants of Popayán achieved in the course of the seventeenth century.

The site of the town of Popayán was selected with considerable care. It was set in the foothills of the central cordillera at an altitude of 5,700 feet, nestling against the Cerro de la Eme (a hill named for its shape, like the letter *m*), whose springs supplied the town with water. A small creek, the Río Molino, ran from east to west, parallel to the town. Drainage could be a problem during the rainy season, but this was offset by the fact that most of the town was built on a ridge that fell off steeply toward the creek. Toward the west and north stretched a plain, broken by numerous gorges and gullies and framed by the distant contours of the coastal cordillera. This broken plain was devoted to the cultivation of maize near the town, the plots of land (estancias) forming a belt around it analogous to the fields (chacras) surrounding Peruvian towns. Farther from the town the plain was used for pasturing cattle.[25]

Beyond the town proper and the maize fields and cattle pastures of its immediate vicinity, the town's territory (distrito) included considerable areas whose Indian population was entrusted in encomienda to the most deserving settlers when Popayán was founded. The extension of these encomiendas (some of them veritable subregions inhabited by separate Indian tribes) also formed the boundaries between Popayán and the neighboring towns of Cali, Caloto, La Plata, Timaná, Almaguer, and Pasto. Not all of this area was under effective Spanish control. Even after the Pijao Indians had been subdued, an area to the south of them, inhabited by the Páez and Toribío, was hardly pacified, let alone settled or catechized. Popayán's claim to Tierradentro, as the area became known, remained tenuous, disputed by Neiva and Timaná. Encomenderos could claim only a reduced tribute there. The area's main value was the inhabitants, who served as a reserve labor force. Sometimes they were forcibly transplanted to encomiendas and estates nearer to town. They could also be lured to work in exchange for cattle and other goods. Their separate existence even today testifies to their resilience and to the settlers' lack of interest in their land.[26]

To the west beyond the coastal cordillera stretched a trackless wilderness that even today has not been opened to settlement. The mining settlements on the coast, such as Micay or Timbiquí, were supplied by coastal navigation from Buenaventura or Santa María del Puerto (Barbacoas). While this coastal zone had always been sparsely settled, the Patía region south of Popayán (the provincias of Bamba and Ceyna) had earlier supported a sizable population that disappeared completely by the seventeenth century. Thereafter the Patía became a refuge for fugitive slaves. Later settlement there bears no relation to an earlier Indian occupation.[27]

Popayán's climate elicited numerous favorable comments. "During the whole year there is no cold that molests nor heat that tires, but rather heat and cold moderate one another," declared Padre Pedro de Mercado, a Jesuit chronicler. In further support of his opinion he cited a saying common to the region, "sky, soil, and bread of Popayán," which supposedly alluded to the excellence of these ingredients of local life. An earlier observer, Fray Gerónimo de Escobar, compared the town's climate to Castile's in May, while calling Pasto's weather a perpetual October and Buga's a permanent August.[28]

Jorge Juan and Antonio de Ulloa, two eighteenth-century Spanish travelers, gave the first comprehensive description of Popayán. Their account, which derives from observations made in the late 1730s and early 1740s, provides a reasonably accurate picture of the town then. It also affords a backdrop against which to set miscellaneous information about the town in the earlier stages of its development.[29]

Juan and Ulloa described Popayán as a medium-sized town with about twenty thousand inhabitants, many of them castas (of mixed African and Indian descent). They noted that it was similar in ethnic composition to Cartagena and unlike Quito with its preponderance of Indians and mestizos. They observed that population was increasing in distinct contrast to other towns they had visited, and went on to note: "The lower class consists of castes resulting from the marriages of the Whites and the Negroes; but very few Indian castes. This is owing to the great multitude of Negro slaves kept as labourers at the plantations in the country, the mines, and to do the servile offices in the city: so that the number of Indians here are very few, compared with the other parts of the province. This government has, however, many large villages of them; and it is only in the capital, and other Spanish towns, that they are so greatly out-numbered by the Negroes." Among the many Spanish families there were sixty in particular who claimed descent "from very noble families in Spain." Since Popayán was a trade center, five or six of its inhabitants claimed fortunes of above 100,000 pesos, while another twenty were worth more than 40,000 pesos. The travelers commented on the town's convenient layout and its clean streets, which were never dusty, its houses of unburnt brick, the better ones two stories high, and its water supply, brought from the hill overlooking the town to supply the religious houses and the houses of the more prominent citizens.

The town had only one parish, that of the cathedral church, which elicited from Juan and Ulloa the comment that the canons could never be brought to allow its subdivision into more parishes because of the loss of revenues that such a reorganization would have occasioned them. In addition to the cathedral there were the churches and monasteries of the Franciscans, Dominicans, and Augustinians, as well as the Jesuit seminary and college. None of these housed many religious —rarely more than six at a time. One of the two nunneries was very large, housing besides the forty or fifty professed nuns nearly four hundred dependents, novices, servants, and other retainers.

The travelers commented on Popayán's role as a regional trade emporium. It was an important point of transit that supplied the mining regions of the Chocó and Barbacoas with foodstuffs, dried meat, salted pork, lard, and sugar and sold rum, cotton, tobacco, and textiles for gold dust. From Quito came textiles and Peruvian silver to be exchanged for the gold and cattle for which Popayán served as a collecting point.

Juan and Ulloa's account provides a vantage point from which to consider the town's development in the two hundred years following its foundation. What began as a series of claims to the land and its people was transformed into a compact town with churches and plazas, monasteries, convents, and substantial houses. The country was made subservient to the Spanish town; rural estates and mining camps were tangible evidence of this fact. A set of relations between conquerors and conquered emerged that involved custom as well as command.

The claims and aspirations of the conquerors and their descendants were expressed in the physical shape of the town. Its focal point was the central square, with streets intersecting it at right angles. The grid thus formed could then, time and means permitting, be filled in with churches, religious houses, public buildings, and substantial stone-built private residences, centering on the plaza, with the town's layout providing a map of social standing, as it were. In Popayán this process took considerable time, reflecting the town's initially precarious situation and late prosperity.

The most imposing structure was the cathedral at the south side of the plaza, built between 1594 and 1610 at a cost close to sixty thousand pesos. It replaced a simple straw-roofed structure. The crown paid for a third of the construction costs, with the remainder provided by the town's inhabitants through an assessment and by the Indian population of the district, who were assessed labor contributions. The building remained unfinished at first; a capilla (interior enclosure) was added later and so was the bell tower, built in the 1670s.[30]

The hospital and cemetery were located in the same block as the cathedral. The hospital was supported by a tithe allocation of one-and-a-half novenos (approximately 9 percent of the tithe), but this allocation was transferred to the seminary founded in the 1640s. Apparently the town had no functioning hospital during most of the seventeenth century; a corner lot of the plaza assigned to it was sold by the cathedral chapter in 1631. In 1673, two generations later, a local petitioner still alleged that, given some legacies, permission to ask for contributions, and the restitution of the tithe allocation, the hospital could be rebuilt and maintained in the future. In the 1680s a private benefactor, Juan de Velasco, who had already built a little church on the outskirts, offered to build a hospital next to it to serve the town's poor. While it is not clear whether anything came of the initiative, this offer does show the precarious state of the town's services.[31]

The town's dead—at least those from prominent families—were better cared for than the sick. In 1570 Pedro de Velasco and Francisco de Mosquera established a capellanía (endowment) designed to support the chapel of Nuestra Señora de la Asunción in the cathedral. The chapel served as a pew and burial place for the founders' families and their descendants. The chapel of Rosario in the Dominican church was endowed in 1605 by Juan de Velasco and Beatriz de Zúñiga (son-in-law and daughter of Pedro de Velasco).[32] Endowments stipulated in wills built up the Church's fortune. Some orders, such as the Jesuits, or specific institutions, such as the town's nunnery, were favored above others. Besides their pious function, these ecclesiastical establishments served utilitarian goals. The nunnery of La Encarnación could be used as a repository for daughters without an avocation for marriage and as an educational institution for girls too young to marry. The Jesuit seminary and college provided instruction that gave access to more advanced studies at the university and to professional careers.

The convent of La Encarnación was founded in 1592 under the joint patronage of the cathedral chapter and the cabildo. The second bishop, Fray Agustín de la Coruña, endowed it with a considerable fortune that included twenty-seven slaves at work in the mines of Chisquío in the vicinity of Popayán.[33] The convent went through considerable vicissitudes in the first century of its existence. In the 1610s a scandal tainted its reputation and nearly led to its dissolution.[34] In the 1660s the nuns requested transfer to Ibarra, alleging the loss of the censos (annuities or mortgages) and of the properties that had secured the censos. The governor, Luis Antonio de Guzmán y Toledo, in an advisory opinion confirmed this sad state of affairs, noting also that with the decline of the Indian population the region had fallen on bad times. He added, however, that with careful management the nunnery's investments could be restored and that meanwhile the nuns could live in decent poverty. The nunnery's removal would be a great loss, since it was the only place where the citizens could provide for their daughters.[35] When a generation later the convent petitioned the cabildo to grant it an additional city block, its difficulties appear to have been surmounted. The institution's growth was such that the sixty nuns with their servants and the many girls entrusted to them simply could not be accommodated any longer in the narrow confines of the old establishment.[36]

By comparison with the nuns' story, the Jesuits' establishment in town is a tale of linear progress, with the conspicuous exception of their unsuccessful missionary enterprise among the Páez Indians. The Jesuits first entered Popayán as Lent preachers during the early 1630s. The great demand for such preaching was rarely met, as the cabildo had noted in one of its petitions to the synod held in Santa Fé de Bogotá in 1624. Scarcely more than a decade passed between the first presence of the Lent preachers and the founding of a seminary and college staffed and directed by the Society of Jesus. Local enthusiasm and support contributed to its rapid success. Bishop, governor, and cabildo jointly urged the crown to permit the full-scale establishment of the order in Popayán. The dean, Francisco Vélez de Zúñiga, donated his fortune, including the mines of Honduras with sixteen slaves. Another thirty-three citizens of the town pledged 1,750 pesos in cash besides promising land, wheat, and cattle. From these modest beginnings the order had advanced by the end of the century to a secure economic position that included the possession of several rural estates, sugar mills, lime and brick kilns, and other income-producing enterprises in the region.[37]

The relative opulence of the Church stood in marked contrast to the penury manifest in what public buildings existed in town. The treasury could not afford an edifice of its own until the 1750s. Until then, official business was conducted in the residence of one of the officials; it also housed the smelter.[38] Efforts to build a town hall, jail, and slaughterhouse substantial enough to withstand the rigors of the weather occupied the cabildo throughout the century without much result.[39] A major problem was the passage over the Río Cauca, two miles north of the town. Until the 1670s the bridge consisted of not more than a few trees and planks that high water would carry away. The risks of passage were such that travelers frequently drowned, once five in a single fortnight. By the 1660s matters had come to such a pass that the cabildo applied to the crown to let it levy a bridge toll to finance construction of a proper bridge. A span was built in the 1670s and permission to levy the toll was given, although apparently it was never levied.[40]

Popayán's basic layout was simple. In the 1660s, according to Governor Díaz de la Cuesta, it still consisted only of four streets that crossed the plaza at right angles.[41] This statement cannot be taken literally, since it is contradicted by other evidence about the town's size and extension. But if it refers to streets with houses of substance it comes close to the truth. These few streets looked like mud lagoons during the rainy season. The attempt to provide them with a gravel foundation and sidewalks was not made until the beginning of the eighteenth century, and actual street paving started in the 1740s.[42]

A stone-built house with a tiled roof was the most visible evidence of a family's social standing. The plaza was surrounded by such houses, which were often two-storied, with shops occupying the ground floor. A section of the plaza in front of Pedro de Velasco's house was taken up by the portales (arcades), a covered section offering protection from the rain and a place to congregate. Away from the plaza, mud-walled houses with thatched roofs prevailed, while farther out were shacks and huts interspersed with open lots. The price for such a simple dwelling with a lot could be as low as twenty-five pesos, but more often it would lie between seventy-five and one hundred pesos.[43] These crude structures needed frequent repairs and often had to be rebuilt completely. Both Governor Sarmiento in 1610 and Governor Díaz in 1671 mention that they had more than fifty houses built and rebuilt by Indian labor they had conscripted for the benefit of inhabitants who could not enlist such help regularly.[44] Land transactions indicate that division into lots had proceeded apace by the beginning of the seventeenth century. No free lots were left for newcomers; instead they had to buy a lot and a house in order to establish a claim to residence.

One derives some idea of what a substantial house was like in Popayán from the building contract concluded in 1631 between Diego Daza, a merchant, and the master carpenter Francisco González Leuro.[45] For 1,600 silver pesos (patacones), plus the provision of building materials, helpers, food, lodging, and clothing, González Leuro agreed to build a house on the plaza similar in specifications to that of Alonso Hurtado, Diego Daza's partner. The house was to be located on a corner lot of the plaza, with four shops on the ground floor, each with a window, a partition, and a storage space in back. A massive door with an entranceway, one large room, storage space, and a staircase with a door at the bottom completed the downstairs layout. The upstairs had five rooms: a sitting room with a balcony and large shuttered windows, and four bedrooms. Neither kitchen nor servants' quarters are mentioned in this particular case; the kitchen was usually a separate thatched structure, as is evident from other descriptions of buildings. In addition, houses of this type included more than one lot, with a back lot sometimes serving as corral and stables. In the early seventeenth century, such a house might be worth between three and four thousand gold pesos.

Building materials are worth separate comment. The adobe, reeds, and thatch used in simple construction were easily procured. Stones were hauled from the river. Lumber needed to be cut, transported, and prepared. In the above contract Diego Daza, who as an encomendero controlled Indian labor, took over the provision of lumber. Bricks, tiles, and lime were items of more specialized production and apparently an ecclesiastical specialty. At the century's end the Jesuits leased the nunnery's brick oven, which earlier had supplied the bricks to build the cathedral. In addition they operated a lime kiln worked with five slaves.[46]

Even substantial houses were only sparsely furnished. One example may suffice, taken from the inventory of don Agustín Fernández de Belalcázar's estate in 1718. The town house was assessed at 6,800 patacones. Of its contents, the silver plate was evaluated at 450 patacones, jewelry at 1,200, and the remaining contents at 591. Among these were paintings, including two large ones with gilt frames and many small devotional pictures, two desks, three chests, many chairs—some of them upholstered in damask—and a large canopied bed. Other inventories give a similar picture. They mirror a style of life that combined austerity in household furnishings (comfort had not yet been invented) with personal display in dress and jewelry. The owner, a distant descendant of the adelantado, belonged to the town's upper class as an encomendero, miner, and estate owner. His whole estate was appraised at 26,000 patacones (exclusive of debts and other obligations). It included the family estate at Guambía, a sugar mill, and forty-three slaves.[47] How were such fortunes created, modest as they were compared with those at the centers of empire, and what were the activities that made this style of life possible? Fundamentally they derived from the town's position as an intermediary between the countryside and the wider world, a role that depended on the inhabitants' ability to compel and cajole contributions from the rural population. It is these activities I will discuss in the following chapter.

2. Estates, Mines, and Commerce

The town of Popayán was the hub of a region supported by mining, ranching, and farming. Merchants and traders mobilized production, serving local needs and creating a system of trade that included Cartagena, Quito, and places beyond. The town was the focus of a network of enterprises, some of them strictly local, others operating on a large scale. All of these were tied together through the efforts of entrepreneurs whose activities had created a market for goods, land, labor, and capital.

The existence of an extensive market produced some degree of economic specialization, such as that between long-distance merchant and local trader. But in Popayán specialization was not advanced. Many of the town's inhabitants combined various activities, whether for short periods or over a lifetime. Encomenderos were also estate owners and mine operators; the operation of an estate usually depended on conscripted Indian labor, which was also used in mining. Estate owners were partners and investors in commercial enterprises. Merchants became estate owners and miners. Ecclesiastics and local officials owned mining gangs composed of slaves. They functioned as real estate dealers, cattle traders, and cloth distributors. By delegating responsibility, a single individual could combine diverse economic pursuits. An encomendero might employ a mine overseer and an estate manager. A merchant could hire a clerk to run his store. Partnerships gave incentive and rewards and allowed a sharing of responsibilities. A partner, whether a relative or not, could manage an enterprise, remitting a fixed income or a share of the proceeds. Since farming, mining, and commerce could be combined in the enterprise of one man, the distinction between them is artificial. But as distinct activities they still required different forms of organization.

The estate of Captain Lorenzo Paz Maldonado, encomendero of Ambaló and Usenda in the province of Guambía, a day's trip (seven leagues) from Popayán, may be considered a characteristic settler enterprise.[1] Paz Maldonado, a native of Salamanca in Old Castile, came to Popayán from Toro, a town in the northern part of the province

17

that he had helped found. In Popayán he married doña Catalina de Herrera, a granddaughter of the adelantado Belalcázar, and became one of the leaders in the intermittent wars carried on with the Toribío, Pijao, and Páez Indians. His territory bordered on that of the warlike Toribíos and also on Guambía, the encomienda of don Sebastián de Belalcázar, his brother-in-law. Although his connection with the Belalcázars did not last—he killed his wife and her presumed lover—it served to establish him locally. A second marriage, to doña Catalina de Zúñiga, brought him a considerable dowry and reaffirmed his local ties, this time with the Velasco y Zúñigas, another prominent family.

A series of maize estancias situated in the Cauca plain near the town belonged to his estate. They included a house inhabited by a caretaker Indian farmer. Higher up, where the farm laborers lived, the captain owned additional maize estancias. In Ambaló, where his encomienda was located, Paz Maldonado owned wheat land. Some of this land had been granted to him by Governor Tuesta y Salazar and some he bought from the cacique of Ambaló. With this property went a house and a grist mill, ten yokes of oxen, several mules, and four hundred head of cattle. In the same area he owned a ranch with corrals stocked with cattle and horses, goats, sheep, and pigs. Labor was obtained on a regular basis from the encomienda. In 1617 Paz Maldonado employed eight hired hands, three vaqueros (cowboys), one helper, and one shepherd. In addition he employed a mine overseer, Gerónimo Pantaleón. The mining and water rights that went with the estate were later sold by his son-in-law and successor. In 1619 Paz Maldonado had to entrust the entire estate to García Álvarez, a merchant, as security for his debts. After Paz Maldonado's death, the estate passed under the temporary administration of Alonso Hurtado del Águila, another merchant, who served as guardian for the encomendero's three daughters. Hurtado in turn soon leased it to Captain Juan de Mera, the oldest daughter's husband. The lease was not onerous: fifty fanegas of wheat, forty fanegas of maize, and one-half the cheeses produced at the ranch. Juan de Mera later became the encomendero of Ambaló, in virtual succession to his father-in-law, and his descendants, the Mera Paz Maldonados, held on to the estate and the encomienda until the early eighteenth century.

The distribution of the various parts of an estate among areas of different altitudes and climates was characteristic of the region. The town's immediate vicinity was divided into numerous estancias that supplied maize to the urban market and the mines. Some of these estancias formed part of larger estates, while others belonged individually to inhabitants of the town, whether Spanish or Indian. Wheat

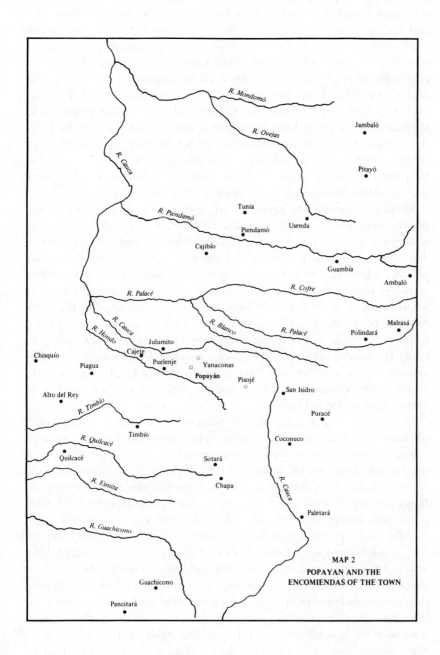

MAP 2
POPAYAN AND THE
ENCOMIENDAS OF THE TOWN

production was concentrated in a series of estancias at a distance from the town, running in an arc from Guambía in the north to Guanacas and Coconuco in the east and Sotará in the south. Potatoes and beans were crops of less importance. While maize production was uncomplicated, demanding little more than human labor, wheat production required yokes of oxen, iron-tipped plows, horses for threshing, and mules to transport the product. A wheat farm also included a grist mill, a granary, and a house for resident laborers, and it might, as in the Gavirías' estate at Sotará, include a smithy and facilities to lodge the owner's family. Wheat estancias tended to form the core of some of the larger estates of the area. Don Ýñigo de Velasco's estancia at Coconuco included forty yokes of oxen, fifty horses for threshing, sixteen plows, and a mule train of thirty animals.[2]

Keeping animals was necessary in both wheat farming and sugar production, but it was often a separate activity as well. Cheese and wool were produced at higher altitudes. Cheeses, together with maize and wheat, were the payments in kind most commonly made by proprietors whose estates were mortgaged to the nunnery. A stock ranch included a house or hut and the corrals needed for the annual roundup, when animals were counted, branded, and separated, for the tithe or other purposes. Although a small ranch contained from fifty to two hundred animals, larger ranches might hold up to three thousand; an estate frequently included several such ranches. People with just a few animals still had their own brand, but they would graze them with larger herds belonging to others. Indian pueblos had their own cattle brand, kept by the cacique.[3]

Sugar mills might form part of an estate complex, or they could constitute an independent operation. They were usually operated with slaves. In one reported case an encomendero secured permission to use Indians from his encomienda.[4] The sugar mill of Bartolomé Sánchez on the Río Esmita was a small operation without estate connection. It was equipped with five copper pans, four yokes of oxen with their plows, five horses to drive the mill, and ten slaves. These mills were usually small affairs located in river bottoms. They could not compare with those of the Cauca valley, veritable plantations prefiguring a later epoch. Preeminent among these were two Jesuit enterprises, one near Buga and the other, Japio, between Cali and Caloto; they employed thirty-eight and twenty-five slaves respectively at the end of the century.[5]

Estates drew their labor from two sources: a small nucleus of resident workers and labor recruited from the Indian communities. Residents might include farm hands drawn from a contingent of Indians from Quito. Blacks might also function as caretakers. Basic tasks were performed by labor recruited from the encomienda on an annual basis. The workers included laborers, cowboys, swineherds, and shepherds. For planting, weeding, and harvesting, the whole population would have to turn out. Pay was regulated by ordinances and ranged from eight pesos (oro común, which was gold dust not yet assayed), for laborers to twelve pesos for cowboys, with maintenance included. These rates applied, with some modifications, throughout the century.[6]

Compulsion was an underlying element of the region's labor system, restrained by custom and patriarchal features. The caciques could join the encomenderos against a change in regulations that prohibited the customary commutation of tribute for labor service. The caciques had as great a customary interest in maintaining this arrangement as had the encomenderos.[7] Bequests by encomenderos and estate owners to Indians from their pueblos indicate a patriarchal dimension. Such bequests differed from the legacies to faithful servants by their collective character. Sometimes they contained an element of restitution. Lorenzo de Paz Maldonado directed the executors of his estate to give three pesos in back pay to each one of his laborers, as ordered by the oidor Armenteros twelve years earlier!

The region's larger estates frequently began as encomiendas, complemented later by actual grants of land. Lorenzo de Paz Maldonado's estate is a case in point, as is don Juan de Gaviría's at Sotará. The process by which an encomienda grant could lead to control of land and ultimately to its legal possession is still not well understood. The Velasco estate at Coconuco, as described in 1559, offers a clue to the beginning of an estate operation.[8] Besides providing tribute in kind (cotton mantles, sandals, mats, chickens), Pedro de Velasco's encomienda supplied him with labor. The Indians of the encomienda were to plant six fanegas of maize and beans in the encomendero's estancia, while in their own pueblo they were to plant two fanegas of maize, two of potatoes, eight of wheat, and eight of barley for him. In both cases the encomendero provided animals and tools for clearing and plowing. The plantings in the area of Indian settlement could turn the encomendero into a land owner. Initially he had to provide implements and animals, keeping them where they would be used. Later he might legalize a de facto presence, either by purchasing land outright, as did Paz Maldonado, or by availing himself of composición (payment of a sum to legalize an extralegal situation).

Land grants appear as estancias, estancias de sembrar mayz (maize-farming), de pan coger (wheat-farming), or de ganado mayor (cattle-raising). These terms refer to the extension of a grant: a property might include many estancias, as did Bernabé Fernández Rico's ranch at Laboyo, which comprised twenty-five estancias de ganado mayor, with 1,500 cattle and 420 horses. The plural *estancias* continued in use, especially in the town's immediate vicinity. Only toward the end of the century did *hacienda* and *hacendado* appear as terms denoting a rural estate and its owner. Earlier *hacienda* had simply meant a property. Doña Francisca Manuela de Belalcázar's estate at Guambía (called the puesto de Guambía) had an administrator of the hacienda (mayordomo de la dicha hacienda).[9] Don Juan de Gaviría's estate at Sotará was referred to interchangeably as estancias or haciendas. The relatively low value of land explains the ease with which land grants were made. Don Yñigo de Velasco's fortune in 1629 amounted to 24,000 gold pesos; his crop land was valued at 2,000 pesos, animals in various locations were worth 9,400 pesos, and his main dwelling with its two lots was worth 4,000 pesos.[10]

The dynamic element in the region's economy was mining.[11] In the opinion of many it was the only profitable enterprise. Gold production sustained everything else. It provided a ready medium of exchange until mid-century, when silver replaced gold dust. Entire towns depended on mining profits. Gold mining also affected the prosperity of such distant centers as Quito, whose textile mills supplied the mines. Yet the full benefits of the expansion of the market, based on the success of mining, were not realized, for neither the Indian miners nor the weavers of Quito participated meaningfully in its results, compulsion and forcible recruitment remaining the norm for their participation.

The uprooting of native Indians to work in areas removed from their natural habitat was one of the basic causes of their decline. As African slaves took their place, after the middle of the seventeenth century, the racial structure of the region was transformed. At the same time the slaves' arrival helped preserve what remained of the native population.

Mining was carried on all over the province. During the sixteenth century the most profitable operations were located in the northern part, principally in Anserma and Cartago, while Caloto and later the Barbacoas region became focal points of mining in the seventeenth century. In the eighteenth century the north again rose in importance, principally the Chocó, which in 1718 became a province independent of Popayán. The most important mining centers in the town's vicinity were Chisquío, Almaguer, and Caloto. Chisquío, fifteen miles west of Popayán, had rich vein deposits that were probably mined even before the coming of the Spaniards. Its native inhabitants constituted a crown encomienda, but the gold was also mined by gangs belonging to other encomenderos. In 1619, for instance, 223 Indian miners, recruited from

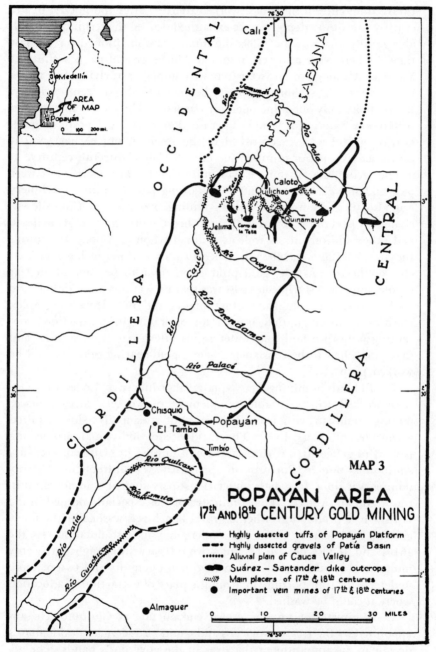

MAP 3

POPAYÁN AREA
17th AND 18th CENTURY GOLD MINING

━━━━━ Highly dissected tuffs of Popayán Platform
━ ━ ━ Highly dissected gravels of Patía Basin
•••••• Alluvial plain of Cauca Valley
⬤⬤ Suárez – Santander dike outcrops
⌁⌁⌁ Main placers of 17th & 18th centuries
⬤ Important vein mines of 17th & 18th centuries

0   10   20   30 MILES

Source: *Colonial Placer Mining in Colombia* by Robert C. West
(Baton Rouge: Louisiana State University Press, 1952)

twelve different encomiendas, worked there.[12] After the middle of the century Chisquío's deposits were exhausted—given the techniques available locally—and in the 1690s the mines were mentioned for the last time.[13] There were also vein mines at Almaguer and in its vicinity at Yscancé. Although there were renewed hopes of reviving the mines there in the 1620s, their prosperity belonged to the sixteenth century. By the 1650s only one mine operator was left.[14] The most stable mining region was Caloto, forty miles north of Popayán. Its deposits of gold-bearing gravel were first worked in the 1610s (if not earlier), and it continued as a major mining zone into the late eighteenth century.

The technology of mining was quite simple. The main tools were pick and shovel, crowbar, and gold-washing pan. Crushing machinery was also used; Pedro de Velasco's mining operation at Chisquío included a wheel drawn by oxen that crushed the ore and a forge, bellows, and other equipment, as well as a miner's house. Among the town's Indian inhabitants in 1607 was a specialist for working such machines.[15] One of the reasons why gold production came to be concentrated at Caloto and along the Pacific coast was that the various kinds of flotation used to separate gold from other matter did not demand complex machinery, although they used a lot of water. In transactions concerning mines we find that water rights often went with a mine and that canals had to be constructed before gold-bearing gravels could be worked properly.

Not all kinds of mining were equally labor intensive. Lodes and veins were worked with a sizable complement of workers. Stream placer mining could do with fewer laborers, but stream diversion required a considerable work force. The incidence of individual prospecting is hard to gauge. It was characteristic of mining in eighteenth-century Antioquia, but in Popayán it apparently was infrequent. Usually mining was done in gangs, under the supervision of a mine administrator and an overseer. The administrator was especially needed in the last stage of production, when a gravel bench was washed or the finely ground gold-bearing paste was undergoing its last flotation. In the 1610s and 1620s the size of gangs would vary from eight to twenty miners and would include one or two pan operators and two or more muleteers for transporting ore from the place of extraction to a location where it could be washed.[16]

An administrator ran the crown encomienda at Chisquío. He was appointed by the treasury officials and could also serve as alcalde mayor de minas, an appointment that was in the governor's hands. The administrator's accounts for the period from 1628 to 1631 and a critique of an earlier administrator's performance—he happened to be the treasurer's younger brother—provide us with some clues about an actual mining operation.[17] The crown encomienda itself comprised 151 inhabitants in 1607, 40 of whom were tribute payers. According to the ordinances, only one-fourth of the tributaries were to serve in mining, yet in 1628 we find twenty-one men conscripted for such work, fifteen as miners, one as panner, one as muleteer, and four as laborers. The laborers tended the maize field that fed the miners. The ordinances settled such matters as pay, weekly rations, and the time to be spent at work. There was no set production quota, but the expectation was that a gang of this size would produce an average of thirty gold pesos a week. Actual production averaged twenty-one pesos between 1618 and 1624, nineteen pesos between 1628 and 1631. During this latter period the enterprise yielded a net profit of 722 pesos to the treasury, a result that may appear small unless one considers that the investment was practically nil.[18] Costs for an integrated estate and mine operation could be reduced considerably because maintenance could be absorbed by the estate, which was served by draft labor. Even after Negro slaves had largely replaced Indian draft labor in mining, Indians continued to be conscripted for agricultural work.

Black slave labor was used on a large scale in the Caloto mining region. The area consisted of a series of mining settlements named La Teta, Gelima, Quinamayó, Honduras, La Jagua and San Antonio, all under the nominal jurisdiction of the town of Caloto. Sometimes a settlement would house several mining gangs—Quinamayó, for instance, contained four slave gangs in the 1660s and five slave gangs in the 1680s—in other cases it would be a simple mining camp. Some of the settlements were called reales de minas, but this label appears to have been nominal, since there was usually no alcalde mayor de minas to exercise jurisdiction. Since neither the alcaldes ordinarios of Caloto nor those of Popayán exercised any effective authority there, control over affairs in the area fell to the mine operators and their representatives. Caloto itself was a town whose thirty-one Spanish householders lived in the country, as Governor Villaquirán noted in the 1630s. With one or two exceptions they had little control over the operation of the mines. The state of affairs in which a few mine and estate owners resident in Popayán controlled matters in the Caloto mining region continued into the early nineteenth century.[19] Rather than being a singular phenomenon it was repeated in other mining regions of the province where slaves furnished the labor force.

The mines of Caloto also attracted mine operators from elsewhere who brought their slaves with them. A case in point was that of Captain Jacinto de Arboleda, a citizen of Anserma, who had served there as alcalde ordinario. In the early 1650s he moved a gang of approximately 50 slaves to Caloto, where he expanded operations until at the time of his death in 1671 he owned 145 slaves, 14 of whom were still working in Anserma. The ground was prepared for Arboleda by his father-in-law, Diego de Victoria (Arboleda had married his step-daughter, doña Teodora de Salazar), who himself had moved from Anserma to Popayán in 1619. He started as a merchant but soon branched out into other enterprises, among them mining. With only 14 slaves in the mining camp of Las Ovejas and others employed on his sugar plantation, Victoria never became a mining operator on a large scale like Arboleda. Two of Arboleda's sons went into mining and expanded the family's operations into Barbacoas and the Chocó in the next generation. In 1633 Victoria and Arboleda had bought the canal and mining rights of Usenda, which Victoria then developed. He connected the canal with other sources of water he had also acquired and made agreements with other mine operators to supply them with water from his canal.[20]

In contrast to native labor, slaves constituted an investment that had to produce a return. Around 1700, slaves sold for an average of 500 silver pesos. Indian labor was not a completely free good. The encomenderos had to make an initial outlay to obtain the encomienda and they had to meet current expenses of pastoral care and of administration. Yet these outlays did not constitute a capital sum that had to be amortized and produce a profit. To cover both the cost entailed in mining and his own purchase price, a slave had to produce 100 to 120 silver pesos yearly. Although considerations of cost and profit affected the employment of slaves, it is not clear how such considerations operated in particular cases. When Diego de Victoria's gang of eight slaves produced only 90 pesos in one year, they were transferred to Victoria's sugar mill on the Río Paila.[21] The returns of other mine operators, although not quite as low as Victoria's, were also insufficient at times. The contador Larrainzar alleged this when pleading with the crown for a reduction of the mining tax.[22]

The mining tax, the assaying charge, and the administrator's share bore no relation to profits after costs. They were simply proportionate to total production. The mining tax was in fact reduced from 20 percent to 5 percent, but it remained proportionate to output. The rationale for reducing the tax was to encourage the miners to buy more slaves and expand production, an acknowledgment of the need for more capital. The transition from a freely available but shrinking supply of native labor to slave labor was not mentioned in the mine owners' petitions. There must have been profits; otherwise enterprises would not have endured nor could they have expanded.[23] The case of Jacinto de Arboleda demonstrates this, both in the substantial increase in the number of slaves he owned and in his ability to provide a substantial dowry for Ana, one of his six children.[24]

Not all mine owners prospered. In the 1680s the Jesuit order, one of the largest mine operators in the region, abandoned mining altogether. Instead, the Jesuits concentrated on ranching and sugar production. An inspector visiting the colegio noted that the mining enterprise scarcely covered its costs.[25] Under these circumstances it is not surprising that the number of mine owners was never great. At the century's beginning all encomenderos had been miners. By the 1650s only six Indian mining gangs remained. There were fifteen slave gangs, while two mine owners, don Joseph Hurtado and Christóbal de Mosquera, used both Indian and Black labor.[26] After mid-century there were never more than fifteen mine operators in town.[27] Many fortunes were indirectly attached to mining. We see this, for instance, when the visitador Pastrana imposed a fine of 8,000 pesos on the town in 1658 for failure to pay the mining tax. Fifty inhabitants were assessed a share of the fine.[28] Some of these men were dealers in bullion. One such dealer, don Sebastián Torijano, was reported (a generation later) to have delivered more than 215,000 pesos to the treasury, where he paid the tax on it, prospering as a dealer rather than as a miner.[29]

But these are mere clues. Without specific knowledge of capital invested—mainly slaves—or of costs and yields, no clear-cut statements about the mine owners' prosperity and the distribution of benefits can be made. One should also note that an investment in mining was usually complemented by other pursuits. Don Lorenzo del Campo Salazar, the encomendero of Guanacas and concessionaire of the route to the Magdalena valley, was one of the more successful mine operators in Popayán. He owned a profitable estate that produced wheat, corn, cattle, leather, and cheeses. He also owned a brickyard and collected rents from his stores on the plaza. In addition he invested considerable sums in commerce.[30]

Although it is difficult to establish the contribution mining made to the prosperity of individuals or groups, it is possible to estimate its quantitative contribution to the region's wealth. The mining tax paid at the treasury in Cali—and later at Popayán—furnishes a way to gauge this production. On that basis, production moved in the course of the century from 100,000 pesos (of 20 carat) at the beginning, to 20,000 pesos annually by the 1630s and a low of 6,000 pesos by mid-century. By the 1680s, production (or collections) recovered somewhat, reaching 50,000 pesos (of 22½ carat). Production remained fairly steady for the next thirty years, with a conspicuous decline around the turn of the century.[31] It is unlikely that these figures reflect actual production with much accuracy. Tax evasion was only part of the problem. Gold produced in the region could be registered and the tax paid at other treasuries. Merchants brought to Quito untaxed gold they had received in payment for their goods.[32] One should also note that the value of gold in relation to silver was rising through most of the period. This explains why silver (patacones or pieces of eight) should have replaced gold as the local medium of exchange by mid-century.[33] To what extent the premium on gold led to an improvement in the region's terms of trade must remain unclear in the absence of comparative price statistics. One may assume that it made some difference in the purchase of European goods, slaves, and Quito textiles.

The most visible signs of Popayán's commercial importance were the numerous stores that lined the plaza and adjacent streets. Some of these were leased on a short-term basis, while others represented permanent commercial establishments.[34] Selling over the counter was not the most respected aspect of the town's commerce. The essence of trade consisted in mobilizing goods over greater or shorter distances, in advancing credit, sometimes for a year or two, and in the trust that made such dealing over time and space possible. Personal ties underwrote trust, but that was not always enough. There were courts in town that enforced contracts and provided a remedy for nonperformance and delinquency. The notaries' registers recorded transactions and provided proof when needed.

At any time during the century Popayán had at least a score of merchants who were busy in the carrera de Cartagena, or long-distance trade. Of these a few usually stood out by reason of their resources and the prominence inevitably attached to their dealings. In the first decades of the century they were Alonso Hurtado del Águila and Diego de Victoria, from Toledo and Zamora respectively; at mid-century, Joseph de Morales Fravega, from Veri in the vicinity of Genoa, and Constantino de Aguiar, a Portuguese; and, at the turn of the eighteenth century, the brothers don Francisco and don Sebastián Torijano, from La Mancha, and don Sebastián Correa, from Cataluña. Most of these merchants made their way to Popayán via Cartagena. Some established themselves by marrying into a local family, while others who could not or did not choose this route relied on connections they had established in the course of their commercial careers. The term *carrera* (route or career) fits their activities quite well, since most of them were frequently on the road, some even combining the merchant's profession with the muleteer's. Throughout the century the town's merchants were immigrants. Expertise and connections acquired in the early stages of a merchant's career with Sevilla, Cartagena, and Quito may have played a role, particularly since imports from Europe formed a large part of the town's trade. Native sons were reluctant to enter commerce, presumably because estate management and mining were traditional upper-class pursuits, as were careers in the Church. This reluctance did not reflect an unwillingness to invest capital in trade, advanced to a merchant for a particular trip or as part of his working capital. The Church also loaned funds to merchants, directly or through intermediaries.[35]

Connections—and the trust they implied—were of utmost importance, since one had to rely on them in order to procure goods and make contracts for future delivery, especially if one could not be present personally. Hence a merchant always was a member of a network of commerce. Connections could be formalized through the device of a compañía (partnership) operating between different towns, but this was rare. It was more frequent to exchange powers of attorney or grant such powers for specific purposes, principally for contracting obligations and collecting debts. Another device frequently used by merchants was the establishment of mutual accounts, which served to reduce cash transactions—with cash often at a premium—and which were liquidated after a period. Commercial networks had both a lateral dimension, uniting merchants operating among Cartagena, Santa Fé de Bogotá, Popayán, and Quito, and a vertical one that tied a series of local and regional traders to a long-distance merchant whose residence and center of operation were in Popayán.

Merchants traded in everything.[36] Differences between them were based not on specialization but rather on their commercial radius. For both the long-distance merchant and the local trader stock items of trade were cloth, both Castilian and local, general merchandise, wine, and salt; they also sold cattle and foodstuffs. The local trader obtained his supplies from a merchant who often had one or two retail outlets himself. Larger transactions were made on credit, although the terms of credit were stated only infrequently. The sums involved in such credit transactions might reach two thousand pesos or more, often with interest previously discounted. It was the local traders' business to supply the miners and encomenderos with textiles, tools, and foodstuffs and to move farm products from the estates to the towns and mines. Estate owners often mortgaged their crops in return for advances of cash or kind. For example, they purchased textiles on credit to pay their workers. Tithe farming and collection frequently complemented the business of dealing in rural produce.

Granting credit and collecting debts were fundamental activities. Diego de Victoria's ledgers in 1620 contained sixty-nine debtors of note, in addition to the many smaller debtors carried on the books of his store. The volume of debts reflected the perennial shortage of cash characteristic of that time and place. It also had a seasonal dimension. Doctrineros, for instance, were paid twice a year, if the corregidor proved cooperative. Until their stipend was disbursed, they could draw on credit, ceding the stipend to a merchant, if need be. Perhaps a merchant would have a better chance of collecting from the corregidor than would a cleric. Gambling, like debts, was ubiquitous. It was no accident that Nicolás de la Rosa, who held the town's playing-card monopoly, was also one of the busiest debt collectors.

Besides their trading activities, merchants perforce had to engage in other pursuits not always directly related to their profession. They not only provided credit for sales they made but also lóaned cash sums. In some cases security was demanded; the curate of Almaguer in 1621 had to put up a slave. Such lack of trust in clerics may appear less surprising when it is recalled that the benefits of the clergy included immunity from prosecution for debts in a secular court.[37] Bullion was entrusted to merchants for safekeeping and cash deposited on loan. Sometimes such loans were in fact commercial investments and approximated the form of a limited partnership; in other cases they were straight loans with a term and interest specified.[38] Merchants were also dealers in bullion and currency. It was standard practice for a mine owner or his representative to sell untaxed gold dust to a merchant for silver pesos (patacones). The merchant was then obliged to pay the tax and have the gold smelted. By mid-century silver replaced gold dust as the local medium of exchange, to judge by its nearly exclusive use as the unit of account then.

The provision of transport was intimately tied to commerce. Some merchants ran their own mule trains between Quito, Popayán, and Honda on the Magdalena River, where goods from Cartagena were transshipped to Santa Fé de Bogotá and other parts of the interior. Other merchants entrusted their goods to professional carriers or to a colleague with mules to spare. Freight costs were high: a mule load of cloth between Quito and Popayán cost ten silver pesos, and a load of wine fifteen silver pesos at the carrier's risk, while rates between Honda and Popayán were double those from Quito. The risks of procuring transport were reduced by contracting beforehand for freight at a determinate time and place or by setting up a partnership with a carrier.[39]

Some merchants attached their fortunes resolutely to the town, buy-ing a house, settling, and marrying into an established family. Others remained on the road, as it were. Their attachment to their hometown was not purely sentimental. Rather they sent remittances, to support relatives and endow local shrines. Their careers appear only fleetingly in the documents, although some of these people may have held public office for a time. Among those who settled in town, none was more prominent during the first half of the century than Alonso Hurtado del Águila, who served several times as alcalde ordinario and governor's deputy.[40] Hurtado del Águila was a native of Toledo in Castile, where he was born around 1583. He made his way to Cartagena, where he married doña Ana de Aranaz, a niece of Francisco de Figueroa, one of Popayán's encomenderos and landed proprietors. By 1616 he was established in Popayán, renting eight stores in the plaza from don Ýñigo de Velasco for a period of three years. In the same year he for-malized an old partnership with Diego Daza, a native of Medina del Campo who had served in Callao and Guayaquil as a soldier before moving on to Quito and Popayán. Daza, four years younger than his partner, later became his son-in-law. He settled in Popayán but held an encomienda in Almaguer as well. Much of the time, however, he resided in Quito as the partnership's representative. Hurtado took care of affairs in Cartagena, where he had relatives (as he did also in Seville and Madrid). Sometimes he would go to Cartagena in person. On other occasions he would dispatch his nephew Alonso Hurtado, empowering him to buy merchandise costing up to five thousand pesos. As addi-tional security Diego de Victoria was empowered to look after the nephew and the goods should the need arise.

Neither holding office nor having an encomienda kept Hurtado from trading on both his own and the partnership's account. In fact, he was alleged to be one of Governor Bermúdez de Castro's close business collaborators during the latter's term.[41] The basis of his business was textiles, wine, and salt consigned from Quito by his partner Daza. Some idea of the volume involved can be gained by noting that the partnership regularly employed eighty mules moving between the two towns. Hurtado dealt in cattle, too, although more as a middleman who advanced funds and cloth to local dealers and contractors. Another line of business consisted of contracts for slaves to be delivered to several local mine operators; the terms were one-half down and one-half pay-able after one year. His business also served as a clearing-house for claims and as a collection agency for debts, ecclesiastics' stipends, and encomenderos' tributes. Selling at retail was an integral part of the enterprise and included woolens from both Quito and Spain, wax and wine, knives, tools, iron, and steel.

Hurtado also dealt in real estate in Popayán. In 1625 he sold a large part of his first wife's inheritance—farms (estancias), herds, houses, and a mine—to Captain Juan de Mera for 2,000 pesos. At the same time he exchanged properties with Christóbal de Mosquera and acquired mining claims in both Caloto (La Teta) and Almaguer. To work these mines, presumably, he acquired a gang of nineteen slaves who were part of a large consignment sold locally, paying 135 gold pesos for each. This enterprise was part of an effort to develop the mines of Caloto and rehabilitate those at Almaguer, a project that at the time dazzled people's imagination.[42]

A merchant's role was not limited to trade. Hurtado's position as a frequent officeholder, mentioned earlier, must have been an outgrowth of his expertise, the trust he enjoyed, and the connections he had established. Other evidence of the esteem in which he was held was the fact that he served as guardian (for instance, for Lorenzo Paz Maldonado's daughters) and was often named as executor in the wills of other merchants. Moreover, he was sometimes asked to serve as bondsman to vouch for the performance of officeholders or the discharge of obligations incurred in private contracts.

No other merchant approached Hurtado's prominence at the time, with the possible exception of Diego de Victoria, whose career was similar. Victoria came to Popayán in the 1610s, married a merchant's widow with two children, and established himself both in long-distance trade and in local retailing business. He became the town's fiel ejecutor in 1624 and ended his days as an encomendero, mine operator, and estate owner. His marriage and the fact that he had fought in the Pijao wars may well have contributed to his social acceptance.[43]

The careers and activities of other merchants, particularly those who worked within a more limited radius, remain rather more obscure. Alonso Belo and Martín de Huegonaga were local dealers, citizens of the town whose activities reached directly into the countryside. Belo was an illiterate immigrant who applied for local citizenship in the 1610s. He conducted a thriving cattle business and served as alcalde de la hermandad for the town in 1621 and 1624.[44] He had his own herd in the Patía region south of the town, but he was more a dealer than a cattleman. His dealings connected him to several merchants, among them Lorenzo Roldán, Hernando Durán, Antonio de Alegría, and Alonso Hurtado del Águila. Transactions with them were in cash and kind, often with generous terms for payment, and included cloth from

Quito as well as silk and taffeta, cotton mantles, domestic wine, machetes and hatchets, wax, and steel. Belo sold cattle on the hoof, sometimes for future delivery, in quantities ranging from two hundred steers to a thousand or more, to Alegría and Hurtado. The evidence makes it fairly clear that Belo was an itinerant trader with his base in Popayán. He rounded up cattle on an annual basis and also served as a distributor of various kinds of merchandise. In 1626 we find him negotiating for the purchase of a house in Quito, where he seems to have moved soon thereafter. Perhaps his case conforms to a pattern as yet insufficiently documented: that of the immigrant who makes a fortune, or at least the beginnings of one, in one region but moves on to another unless strong ties, such as marriage, keep him in his previous location.

Martín de Huegonaga did not even live in Popayán.[45] Although he was at times described as a vecino morador, at other occasions he appeared either as a morador in the mines of San Antonio or as with his herd at Esmita. Huegonaga's main business was moving supplies among the town, the estates, and the mines. He had dealings with such merchants as Diego de Victoria and Diego Sánchez de Luna, who sold him cloth, wax, and steel. He may have started out as a steward of don Juan de Gaviría's estate, which was certainly his stronghold between 1614 and 1624. He gave permission to sell produce (as don Juan de Gaviría's creditor), received wheat and cheeses in payment for debts, and took over debts the Gaviría family owed to other merchants. He advanced the money for Gaviría's daughter to make a trip to Pasto. By 1621, when don Juan de Gaviría died prematurely, the estate was mortgaged to Huegonaga for 4,800 gold pesos (the haciendas of Sotará had been sold to him in 1618, perhaps in fictitious fashion). The heirs—don Juan's mother, wife, and minor son—agreed, after some wrangling, "considering the worry caused by lawsuits, their doubtful outcome, and their costs," to cede the haciendas and the encomienda of Guachicono to Huegonaga for three years, giving Huegonaga the usufruct of the Indian miners' labor and of four harvests. Huegonaga's nephew, Captain Juan de Huegonaga, inherited and expanded his uncle's position. In 1634 he became a citizen (vecino morador), and in 1636 he was even elected as alcalde ordinario. His son, Juan de Huegonaga Salazar, served as corregidor de naturales and also as alcalde ordinario, and in 1677 he bought the office of alguacil mayor. His prestige was enhanced by his marriage to doña Ana de Deza Fernández Rico. Her brother, Captain Bernabé Fernández Rico, with whom Huegonaga entered into a partnership, had married doña María Manuela de Belalcázar y Aragón, of the adelantado's family. Huegonaga's three daughters—he had no sons—joined the convent of La Encarnación, and with his death in 1679 the family came to an end. Nevertheless, the Huegonagas had nearly completed the cycle of social ascent characteristic of the town's more successful merchants. What was the society they joined like?

3. Spaniards, Indians, and Negroes

Estate owners, miners, and merchants, along with the higher clergy and crown officials, ran the town. They were members of the república de españoles—the Spanish community. The Indian population was divided into a rural and an urban component. As the república de indios the Indians formed a separate and unequal community that nevertheless was joined in multiple ways to that of the Spaniards. But these official divisions ignored the presence of new social groupings that did not fit the old categories. As slaves, the Blacks who worked on estates, in mines, and in households were the easiest element to deal with. They formed a growing part of the working population. More important still, there was a group not easily defined, the mixed bloods. Their status was ambiguous, described by its imprecision, as it were. Spaniards married and cohabited with Indians and Negroes. Their descendants were not Indians (and would not pay tribute as such) nor necessarily slaves. Some were vecinos. Others with houses in town were simply moradores. There were also many temporary residents (estantes). This chapter describes the circumstances, status, and relative position of these ethnic and social groups, albeit with greater attention to those at the top.

During the seventeenth century, Popayán had approximately 150 permanent Spanish households. A household could include, besides the immediate family, a large retinue of servants, either recruited from the native population or Black slaves. Women were needed for daily chores and men for such work as taking care of horses and mules. The number of domestic slaves was high. Where they were encountered as part of a household, four was a typical figure and eight or ten no rarity. A nun's dowry could include a slave girl. In the absence of a census, only these impressionistic figures were available.[1]

How many people lived in Popayán? If we assume the generous figure of 10 people attached to each Spanish household (5 would be too little, given the number of servants; 10 may be too large), we arrive at a figure of 1,500. To this we must add the clergy, the moradores not counted as contributing vecinos, and a number of floating residents.

Then there were three groups of Indians attached to the town although settled separately. In 1607 there were 350 of them. A conservative estimate thus yields approximately 2,000 inhabitants of the town itself.[2]

The Indian population of the countryside numbered about 10,000 in 1607. They lived in some thirty-five villages and were allotted to twenty-four encomenderos. By 1637 their number had fallen to less than 6,000.[3] African slaves replaced Indian labor but did not compensate for the loss in numbers. In 1628, 250 slaves were reported working in the mines. An incomplete census of the mining district around Popayán, made in 1659 and more to be trusted than the earlier figure, listed 313 slaves.[4]

A realistic picture of the town's hinterland must include the two satellite towns of Caloto and Almaguer and the mountain region of Tierradentro, inhabited by the Páez Indians. Caloto and Almaguer had scarcely thirty vecinos, some of whom in fact habitually resided in Popayán. Caloto had no Indian population worth mentioning, aside from the Indians on encomiendas in Tierradentro. On the other hand, it included a growing Black and half-caste population scattered in the mining settlements and attached to them. The district of Almaguer counted 1,500 natives in the 1630s. In sum, the area of the three towns of Popayán, Caloto, and Almaguer—essentially the present-day departamento of Cauca—had then approximately 200 families of Spanish extraction. The urban population of 2,000 to 3,000 inhabitants was complemented by a rural population of 10,000 to 15,000 inhabitants.[5]

The dualism of the two separate yet complementary republics of Spaniards and Indians was the dominant ordering ideal of society in the Indies. The Indians provided the material support for the Spaniards, who in turn supplied spiritual sustenance, the "pasto espiritual," in the telling phrase of the period. This image of separation and mutual dependence does not falsify the ordering ideal of crown and Church frequently invoked in royal cédulas, yet it hardly does justice to the complexities of colonial society in town and countryside. The lines of demarcation among the racial categories of Spaniard, Indian, and Negro were blurred. Members of each group resided as neighbors in the same section of town. In the countryside, residential restrictions on Spaniards or Blacks were not enforced. They applied, at any rate, only to the area proper of an Indian village.[6]

Estates and mines contributed to the breakdown of segregation. By the eighteenth century the shrinking Indian settlements offered little resistance to penetration by non-Indians. Reconstitution as resguardos (reservations) had not halted the process. Especially in the lower Cauca region, such Indian settlements had become mere shells by then, inhabited by non-Indians who leased the land or simply used it.[7] In town, individuals of each race practiced trades and crafts without distinctions. Concubinage, as well as marriage across racial lines, was a fact of life in Popayán. The frequency of concubinage is documented by the repeated accusations against officials who did nothing to prevent it (how should they have done it?). In more telling fashion it shows in the recognition extended in a will or in bequests made to illegitimate offspring. Intermarriage was no rarity either, as is evident from marriage and baptismal records, although its frequency remains to be studied. In 1646, for instance, Juana Rodríguez, india, widow of Lucas de Ortega, color pardo (colored), set up a capellanía under the auspices of the Dominican monastery. Some sodalities (cofradías) recruited members without regard for race or social station.[8]

There were no clear-cut racial boundaries. Still, the town was characterized by legal and social distinctions, expressed in obligations, privileges, and exclusions that were formulated in terms of racial identity. In this sense the terms *Spaniard* and *Indian,* despite their ambiguity, retained their significance.

The town's Spanish population consisted of vecinos (town citizens), a vague category in which one might include all those called up in a muster or the heads of households contributing to a levy or making a contribution to the cathedral's construction.[9] There was apparently no official register of vecinos. Among these vecinos were mestizos, offspring of a mixed union (legitimate or legitimized), a fact of no legal bearing but not overlooked. For instance, don Francisco de Belalcázar was a legitimized son of the province's founder. The chronicler Fray Pedro de Aguado commented on his tardiness in aiding Spanish settlements under Indian attack by noting that he was a mestizo and did not have his father's sense of honor.[10] It is characteristic that a Basque immigrant, defendant in a lawsuit, belittled a witness's deposition by noting that he was mestizo, although he happened to be an encomendero.[11]

The division of the town's Spanish inhabitants, at the beginning of the century, into vecinos encomenderos or feudatarios and vecinos moradores was reflected in the elections of alcaldes ordinarios. This division still prevailed toward the end of the century, but by that time the vecinos moradores were called domiciliarios. A merchant was often called a vecino mercader, although for practical purposes he was a vecino morador. Quite a few merchants were not vecinos. In 1676, a governor ordered a score of merchants to leave town within six days because they, as natives of Spain, held no license to be in the Indies. Their appeal to the audiencia of Quito pointed out other Spaniards in town who suffered from the same defect. The tribunal resolved the matter by asking each one to post guarantees and pay for the requisite license and exemption, as Joseph de Morales Fravega, a Genoese, did in 1680.[12]

Within the Spanish stratum the encomenderos constituted a privileged rank. Their privileges and duties included preferential access to native labor, a claim to Indian tribute (five silver pesos per tributary in 1668), and a special military obligation. The position could be transmitted to an heir only once, that is, it was good for two lifetimes, but this limitation could be waived. Because of the exalted position of the group, we know more about them than about any other part of the town's population. An encomendero was supposed to be equipped with arms and a horse and to serve in time of attack. This obligation was affirmed in Popayán as late as the 1670s, when an English invasion appeared to threaten the coast. By that time the encomenderos were nearly worthless in a military emergency, even though most of them were militia captains. Two generations earlier, during the Pijao wars, there were few captains but many encomenderos equipped and ready to serve. But in the 1670s nearly all of them claimed various ailments that impeded their personal participation in the defense of Buenaventura. A cabildo abierto was held to discuss military preparations. The town's procurador general stressed that only men apt for work and resistant to disease should be sent. The order would have excluded the encomenderos and merchants, who because of their delicate constitutions easily fell sick. The maestre de campo, who was to lead the expedition, asked for at least some encomenderos to serve under him, adding that "despite their delicate physique they make up in presumption what they lack in military training."[13]. While they held no fief, they were called vecinos feudatarios because of their military obligation. One of their number was customarily elected senior alcalde, but late in the seventeenth century the practice fell into disuse. Besides commanding prestige, encomenderos held a privileged economic position. They could directly use the labor of the Indians entrusted to them. This practice, known as servicio personal, was prohibited early in New Spain and elsewhere but continued in the province throughout the century, even though ordinances prohibiting it had been issued in 1637.[14]

The encomenderos' privileges did not lead to the formation of an aristocracy. Encomienda proved too infirm a foundation. One reason was the decline of the native population. Encomiendas shrank in size; some villages disappeared completely. Encomiendas differed greatly in size, so that some produced sizable incomes, others only a pittance. Hereditary claims existed, but their consideration was not automatic.

In theory, succession was possible only for two lifetimes, with one extension. But more extensions could be arranged, even in advance, for payment of a fee. Doña María Magdalena de Noguera in her will recounted her efforts to preserve her husband's "inheritance"—his encomiendas of Guambía and Carlosama—for her son don Francisco Ventura de Belalcázar. The effort was successful, at a cost of 4,700 gold pesos. Her husband at his death left more than 30,000 pesos in debts. Her own fortune went to preserve his, at the expense of the children of her first marriage. If a confirmed heir to an encomienda died, the expense was for nought, since the encomienda would be vacant again. To hedge against this eventuality, clauses that allowed the designation of an heir would be admitted, for a fee. Since encomenderos were habitually in the clutches of creditors, ways were found to create negotiable assets. The usufruct of encomiendas, that is, of the Indians' labor, could be transferred temporarily, to pay for debts.[15] Yet none of these devices were of much avail.

No self-assured aristocracy could exist where there was no military challenge, too little security, and a need for unremitting entrepreneurial effort. What survived was aristocratic claims. These claims were not inherent in a status group: they were invoked individually, not defended collectively. The long-term importance of the institution of encomienda rested, then, on individual claims to consideration and the uses they were put to.

An encomienda would remain in the same family for several generations, passing from father to son or son-in-law. A conspicuous example was the Velasco family, which held the encomienda of Coconuco for five generations by direct male succession, from the 1550s until 1706. The Belalcázar family held on to the encomienda of Guambía in less direct fashion.[16] Occasionally fierce competition would ensue when an encomienda fell vacant. In other cases someone would quietly amass several encomiendas, as did Captain don Joseph Hurtado del Águila. He acquired three for his son, don Lucas Gonzalo del Águila, in a short while.[17] That he could do so demonstrates don Joseph's local standing and his ability to persuade the governor of his son's merits. It also shows the difficulties the Council of the Indies had in keeping track of such local transactions: the Council invalidated two of these grants, after nearly twenty years had passed. As late as the 1710s a long-drawn-out competition was waged over possession of the encomienda of Ambaló, which was held by the Mera Paz Maldonado family until 1706. The struggle was between Captain Juan Álvarez de Uria, a Spanish immigrant who had married doña Ysabel de Torijano y Ubillus, and don Martín Prieto de Tovar, a newcomer from Tunja and Muzo in New Granada but well-connected locally. He was the son-in-law of don Francisco de Arboleda and also the father-in-law of don Christóbal de Mosquera. As credentials Captain Álvarez offered his wife's merits in lieu of his own. He asserted in his probanza (attested proof of merits) that her "relatives and ancestors the Velascos, Belalcázares, Aragones, Nogueras, and Ubillus . . . are among the first and principal personages" of the town. In due time Governor Bolaños awarded him the encomienda as "benemérito competente," over the opposing faction's protests.[18]

This battle points up a phenomenon characteristic of the town's Creole society: its continual replenishment by immigrants. Most of them came from Spain, some from other parts of the Indies. They married into local families and were absorbed into local society. Most of these men (there were no women, apparently) came as merchants or officeholders, accompanied by relatives and hangers-on. Not all of them were successful and not all of them managed to found families that endured over several generations. But quite a few did. Around 1700, members of the town's upper stratum included several first-generation immigrants. Others were descendants of earlier immigrants; only a few were direct descendants in the male line of conquerors and first settlers.[19]

However, this apparent discontinuity in the town's upper stratum is deceptive. Descent was reckoned bilaterally, in both the male and the female line. Probanzas and the choice of names indicate this clearly. The merits of the first generation thus accrued to a host of descendants, of whom only a few could be rewarded suitably with the grant of an encomienda. Other pretenders to lineage would have to be content, unless given an office or some other recompense, with being "noble" citizens and with the title of don, a form of address increasingly adopted by mid-century. The phenomenon is revealing because until then this form of address was extremely rare. Among the town's encomenderos, for instance, only don Juan de Gaviría and don Ýñigo de Velasco (but not his father) had laid claim to it earlier, aside from the adelantado Belalcázar's descendants.

Wealth contributed in many ways to the definition of status. A position, whether an office or even an encomienda, could be bought. Buying or building a house on the plaza also enhanced one's standing. Bestowing a substantial dowry was less reliable: a father could not know if his son-in-law would turn out to be a good investment. The sumptuous funeral of don Francisco Ventura de Belalcázar y Aragón, last descendant of the adelantado in the male line, gave status where it might seem no more was needed. Beyond the grave, there were endowments to speed a soul's redemption—but also to secure the position of the living. Churches and chapels were built to honor a benefactor's name and his lineage. Endowments of masses (capellanías) for the benefit of a soul were designed to yield benefits for one's descendants also. The family's standing could not be maintained on the basis of past accomplishments alone. Even descendants of conquistadors were imprisoned for their debts, as was Captain Diego de Alvarado Ampudia, great-grandson of one of the town's founders. He was clapped into jail several times as a hardened debtor, over his protest.[20]

Below the class of noble, wealthy, and "well-deserving" citizens came the mass of the town's Spanish population, not undifferentiated, to be sure, but less visible to us in their activities. Partial exceptions to this were the merchants and the clergy. The former were an important and conspicuous element in town, but they were not a cohesive group and displayed little continuity beyond one generation. In this setting wealth translated rather easily into rank, as was evident in the careers of Alonso Hurtado, Diego Daza, and Diego de Victoria, who were all of one generation.[21] But the socially mobile merchant did not apprentice his sons to trade. Evidently sons-in-law or nephews did not take over the business either, although this was a common enough pattern in Spanish America.[22] Generally, merchants who did not personally engage in retailing were most likely to improve their social standing. Storekeepers, peddlers, and petty dealers belonged to a different social category, even though there were numerous transactions, based on a familiarity with business dealings and common usage, between them and the bona fide merchants. Many of the smaller merchants who ran businesses in town did not have strong ties to the community. The testaments made by a few of these men may give us some idea of their lives.

Lope de Labayen, an unmarried merchant and muleteer from Navarre, owned a house, two town lots, six slaves, and a mule train of forty-one mules. He left his fortune to revive the defunct cofradía of the Holy Sacrament in the Cathedral, together with a capellanía of thirteen masses sung each year for the benefit of his soul and the souls of his brothers in the cofradía.[23] Another merchant, Gerónimo Potes, from Old Castile, also a bachelor, who traveled customarily between Cartagena and Popayán, carried his entire capital of 5,700 gold pesos in merchandise. His executors, two other local merchants, Pedro Muñoz and Gerónimo de Toro, were to forward the proceeds to his home town with legacies destined for his brothers, the town's orphaned girls, and an endowment of masses.[24] Hernando Durán, from Cáceres in Extremadura, held most of his capital in goods and cash, but he also owned a small house in Popayán, where he kept a housekeeper. For one year he even served as alcalde ordinario. His parents, who still lived in Cáceres, were to be his heirs. For the benefit of his soul he instituted twenty-nine masses in eight different towns in Spain and the Indies.[25]

The clergy played a vital role in the town's daily life. It did not constitute a uniform element in the population, even though it was a legally distinct group with its own special privileges.[26] There were secular and regular clergy, those recruited from afar and native sons (hijos de la tierra), priests who held a benefice and others who did not. At the beginning of the century they were hard-pressed financially—at least this was their common complaint.[27] The limited yield of the tithe in the bishopric and a declining native population, a portion of whose tribute supported the doctrineros of Indian parishes (doctrinas), would seem to bear out the complaint. In addition, the income of many priests and sacristans in the diocese had to be supplemented by the provincial treasury to bring it up to the level guaranteed by the crown. As clergy, then, they were poverty-stricken. But clerics were also men of affairs who could better their condition.

At the beginning of the century, the local clergy included such men as the dean don Francisco Vélez de Zúñiga, noted earlier as a mining entrepreneur. The beneficiado Alonso de Belalcázar made a living by dealing in real estate, aided no doubt by his position as cura doctrinero of the Indians attached to the town. Some of his income was bequeathed to him by his parishioners.[28] Many ecclesiastics hustled to make ends meet. As the cabildo complained, they charged fees for burials up to what the traffic would bear and beyond what the fee schedule of New Granada permitted.[29] Priests also dealt in cloth and cattle and acted as local retailers.[30] Such activities were inevitable as long as the religious life did not provide a sufficient livelihood.

The clergy's material independence increased in the course of the century. This is evident from the mortgages the Dominicans and Franciscans held on urban and rural real estate. The Jesuits, instead of seeking a fixed income, acquired and managed properties that would yield a profit. Individual income among the clergy also increased as the volume of endowments rose. The cathedral chapter in 1625, for example, disposed of four capellanías that yielded an income of 142 gold pesos. In 1701 the chapter as a whole held thirteen capellanías worth 883 silver pesos a year, a fourfold increase in value.[31] Some patrimony was of course a precondition for taking holy orders, as was a dowry for entering the nunnery. But the sums involved or the property set aside for the purpose rarely exceeded 1,000 pesos, which would yield only a pittance at 5 percent.[32] The gap between aspirations and income, exacerbated by the low tithe yield and the shrinking number of Indian contributors, was filled in the course of the century by capellanías, endowments that stipulated a certain number of masses to be said by the material beneficiary in return for a specified annual income, the principal of which was usually secured by a mortgage. These mortgages on income-bearing property could also serve to keep estates intact, as units of management, supporting the ecclesiastical career of heirs through annuities in the form of capellanías.[33]

The town's Spanish population merged at one end of the spectrum into the half-caste and Indian population. Artisans and small farmers were of both Spanish and Indian extraction. Simón García de Santa Cruz, a vecino born in Quito who was married and had six children, owned an estancia in Quilcacé and a potrero (cattle pasture) in Calocé. The potrero was cared for by Juan, an Indian who lived there with his wife and four children.[34] We do not know how many ostensibly Spanish small holders of this type there were. A considerable number of Indians also held land in this outright fashion, some in the immediate vicinity of Popayán—for example, next to the ejido—others near such Indian settlements as Chisquío or Timbío. Don Andrés Ambito, cacique of the locally-born Indians of Popayán, owned a cattle estancia stocked with fifty head of cattle and a quantity of horses with his own brand. The estancia was bordered by a property belonging to María, a mulata. Don Andrés owned other pieces of land too. So did Diego Sinay of the parcialidad of indios yanaconas. He also owned horses and a yoke of oxen marked with his own brand.[35]

Among the artisans were shoemakers and tailors, carpenters, masons, blacksmiths, silversmiths, and locksmiths. Some artisans, such as the silversmith Juan Álvarez Quiñones, were men of substance.[36] They were sometimes described as master carpenter (Francisco González Leuro) or master tailor (Gerónimo Garrido). In other cases, they were labeled as journeymen. A person's trade might simply be added after the name—Juan Criollo, herrero (blacksmith); Miguel Ortiz, platero (silversmith)—or might even provide the surname, as in Marcos el sastre (tailor) or Martín Zapatero (shoemaker). A person so named was most likely of Indian origin. Among the town's Indian population were a number of artisans, most of them journeymen, although several worked on their own account.[37] As well as the customary tailors and shoemakers, there were chair makers, brick makers, button makers, bricklayers, a silversmith, and a carpenter. Artisans had their helpers. Master carpenter Francisco González Leuro, when building a house for Diego Daza, hired Agustín Hernández as his assistant for two years.

He promised to pay him two hundred pesos and to give him a suit made of Castilian cloth, a pair of shoes, silk stockings, ten yards of local wool cloth, and a bull (indulgence) of the Santa Cruzada at one peso. He also agreed to maintain him and care for him in case of sickness. In addition, the carpenter used the services of Luisillo, an Indian helper, and promised to teach his trade to Diego Daza's slave Bartolomé.[38]

The town's Indian population was assimilated to the Spaniards' ways. Indians held property outright and worked in many trades. In other respects, Indians led a separate existence. One group, belonging mostly to the parcialidad of the mitimaes, lived in La Rinconada, a location one-quarter league from town. Today it is still known as Yanaconas. Others lived in the town proper or dispersed over the countryside, some as resident laborers in the estancias of Spaniards and others with their own herds and estancias. Many came to Popayán in the 1560s from the area of Quito, Latacunga, and Riobamba and had been given land to settle on by Bishop Juan del Valle. Common to the 344 individual Indians counted in 1607 and included in the three parcialidades of indios yanaconas, mitimaes, and criollos was the fact that they were not subject to a cacique or an encomendero. Each of the 94 tributaries was liable to pay a tribute of two pesos set in 1607, to be collected by their own officials, who were appointed by the visitador at the same time. The appointed Indian officials included two caciques and one gobernador; there were also a number of lesser officials, such as two alcaldes de los naturales, one alguacil, and one mandón (orderly).[39]

The town's Indians were new to the region, like the Spaniards. They had come to Popayán as their auxiliaries. Some of them were recruited in organized fashion, like the indios yanaconas and mitimaes. Their name indicates their origins in the former Inca empire, as yanaconas (serfs or servants unattached to a territorial kin group) or as mitimaes (transplanted colonists). Others had drifted into the area. These were thrown together into one comprehensive parcialidad, for the corregidor's convenience, since he had to count them. All these Indians were connected to the Spaniards through their occupations as workers, farmers, and artisans and their participation in the town's life. The tailor Diego Sinay, for example, was mayordomo to the cofradía of Rosario. They also shared the Spaniards' notions of civilization and civilized life, as is evident from their making of testaments. Besides providing the Spanish settlers with trained and docile workers, they were a kind of contact group that facilitated the acculturation of the region's native Indians. Multiple ties of marriage and business linked the "urban" Indians and the area's native population. Don Diego Guamán Pichuchu, the head cacique of the indios yanaconas, married doña Ana Coconuco, whose name indicates her origin in the tribe and encomienda of Coconuco. At least eight of the thiry-five married men in the parcialidad of yanaconas took wives from the town's district (most likely there were more, since in many cases the wife's surname is not indicated). Diego Sinay the tailor dealt with many encomienda Indians, among them the caciques of Cubaló and Coconuco. He sold them horses, cattle, clothing, furniture, and salt. Despite such ties and many similarities of actual and legal condition, the rural Indian's situation was different from his urban cousin's. The difference lay in the institution of encomienda and the host of customary arrangements that accompanied it.

Another new ethnic group was the Africans, whose lives were commonly circumscribed by the institution of slavery. The number of slaves was constantly augmented by new arrivals, although it was also diminished by manumissions, which were often motivated by sentiment.[40] The slaves formed the true permanent "working class" of the town and the countryside. In town each respectable household had slaves, as much by necessity as for pretension. In the countryside slaves occasionally served as caretakers on rural properties or provided labor for sugar plantations large and small. But their main contribution lay in mining.

The large-scale use of slaves to work the mines of Popayán cannot be dated with certainty. The example of Bishop Agustín de la Coruña, who invested in slaves so as to bequeath them to the convent of nuns in 1592, apparently was not followed at the time. Christóbal de Mosquera was one of the town's first encomenderos to shift to slave labor in mining. In 1626 he bought thirteen slaves who were part of a larger consignment then being sold in Popayán. This was the largest number of slaves bought in the town until then.[41] By 1633 he had a fully developed mining operation with waterworks and canals at La Teta, where forty slaves worked. In his house he kept six slaves. In his will he exhorted his wife not to sell the enterprise but to consult with the coexecutor, the dean don Francisco Vélez de Zúñiga, about hiring a mine administrator. Apparently Mosquera was his own administrator. He suggested she place five thousand gold pesos in the dean's safekeeping to purchase yet more slaves.[42] The dean himself was no stranger to mining. In 1634 he entered into a partnership with Andrés Martín Rayo. Each invested twenty slaves in a mine in Gelima that Rayo was to manage. The dean's slaves later formed the basis for the Jesuits' mining enterprise in the region.[43] The transition from Indian to slave labor can be seen in the partnership between the merchant Lorenzo Roldán and Captain Juan de Mera, encomendero of Ambaló. While the former contributed twenty slaves with their tools, the latter provided ten Indian miners and the mining and water rights he held at La Teta.[44]

Without greater knowledge of the internal organization of mining, it is difficult to describe precisely the changes brought about by the shift to slave labor. Still, a few general points can be made. Technology was not much affected, except that a larger and more mobile force could undertake such projects as stream diversion and large waterworks. The availability of slaves and their mobility meant that expansion into the sparsely inhabited coastal zone became possible. Earlier coastal incursions did not lead to permanent settlement. The arrival of slaves in large numbers was a cause as well as a consequence of expansion.[45] The organization of mining itself did not change much, but since the mine owner lived further from his mine, greater responsibilities fell to his administrator. In quite a few cases, relatives of the owner held this position. Slavery made the mining camps more self-contained both economically and socially. Often they produced their own food supply of maize and plantains on local plots, supplemented by meat and salt brought in from the outside. Slave women cooked and did planting and harvesting. The ratio of women and children to men was higher than required by these needs. While sex ratios were unbalanced and some mining camps were almost entirely male, the overall proportion of women to men was about one to three.[46] Marriage between a free Black or mulatto woman and a slave miner was not uncommon. Separation between work site and residence was less frequent for slaves than for Indians, who had to leave their settlements periodically to work in distant mining areas. Slave camps, it appears, had some degree of social stability. But how did the slaves' lot compare with that of the rural Indian population?

Spanish settlers saw the Indian population as a source of cheap labor. The crown took its obligation to the Indian community seriously, as an undertaking that engaged the king's conscience and his sense of what was his own. His officials were to look after the Indians' spiritual well-being and provide for a well-ordered life, to say nothing of the more mundane interest of keeping the settlers in check. The conflict between crown and colonists was resolved by a series of decrees that tried to protect the Indians. This "native" legislation gives us only a limited view of Indian life—its traditions and customs—and the effect on it of the Spanish presence. Still, the ordinances throw some light on Indian life. In particular they describe the relation between the town and the countryside, indicating the presence of the Indians and their functions within the region, although not saying much about daily existence.[47]

Compact settlement was a prime concern. The natives were to settle in compact settlements (pueblos), in "houses with a cross over the door, with courtyards, gardens, and streets in the manner of the Spaniards, a church, a plaza with a cross in its middle and a stream of water running through." What was the rationale for this order of things? Confined to towns, the Indians could be maintained in "Christian order" (policía). This meant religious instruction twice weekly for children and once a week for adults. Their vices could be curbed, in particular drunkenness; idolatry could not return. Nor would they die without benefit of confession. In this, as in many other regulations, laws reflected general postulates of crown policy vis-à-vis its Indian subjects. A corollary of this policy was the separation of the Indian and non-Indian population. Spaniards were not allowed to enter Indian villages except in passing, nor were mestizos or mulattoes permitted to live there, to say nothing of Negroes.

Not all rules about settlement or segregation were carried out in practice. In Tierradentro, on the fringe of the area under Spanish control, Indians still lived in a dispersed fashion. Some Indians were permanently settled on Spanish estancias. In a number of cases these estancias were in close proximity to Indian villages, thus directly violating the law. Communal lands were supposed to extend one league from the village, and cattle herding was prohibited within a radius of a league and a half. Yet another exception to the policy of separation was made by encomenderos who had fields inside Indian settlements.[48] In actual fact the two phenomena (Spanish presence in an Indian village and Indian proximity to or presence in a Spanish estancia) are hard to distinguish except by their antecedents—for example, the transplanting of an Indian community or group from one area to another by an encomendero.[49]

In its consequences the system of labor conscription also ran counter to the policy of concentration. Its effect was that Indian miners were often scattered over the countryside instead of doing their stint in mining settlements. In many cases labor service involved the families of those conscripted, too, and as a consequence children born on estancias were never registered with the doctrinero of the settlement. Proprietors often proved reluctant to part with their workers so that others could take their place as the law stipulated. The ordinances recognized that Indian workers on distant estancias could not attend church or receive religious instruction. Consequently, they entrusted responsibility for religious instruction to the proprietor or his administrator, making him, as it were, an honorary doctrinero.

Dress regulations also segregated the Indian population. "If Indians are allowed to dress in the Spanish manner, with long hair, and to carry knives and other weapons, they will turn out haughty and hard to subject to serfdom [servidumbre] . . . going to other places they become indistinguishable from mestizos since they are fluent [muy ladinos] in Spanish." Hence, they were forbidden to wear Spanish dress. They were instructed to wear white trousers and shirts, to go barefoot, and to let their hair reach only to the ears, "as in Peru." Nor were they to carry knives or to have weapons in their houses. The tenor of the regulation indicates that the phenomenon of "passing" was common. It also reflects the frequency of absenteeism—that is, of Indians removing themselves permanently from the place where they were supposed to pay tribute.[50]

The basis for the continued and separate existence of Indian communities was possession of land. Each village controlled an area within a radius of one league from its center, with the boundary of the reservation (resguardo) shown by markers. The land had no proprietor and could not be alienated. As stated in the 1692 ordinances, Indians could sell land only with audiencia approval. Before that, license to sell from the corregidor or governor was deemed enough. Such sales, especially by caciques, were not infrequent, but they required a license, testimony about the land's value (small), and its utility (little).[51] Land sales show, despite the possible element of fiction involved, that the encomienda Indians understood and used the concept of private property. This fact was recognized in legal transactions. Deals indicate as much: the cacique of Piagua, for instance, sold land he had inherited from his father, who in turn had bought it from don Andrés Cobo de Figueroa, an encomendero.[52] In another case García Chapa endowed a capellanía with the proceeds from the sale of a herd of cattle and a piece of land he owned in Chisquío.[53] Hence we find that among the Indians "communal" possession of land coexisted with private property outside the reservation. The extent of such individual holdings and the effect they had on land use or the cohesion of the settlements are not known.

Tribute and labor obligation were the hallmark of Indian status. They were distinct obligations, settled in law and regulated by a succession of legal ordinances. Regulations did change with circumstances, yet the progression of encomienda, repartimiento, and peonage thought to be characteristic of the centers of empire did not exist in Popayán. From the settlers' perspective, customary claims to Indian labor existed and were defended tenaciously as usage. From an Indian perspective (or that of the caciques), there were also time-honored and convenient ways of allocating labor and of handling obligations. What is missing, here, is the evidence that would allow us to understand the functioning of the system in detail. Yet, even so, regulations do give some idea of what things were like.[54]

Labor conscription was only one means to obtain workers. Another means was slavery; a third was the market with its free exchange of goods and services, in which Indians participated, as in the land market. It is the coexistence of these three systems that occasionally appears confusing, since one household might contain at the same time slaves (perhaps both Indian and Black), Indian servants doing their stint, and people working under a free contract. The system of tribute and draft labor was important because it distributed status, burdens, and benefits in a specific way and produced a vested interest in maintaining separate Indian settlements. Its justification rested on what was considered the Indians' natural leisure and laziness, which would lead to other vices and a return to idolatry if not checked. Its economic rationale was that Indians did not produce a surplus that could be appropriated and marketed. Hence they had to be compelled to do so, under settler management.

The ordinances established a series of vital distinctions, governing who was in charge, who was to work and when, how much work was to be done, and what the pay was to be. As to the beneficiaries, there was a margin of discretion. Initially the encomenderos were the automatic beneficiaries, later the customary ones. It is clear that there was some room for adjustment among corregidor, settlers, and even caciques, particularly in regard to the allocation of labor. The most important group was the useful Indians, that is, all males between eighteen and fifty years of age who paid tribute and hence belonged to the pool of labor available to be drawn on. Caciques and a few other officials were exempt and were not counted as a part of the labor pool (gruesa) to be drawn on. Repeated and precise counts of population were fundamental for the functioning of this system, with corregidor and cacique presumably in possession of the figures and the doctrineros responsible for keeping matters up to date between counts.

A second important part of the ordinances was the tasa (schedule), which stated specific work obligations and tasks, the rate of pay, working conditions, and the proportion of useful Indians to be allocated for different purposes. The tasa shows the declining importance of mining in comparison to agriculture. In 1607 every encomendero still had a specific quota for mining that took a fourth of the labor pool.

By 1668 this had shrunk to one-tenth of the pool, and by 1692 it disappeared.[55] In agriculture, draft labor continued to be important. In 1607 the corregidor could simply assign three men for each fanega of wheat sown and twenty men for each fanega of maize, with no limit. In 1667, one-third of the labor pool could be assigned to work in agriculture. As we have seen, agriculture functioned with a nucleus of resident labor. But this was insufficient, so laborers, cowboys, shepherds, and swineherds were drafted from the pool. During the planting and harvesting season more people were needed. For a maximum of seventy days (the length of period was a matter of contention, since it obviously coincided with the harvest period in general) all useful Indians might have to come to do weeding, threshing, and so on. Young and old were also welcome but could expect only food, not pay (in 1668). Clearly this was not attractive enough, and by 1692 they were to be paid one-half real daily.[56]

Tribute was a separate matter. It was in effect a head tax collected from all who belonged to the pool. It was stated in money, although in 1607 it still included two hens and one pound of cabuya as a relic of earlier tribute schedules. Yet the money amount (four gold pesos in 1607, seven silver pesos in 1668 and 1692) served mainly for accounting purposes. Ordinances included price schedules for items of local production, to serve in lieu of cash; they also included wage schedules that stipulated the mode of payment. Occasions are documented when cash changed hands (in the presence of a notary), yet the tendency to do without cash, to discount payments against one other, must have been strong. Notions of what is fit and due depend not on an exchange of cash but on a system of accounting that need not be on paper. It is not the worker who is shortchanged necessarily, but the historian.

Under local conditions it would have been difficult to move Indians into an exchange economy based on money, through tribute and wages. Cash was often scarce. The coming of the silver peso may have made a difference, but smaller units were actually more important. How current they were we do not know. It is clear, however, that Indians were participants in an exchange economy beyond their status as draftees. Some became gold miners on their own account. Others owned cattle herds or grew sugar cane (and manufactured guarapo as a potent drink for sale as well as for their own consumption). They baked bread at home under the auspices of the encomienda and then sold it over a wide area for cash.[57] What remains unclear is the extent of their participation and the degree to which it was systematic rather than incidental.

Besides conscription for mining and agriculture, the Indian com-

munities were burdened with additional obligations. Each was supposed to maintain roads, bridges, and tambos (roadside hostels) in the
area. In the encomienda of Guanacas, this was the inhabitants' main
responsibility. There the encomendero became the concessionaire of
the pass route and charged a fee for its use. A variant of this obligation
was recruitment for public works in town. The arrangement current
at the end of the century was for the corregidor to call up men for one
week's work. Earlier (1668), one-tenth of the labor pool was destined
for this purpose and was to be assigned by the corregidor without
favoritism. In an earlier arrangement, favored vecinos could claim the
one-week services by virtue of being included in a listing established
at the time of the visita. Sometimes new beneficiaries who could procure royal cédulas in their favor were added. Only on occasion was
cheap labor available to all vecinos, as when a governor would recruit
Indian labor to rebuild the houses of the town's poor and needy.[58]

To what extent did the actual tribute and labor arrangements follow
regulations or diverge from them? One has to distinguish here between
arrangements that became customary, although they contradicted regulations, and those that were considered abuses, although the distinction
in fact may be difficult to make. The substitution of labor for tribute
was one custom that proved difficult to eradicate, although it was
equated in legislation and ordinances with servicio personal, work performed by a tributary for the encomendero without the corregidor's
intervention or a formal contract and hence liable to lead to excesses
by the encomendero. The persistence of the practice is attested in a
petition of 1669 from the caciques of Popayán to the Council of the
Indies, asking it to sanction the continued commutation of tribute for
labor in the encomenderos' fields, as was the custom until then.[59] The
vacillating and somewhat resigned attitude of the Council itself emerges
clearly from its sentence in Governor Guzmán y Toledo's residencia.
It revoked a fine imposed on him for tolerating the abuse of servicio
personal and instead decided to have a cédula dispatched to the governor of Popayán, leaving the decision in the matter to him but
making it depend on the Indians' consent.[60] Paying miners in kind—in
cloth—was another practice that could lead to all kinds of abuses and
undesirable consequences, as the oidor Diego de Armenteros stated
emphatically in 1607, prohibiting it in the future. The audiencia,
nonetheless, again sanctioned the practice after a lapse of twenty years,
giving in to pressures from merchants and mine operators.[61] Substitution of labor for tribute and payment in kind were pernicious practices
precisely because they could easily lead to outright abuses, such as
refusal to pay the Indians wages at all or the encomenderos' failure to

remunerate the doctrineros.[62] It was the crown's intent to introduce the cash nexus between employer and worker under the corregidor's vigilant supervision, while the tendency of the encomenderos, as estate and mine owners, was to short-circuit this supervision and evade the cash nexus. The outcome of the contest depended on the structure of authority in the region, especially in the countryside. Since this is one of the topics that runs through the coming chapters, I shall only allude to it here.

Formal authority over the Indian population was vested in the office of corregidor de naturales, although in fact it was divided among corregidor, caciques, encomenderos, and doctrineros.[63] The corregidor's formal powers were considerable. His functions were so extensive that he must have delegated quite a few of them or foregone their exercise altogether. He was supposed to collect tribute and to hand their respective shares to the encomendero and doctrinero, retaining a small fraction for his pains. Similarly he was to assign Indian labor for public and private purposes. Successive ordinances tended to strengthen the corregidor's formal position and expand his responsibilities, yet many corregidors failed to exercise their authority. This seems evident from the caliber of persons who held the office. The caciques were in theory merely the corregidor's executive assistants, but in practice their power was more extensive. They were addressed as "don" and were exempt from tribute. They could appoint other officials—alcaldes and alguaciles—who were also exempt from tribute during their period of service. As part of their prerogatives they could claim an allotment of Indian servants. In addition, the Indians of the pueblo were to till a plot of maize for them. The formal attributes of the position were limited. Caciques were supposed to set a good example and to make rounds in the manner of Spanish alcaldes. That they were allowed to imprison culprits and suspects for only twenty-four hours before handing them over to the corregidor shows the limited discretion they were allowed.[64]

The official position of encomenderos and doctrineros was characterized by a series of prohibitions that enjoined them from substituting labor for tribute, collecting tribute themselves, retaining Indians on their estancias, employing them without a contract, or hiring them to others. In similar fashion the doctrineros were not to claim services, housing, food, and servants (beyond those allotted), nor were they to claim inheritances or influence the making of wills in their favor. The injunctions were not merely ritual in character. The chance of implementing them depended on the corregidor's and the governor's authority. Besides, the prohibitions concerned not mere infractions but rather various customary practices that had been sanctioned earlier and could not be eradicated by decree, especially if such decrees were enforced by men who grew up with the customs or shared the assumptions underlying them.[65]

The social and economic structure I have described in this and the preceding chapter had its beginning in conquest. Indeed, at the fringe of the region, conquest continued during the seventeenth century. This hierarchy of European over non-European, of town over country, was tied to the social and economic features described earlier. But was it derived exclusively from them? Or did this structure include institutional and political elements that gave it the durability and flexibility to adjust to new circumstances without losing its fundamental features? The following chapters will be devoted to an examination of this question, through an analysis of government in its local setting.

4. Cabildo Government

The cabildo governed the town of Popayán. Its authority was far from complete, since it formed part of a larger framework of government that gave the governor and the treasury officials important local roles. The governor, as the crown's representative, was the supreme authority in the whole province. He also had local responsibilities that he could either discharge personally or delegate to a deputy. The deputy—or the governor himself, if so disposed—presided over the cabildo's sessions, held court as justicia mayor, and took care of public order, administration, and welfare. The deputy was a governor's alter ego. The treasury officials, too, took a hand in local affairs. Their administration of the crown's finances in the province, including local taxes, could bring them into conflict with the cabildo and its individual members. Their authority extended over the whole region. Instead of employing local deputies, however, they either went on tours of collection themselves or entrusted the task to ad hoc collectors (jueces de cobranzas), who were empowered to imprison tardy debtors.

The audiencia and the Council of the Indies were the most important imperial institutions in the Spanish world. The audiencia of Quito served as a court of appeals for Popayán. It not only acted in a strictly judicial capacity but also had the power to review, confirm, or rescind a governor's actions. The journey from Quito took anywhere from two weeks to one month. The audiencia was hence reluctant to send judges to investigate and rectify matters, except in extreme cases. From an even greater distance the Council of the Indies appointed the governors and treasury officials, as well as the residencia judges who reviewed performance. The Council reserved the right to confirm encomienda grants and the sales of offices made locally. In extraordinary cases, the Council would send directives of its own. These cédulas reales, as they were called (in contrast to the provisiones reales that emanated from the audiencia), were addressed to audiencia, governor, bishop, and treasury officials, and to the cabildo as well. The cabildo appears as simply one unit in an imperial system of government.[1] How systematic was this government, when it came to local matters, and how effective, considering the need for local support? An answer hinges on the cabildo and its place in local affairs.

The cabildo of Popayán had strictly local responsibilities. Its members were recruited from the town and their attention was usually directed to local matters. The cabildo's role was not well defined either in its relation to the system of imperial government or as a corporation that virtually represented the town. It possessed neither statutes nor bylaws of its own. Yet, despite the absence of explicit and consistent regulation, government usually moved in orderly and regular tracks, conforming to patterns general in the Indies. Legislation, such as that of the Recopilación of 1681, is an uncertain guide to the performance of the cabildo. Local practice not only indicates conformity with or deviation from abstract legal norms but also in many cases indicates the norms themselves. Hence my purpose here and in the following chapter is to describe town government in Popayán by looking at its organization and routine activities.

Municipal government lacked definition in regard to its range and responsibilities. This was true not only in the Indies but also in Europe, where the jurisdiction and scope of offices and governmental bodies were not clearly separated in modern bureaucratic fashion. The Castilian state had developed a bureaucracy of sorts, competent to deal with domestic affairs and also adaptable to overseas expansion. Such a government, with a clear set of objectives and procedures, was hardly in evidence in Popayán. Its absence appears most clearly in the cabildo's inability to draw up ordinances and to keep its records in order.[2]

The town tried to frame ordinances and rules to fit its circumstances, but they proved abortive. In 1624 the lieutenant governor insisted on the town's need for ordinances of good government, as specified in the capítulos de corregidores of 1500. In response the cabildo appointed three members to draw up ordinances for discussion at its next meeting. In fact, the ordinances were not forthcoming until nine years later, when two regidores were selected to prepare the definitive version that was to be submitted within the week. There the subject came to rest, never to be mentioned again in the minutes.[3] Two generations later, in 1696, the fiscal (crown attorney) Sarmiento y Huesterlin drew up a fourteen-point program of improvements in procedure that amounted to a set of municipal ordinances. The fiscal criticized a variety of shortcomings and abuses in the town's administration he had encountered while undertaking several residencias and a special investigation. In its reply the cabildo indignantly rejected these suggestions, asserting that it needed no instruction in good government.[4]

Conscientious record-keeping might have compensated for the lack of explicit regulations. Once records were available, precedent could be invoked and custom could be based on more than memory. But the papers of the cabildo were in disarray during most of the century. This sad state of affairs cannot be attributed simply to lack of interest or the town clerk's negligence. A major reason was the absence of clear-cut control over or functional responsibility for the cabildo's papers, illustrated by the governors' tendency to appropriate these papers.

In a meeting in 1664, the cabildo resolved that, "inasmuch as this town is without its old *libros capitulares, reales cédulas, provisiones,* and other decrees that it always has possessed and must possess to maintain its authority and preserve its jurisdiction," the cabildo of Cartagena should be approached and asked to remit a copy of the "preeminences it possesses and all its other privileges."[5] The papers were lost because Governor Fajardo y Valenzuela had taken and never returned them. This resolution shows the haphazard way in which records were kept. The cabildo apparently assumed that privileges and preeminences were exchangeable as a set of general formulae, instead of being tied to the town's foundation and history. Nothing further was heard of the resolution. The same problem came up in 1671, during the residencia of Governor Guzmán y Toledo. He was fined for losing the cabildo's papers. The sentence also carried instructions to future governors. They were to keep an inventory of the town's papers and hand it over to their successors. Papers were to be kept in a strongbox, with three officials (governor, senior regidor, and escribano) having each a key.[6] To judge by later admonitions and instructions—for instance, never to hand over originals but always to make copies—record-keeping did not become a matter of routine. None of these regulations was anything new at the time. The capítulos de corregidores of 1500 already stated the need for an archive and the responsibility of the corregidor for maintaining it.[7] The problem was not the absence of principles, or even ignorance of them; it was rather the absence of an appropriate apparatus and of trained functionaries.

Much of the blame for the state of the town's papers rested with the escribanos. Easily the worst on record was Bernardino Blanco de Toro, who bought Diego Gómez de Morcillo's escribanía in 1650 for twelve hundred patacones. He fled the town in 1658, leaving his papers with the clergy. He appeared again after fourteen months and even tried to nullify all transactions that had occurred during his absence. During Governor Valenzuela's residencia in 1660, the fiscal Andrés de Rocha of the audiencia of Santa Fé deprived Blanco of his office: pages in the registers were left blank, signatures were omitted, and the cabildo's elections went unsigned. Nevertheless, Blanco remained in town and apparently even continued to exercise the office until 1668, when he was deprived of it a second time by the oidor and visitador Ynclán y Valdés.[8]

There were two notaries' offices in town. One of the incumbents also served as clerk of the cabildo. He was entitled to "have all business of the cabildo transacted before him and nobody else." The other position was that of a simple notary.[9] For a time there were also two procuradores de causas in town. They could draw up petitions, handle legal papers, and engage in litigation. Their task was similar to that of an attorney. They also served as collector of the sales tax and mayordomo of the cabildo. The office served as a stepping stone to that of notary public. The Church also required the services of notaries. When Miguel Sánchez d'Alava became an ecclesiastical notary, the Church's gain was the town's loss. His was the best pen, by far, in the whole province.

The escribanos' compensation was regulated by the arancel real, which set a fee schedule for every service they performed. A regidor's reception cost one thousand maravedis; drawing up a power of attorney cost five hundred maravedis. The escribanos were to record the bidding for the town's meat supply gratis, as a public service. Their fees in the Indies were in general five times those applicable in Castile. In Popayán the fee schedule was inserted in the cabildo minutes of 1637, after a complaint that escribanos charged as much as four reals for one sheet of paper.[10] How the schedule came to be published illustrates the roundabout way legislation could arrive locally. The schedule had been published under the auspices of the audiencia of Santa Fé de Bogotá in 1589. A decree reiterating the original decree was sent to Timaná in 1636. The cabildo of Popayán appropriated this decree a year later and sent it to Quito for confirmation. Without the audiencia's approval it would have no legal bearing in Popayán. The episode shows the extent of jurisdictional casuistry that could develop over as seemingly simple a matter as a fee schedule.

A proprietary escribano served the cabildo for only short periods: before 1610, between 1624 and 1654, and for a while in the 1670s. At other times, interim escribanos or the second notary public served. When there was no notary at all—during the 1660s and 1670s—a scribe (escribiente), who would also handle the notarial registers, would have to suffice. A magistrate, commonly an alcalde ordinario, would then have to certify matters. Business was handled sometimes by transitory notaries, at other times by an interim escribano de gobernación, who in theory was responsible only for business transacted before the governor.

Prices paid for the office measure its declining attractiveness. The escribanía del cabildo fetched 2,400 patacones in 1624; Juan de Correa, who soon disappeared from sight, paid 1,000 patacones in 1676. He may never have paid up or failed to obtain confirmation. The second notary fetched 1,600 patacones in 1618 and 500 patacones in the 1680s. The procurador de causas disappeared completely.[11]

The simplest conclusion is that the volume of paperwork could not support one notary, let alone two. Testimony before the audiencia of Quito in 1700 asserted that "the notary public of the said town has very few emoluments because of the limited business, lawsuits and writs, and also because it is poor country."[12] One may admit the self-serving tendency of such testimony, as the crown habitually did. Yet how does one explain the high prices early in the century? Business may have been better then, and expectations better yet. Clerking offices (oficios de pluma) may have carried a prestige they lost. Whatever the reason, it seems clear that at the margin of the empire the "chains of paper" that held it together became rather thin. The supply of notaries may once have been plentiful, but in the end it became a trickle or even a drop. The absence of lawyers and their ilk may have been a boon to the inhabitants; on government it had a negative effect.

The cabildo of Popayán was composed of proprietary members who purchased their seats from the crown. It also included three elected members: the two alcaldes ordinarios and the procurador general chosen annually by the proprietary members. The proprietors included simple regidores as well as officeholders who had purchased the municipal offices of alférez real (standard bearer), alguacil mayor (chief constable), depositario general (public trustee), fiel ejecutor (inspector of trade), and alcalde provincial de la hermandad (rural magistrate). The proprietors of these offices were members of the cabildo as regidores de oficio. The enlargement of the cabildo modified the simple division between regidores, who administered the town, and alcaldes ordinarios, who administered justice. The crown inflated the size of the cabildo so it could offer for sale offices that had the added attraction of membership in the cabildo. This was true of the office of alguacil mayor. In the case of the fiel ejecutor, an office was created out of a function previously exercised by the cabildo as a whole. In this way the cabildo changed from an institution whose business was conducted essentially in corporate fashion to an umbrella institution shielding a congeries of offices with disparate functions.

The three avenues to cabildo membership were purchase, election, and appointment. Purchase was regulated in detailed fashion by the crown, although these provisions did not always prove adequate, given local conditions. Purchase could involve either buying a vacant or newly created position from the crown or purchasing an office from its previous occupant. In the former case, the office was put up for sale by the appropriate authority; bids were made and published over a thirty-day period. If the price offered and the conditions of payment proved acceptable, the title was awarded and later presented before the cabildo. A record of the reception, together with the title, was then forwarded to the Council of the Indies for confirmation. An office so acquired could be held for life and bequeathed to an heir, or the purchaser could sell it again, by renouncing the office in favor of a stated beneficiary. In both cases certain conditions had to be met for the crown to recognize the transfer. A transfer fee had to be paid, also, of one-half the original price at the first transfer and one-third thereafter.[13]

Of the three elected members only the two alcaldes held full membership with both voice and vote; the procurador general had only a voice in the deliberations. In the annual elections, both proprietary members and the alcaldes ordinarios of the preceding year cast a vote.[14] In theory, all local citizens (vecinos) were eligible; in practice, certain conventions and restrictions existed. One custom that continued long into the seventeenth century was to take the senior alcalde from the encomenderos' ranks. The junior alcalde was often a merchant. By the beginning of the eighteenth century only a limited number of citizens were deemed eligible for the office, with a list drawn up of those who could be considered.[15] After the election was held, its results had to be confirmed, either by the governor himself or by his deputy. Confirmation was not necessarily automatic. Besides their role in granting or withholding confirmation, governors also influenced elections directly, by advancing nominees of their own.[16] The term of service in an elective office was one year, with reelection permitted only after a lapse of years. In fact, reelection was quite frequent, without much observation of the required interval. Alcaldes were also sometimes elected from among the proprietary members, despite the prohibition of that practice.

Appointment was not, strictly speaking, an avenue to formal membership in the cabildo. But, since the governor's deputy commonly presided over the cabildo's meetings—and cast a deciding vote in a tie—it ought to be discussed. Governors appointed deputies as soon as they themselves had been formally received. The newly appointed deputy then presented his title to the cabildo, also offering the required bond. The audiencia of Quito had to approve the appointment within six months. Governors also appointed alcaldes ordinarios when an incumbent died.

The cabildo's most substantial privilege and its most important function was the election of the annual members and the formal reception of permanent ones. In this way the cabildo retained some control over its own membership. All permanent and temporary officials with business in the town had to be formally received and might have to post bond. This reception—in effect an accreditation—although usually a formality, gave the cabildo a measure of control over officials outside its own sphere. These occasions when the cabildo sat in its corporate capacity were sometimes the only meetings recorded during a given year. Attendance at elections was required. Once some members went into temporary hiding in order to sabotage an election. After a prolonged search the election was held, but first the efforts to find the members and their failure were recorded *in extenso*. Members who were imprisoned had to be released' so that they could participate in an election.

Elections occurred on the first day of the new year.[17] The election of the procurador was frequently held at a later date, with minor appointments also made then. The weighty character of the occasion was underscored by the mass attended before the business of the day began. An election could be a simple or a complicated affair; in both cases the purpose was to minimize conflict. A slate could be elected by everyone voting for it "unanimously and in conformity." In this case the rules were suspended, as it were, whether they related to matters of substance—such as the prohibition of reelection—or to the prescribed procedure for an election. But rival candidacies could occur. In this case the formal procedure for holding elections tended to eliminate personal preference and institute chance in the selection of officials. This was achieved by having three candidates for each office nominated by each member; those with the highest number of votes then got another turn; their names were put on pieces of paper, and the one whose name was drawn was declared "elected" to the office. The procedure had a quaint aspect; it was called elección a cántaro, because of the clay pot in which the papers were deposited. When everything was ready, a boy was called in from the street to pull out one of the papers. Further refinements existed, to deal, for instance, with the complications when too many candidates obtained a qualifying number of votes. Only when elections were contested was this procedure mandatory. In 1627 the cabildo proceeded unanimously; the deputy protested and suspended the elections—for reasons of his own, so the cabildo alleged. The governor, when appealed to, upheld the cabildo.

Despite this elaborate system of precautions, discord was not eliminated. The procedure itself was not quite tamper-proof, as is evident from a complaint by Diego de Victoria to the audiencia. The deputy, for instance, was in the habit of reading the names of those elected and then destroying the papers before the results could be checked. Also, names were made out in duplicate and then put into the clay pot, Victoria alleged. In this fashion people were elected at the pleasure of the deputy. To stop these abuses, Victoria asked that the town clerk read aloud the names of those elected and that all members be allowed to scrutinize the papers.[18]

Did the mere presence of the governor during an election constitute interference? The cabildo certainly thought so at one time. In a petition of 1627 it asked the audiencia to send instructions prohibiting governor and deputy from being present during elections! Instead the alcaldes should preside and hand over the staff of office to their successors.[19] Either governor or deputy was usually present, during deliberations as well as during the election.

Overt interference by the governor or the deputy was no rarity. In 1619, the audiencia insisted, upon the complaint of a regidor, that imprisoned members retained their voting rights.[20] Incarceration to make a cabildo pliable was strong medicine when written instructions might be sufficient. Governor Guzmán y Toledo sent a letter to the cabildo in 1664 in which he stated his desire for peaceful elections and for the choice of citizens worthy of selection. To reinforce his point, he appended a list of his preferred candidates. If difficulties should perchance arise, last year's incumbents were to be reelected.[21] One may surmise that instructions of this sort were not uncommon.

Governors could delay or deny confirmation. The elections of 1631 and 1632 were notorious examples of this kind of interference. The first year the governor refused to approve the election of those he considered unfit. He claimed that they were either too old and decrepit or had their residence in a neighboring town. Hence the incumbents continued in office. Next year the governor again refused to ratify the election. This time everybody had voted for relatives, a practice prohibited in explicit fashion. The alcaldes, who had already served for two years, continued in office until the audiencia broke the deadlock between governor and cabildo by ordering new elections.

The vote for relatives had been an issue before. In 1592, Captain Pedro de Velasco, father of the alférez real don Ýñigo, obtained a decree from the audiencia stating that, in such "matters of honor and courtesy" as the elections of alcaldes and regidores (regidores were then still elected), relatives could vote for one another. In 1616, don Ýñigo de Velasco himself petitioned the audiencia for redress, claiming that members of the cabildo continually elected relatives to all the offices and excluded many citizens from the "honors." The audiencia responded with a decree forbidding fathers to vote for sons and vice versa; brothers were also forbidden to vote for each other. But the cabildo appealed the decree. In 1623 the appeal was still pending. Only the renewed clash between opposed factions on the cabildo prompted the audiencia to resolve its incompatible decrees of 1592 and 1616. In a Solomonic decision, the audiencia in 1632 decreed "that such elections can be done with relatives voting for relatives if they are not fathers voting for sons nor sons voting for fathers nor brothers." [22] That decision left unanswered the question whether in-laws were included in the prohibition. For the moment this was decided in the affirmative by a ruling of the two alcaldes.

Neither this particular episode nor its antecedents tell us what rules were really followed. Past elections had not conformed to the standards set down in 1632, nor did future elections adhere to them. The episode is nevertheless informative. It shows how rules reflected local politics. Were the Velascos inconsistent in appealing to different principles in 1592 and 1616, returning in 1631 to their first preference? For them the only inconsistency was that they were in a minority in 1616. Appeal to the audiencia for a ruling was the resort of a party at the losing end of a conflict. When there was no conflict, no rules had to be supplied from outside or from above, because custom supplied them. Custom consisted simply of the prevailing practice of the majority that, at least for the moment, encountered no opposition armed with rulings to the contrary. Only explicit and repeated rulings, backed by local support, could be expected to change what were judged abuses by general norms. Voting for relatives, for example, continued after the decree was received, ostensibly because the matter was on appeal. When the issue was decided, the previous practice was nevertheless soon resumed as if nothing had happened.

Formal reception by the cabildo comprised a series of separate functions. It included the seating of its own members, the registration of officials' credentials, the recording and implementation of decrees emanating from the governor or other, superior, bodies, and the reception of new local citizens (vecinos). Usually new regidores were received without difficulties. In one case a minority opposed the reception of a new regidor, alleging his unfitness for office, his low occupation, and the fact that rival bids for office had not been considered. The matter dragged on for months. Before the annual election, a decree from the audiencia ordered the cabildo to cease its obstruction, and the new member was duly sworn in.[23]

The reception of a new governor was a solemn occasion. The escribano presented his patent of office and read it to the assembled cabildo, which then received and obeyed it. At the same time the cabildo required the posting of a bond by the governor. Once this request was complied with, the oath of office was administered and the governor was given his staff of office. He thus entered into "actual and corporal possession of the government." On two occasions incoming governors were denied reception by the cabildo. In 1701, the cabildo, acting in league with the incumbent governor, refused to receive don Juan de Miera Ceballos, and again, in 1704, it refused to receive don Juan's successor, don Pedro de Bolaños. These refusals occurred under singular circumstances. The incumbent governor wanted to keep his dearly bought office, in spite of a waiting line of aspirants. The cabildo was alternately dominated by quarreling local factions, and Spain was in the throes of the War of Succession (1701-1714).[24]

On occasion, governors' deputies ran into opposition. In 1615, Juan de Berganzo, appointed deputy by Governor Lasso, faced determined resistance from some members, ostensibly because he was a local encomendero and thus unfit to hold the deputyship. Five members and the junior alcalde favored reception, two members and the senior alcalde opposed it. In order "to avoid trouble and scandal," the alcaldes then remitted the matter to the governor, who commissioned the depositario general, Ortíz, to break this "deadlock" and invest the deputy with the office, a task normally in the hands of the senior alcalde.[25]

An important aspect of official reception by the cabildo was the demand for bond to be posted by officials who were subject to the residencia or who handled public funds. It was the cabildo's duty to exact such guarantees. Should it fail to do so, it could be held responsible for the fines an official incurred in a residencia. Wealthy citizens either acted as guarantors or vouched in turn for other guarantors. The cabildo usually made no difficulty about guarantees. In one case, however, it dragged out reception over three years, supposedly because the guarantees offered by the new contador, don Juan de Larrainzar, were insufficient. Actually the cabildo, with only four members then, acted on behalf of two local worthies, don Joseph Hurtado and don Fernando de Salazar Betancur, who both had wanted the post. The barrier was broken only when the audiencia of Santa Fé authorized the treasurer, don Bernardino Pérez de Ubillus, to bypass the obstructionist cabildo by ruling on the quality of the guarantees.[26]

The cabildo functioned as a body when it formulated petitions or provided instructions for a specific purpose, but, when it brought suit before the audiencia or pursued a petition through the Council of the

Indies, the cabildo necessarily employed agents. The minutes contain a detailed set of instructions to the cabildo's emissaries before the synod sitting in Bogotá in 1624.[27] In other cases instructions were handled in routine fashion, for instance, by the cabildo's agent before the audiencia of Quito. These agents, commonly procuradores de causas, received commissions from case to case. For its local business, the cabildo used ad hoc "diputados"—often forming a committee—who would investigate a matter and then put it before the cabildo for resolution. Diputados might be appointed from among the members to negotiate the commutation of the sales tax, establish the best location of a bridge, or receive a new governor at the town's limits. Sometimes they would in turn co-opt a specialist in the matter at hand. There was also one standing committee, appointed at the year's beginning, whose duty it was to take the mayordomo's accounts. Other permanent business was handled by officials whose offices had been incorporated in the cabildo but over whose performance the corporation had no jurisdiction.

The alferazgo was the most prestigious of these offices. It was held continuously by one family during the century. The office drew no salary, although in one instance the title contained the statement that the holder was to be compensated for his services beyond what was "ordinarily" paid him, presumably a reference to the ordinary remuneration of regidores. In Popayán, however, neither alférez real nor regidores received any compensation. The price of the office went down in the course of the century: it cost one thousand pesos in gold in 1594, while its assessed value in 1690 was eight hundred silver pesos, less than half the earlier price. Before that price was agreed on, the audiencia objected to the evaluation of five hundred pesos made by witnesses. In the end the treasury officials set the price at the level that prevailed in 1662, at the time of the last transfer.[28] The alferazgo was in essence a ceremonial office with few tasks, bearing prestige in an inverse proportion to its burdens. The alférez real held precedence over all other members, ranking just below the alcaldes ordinarios. In the deliberations of the cabildo of Popayán, the incumbents—in particular don Ýñigo de Velasco and, in later decades, his son don Diego and his grandson don Diego Joseph—frequently exercised considerable influence. This influence derived from their local position rather than from the possession of the alferazgo, which simply gave expression to that status.

The alguacil mayor's main duty was to keep order in town. He executed court orders, made arrests, and was supposed to make rounds at night. He was also responsible for the jail and appointed the jail keeper (alcaide). He could appoint deputies (alguaciles menores), but he could not share in the fees they collected. The Council of the Indies, notoriously lenient in its attitude toward local infractions, upheld a stiff fine imposed on the alguacil Cabrera for indulging in this practice.[29] Interest in the office was keen for a while, as is evident from contested renunciations in 1617 and 1636. In neither case did the intended beneficiary obtain possession. Despite the drop in prices (see table 1) aspirants became scarce, and prolonged vacancies resulted.[30] The town had no proprietary alguacil mayor between 1663 and 1675, and after 1680 the office was again vacant. Interim appointments by the governor may have filled the gap; in 1668, Diego Gómez, a native of Spain and resident of the town, was appointed in this fashion to the job.[31]

The office of the depositario general (public trustee) was in effect a sinecure. He took charge of goods and funds under the administration

TABLE 1
PRICES PAID FOR LOCAL OFFICES

	Popayán			Potosí		
Regidor	300	gold pesos	(1594)	10,000	patacones	(1593)
	550	patacones	(1609)	8,000	"	(1602)
	400	"	(1620)	6,000	"	(1613)
	400	"	(1636)	9,000	"	(1622)
	300	"	(1673)	9,000	"	(1631)
	220	"	(1701)	5,000	"	(1644)
Alférez real	1,000	gold pesos	(1594)	20,000	"	(1604)
	800	patacones	(1664)	8,000	"	(1659)
	800	"	(1690)			
Alguacil mayor	2,500	gold pesos	(1621)	100,000	"	(1603)
	1,210	" "	(1636)	60,000	"	(1628)
	800	patacones	(1675)			
Fiel ejecutor	3,000	"	(1624)	20,000	"	(1592)
				18,000	"	(1619)
Escribano público	3,000	"	(1604)			
	1,200	"	(1650)			

Sources: ACC, LC passim; AGI/AQ 35-44; Inge Wolff, *Regierung und Verwaltung*, Appendix.
Note: In Cali, the office of alguacil mayor cost 450 patacones in 1633, and that of fiel ejecutor cost 750 patacones in 1680; in Quito, the office of regidor cost 1,300 patacones in 1630, and that of escribano público cost 10,000 patacones in 1617. A gold peso was approximately double the value of a silver peso, or patacón.

of the courts. His reward was two-and-a-half percent of the income produced by such deposits. The price of this office remained relatively stable and interest in it was sustained.[32]

The fiel ejecutor had extensive duties. His main task was to inspect and set prices for all foodstuffs brought into the town. The only exception was the supply of meat, which remained the cabildo's responsibility. Since the fiel ejecutor exercised jurisdiction, he carried a staff of office that was handed over in ceremonial fashion to a successor or deputy. Appeals of his decisions went to the governor's court. Diego de Victoria held the office for nearly forty years. Before he purchased it in 1623 for three thousand silver pesos, the function had been annexed to the cabildo and rotated among the members every four months. Its fees and prerogatives made it an attractive duty. When the office was put up for sale, the cabildo challenged the crown's action, arguing that the function was a constituent part of the members' privileges that could not be diminished unilaterally, but to no avail.[33] After Victoria's death in 1661, there was to be no proprietor until 1732. The vacancy was at first accidental, since the renunciation in favor of the younger Victoria was rejected as being too late. When no bidders appeared after the office was declared vacant, the cabildo again exercised the function by rotation. Complaints by the procurador general about the lack of a fiel ejecutor made no difference.[34]

The honorific connotation of these offices (cargos) derived from their incorporation into the cabildo. Prestige, functions, and emoluments varied, and so did performance and interest. Indifference and low prices do not necessarily indicate municipal decadence. They also can mean that a standard version of the municipality, with one set of offices, was not necessarily appropriate to a given town. By contrast with the offices described above, alcaldes ordinarios were needed as magistrates under all circumstances.

The alcaldes ordinarios were magistrates and judges. Their duties were wide-ranging. They presided over the cabildo in the absence of the governor or the deputy. Aside from criminal and civil litigation, their duties related to wills and successions, opening testaments, making inventories, and awarding inheritances. They also might have to act as notaries. They either did not impose fines or did not report them. Their emoluments consisted in the fees they collected. To judge by the media anata they had to pay, their import was small.[35] As judges, the alcaldes had to be available to the public. In 1629, Governor Bermúdez de Castro decreed that the alcaldes were to hold hearings every day at eleven in the morning at the residence of the town clerk, an old custom that had fallen into disuse. The residencia records give little indication of the alcaldes' duties aside from the recurring charges that they did not guard enough against nor penalize public sinfulness—for instance, concubinage—and did not keep the roads in good repair.[36]

A few cases may illustrate the alcaldes' judicial activity and throw some light on their position, particularly the relation of their jurisdiction to that of governor and deputy. In civil suits—for example, the recovery of debts—individuals could sue either before one of the alcaldes ordinarios or before the deputy. In 1620, Lorenzo Roldán, a merchant, presented a petition before the deputy, Alonso Hurtado del Águila, asking that Agustín Arias Zambrano, encomendero of Puracé, pay a debt of thirty-one pesos for merchandise bought in his store. The latter was notified, recognized the debt, but still did not pay. Roldán therefore asked for an order compelling payment, and the deputy complied with the request. Whether the debt was in fact paid is not clear from the evidence. In the same year Pedro Muñoz, another merchant, presented a note in his favor from Antonio Valencia before the alcalde Agustín Arias Zambrano. He, too, was given an order requiring payment.[37]

Two other cases show the value of being able to choose between judges. In one, Antonio de Alegría petitioned the alcalde Belalcázar, who had just freed him from jail, to prevent the other alcalde, Quintero Principe, from clapping him into jail again simply in order to satisfy his lust for revenge. In another case, Lorenzo de Anaya, who temporarily filled the office of alguacil mayor, petitioned the alcalde Belalcázar to have the mulatto slave Antonio imprisoned. The latter, although accused of murder, had not been jailed, since he was under the protection of Quintero Principe, the other alcalde.[38]

The usefulness of the governor's intervention in a case is demonstrated in the complaint made by the merchant Antonio de Valderrama against the alcaldes of Cali, who had embargoed his merchandise and mules and imprisoned his son. The son had been surprised *in flagrante* with a woman he was now supposed to marry. Valderrama reclaimed his goods after the governor granted his request for restitution and sent an appropriate order to Cali.[39] In minor cases, appeals from an alcalde's judgment could be lodged before the cabildo. In 1625 the cabildo appointed Juan de Angulo and Miguel Rojo as diputados to revoke a previous sentence.[40] In cases of more than fifty pesos, appeals could be made to the governor, who would pass final sentence in cases up to five hundred pesos. In a bankruptcy case of 1635, for example, the creditors appealed the alcalde's sentence. The governor revoked it, ordering payment without delay.[41]

Twice during the century the alcaldes acted in the capacity of interim governor, once when a governor died and again when a governor was suspended from office. Did the deputy's commission expire automatically in such a case? The cabildo debated the matter in 1627, instructing the deputy, as the object of the discussion, to leave the meeting. The alcaldes finally ruled that, until the audiencia had decided the matter, the deputy was to surrender his staff of office. No such doubts about the locus of authority arose in 1682, when the suspension of the governor decreed by the president of the audiencia of Santa Fé included the order that the cabildo was to assume the interim governorship.[42]

The procurador general was a constituent member of the cabildo, without voting rights.[43] It was customary in Popayán to elect one of the alcaldes of the preceding year, so as to provide continuity or avoid recriminations. The procurador sometimes would draw up a detailed petition at the year's beginning, listing the unfinished business of the past year. A set of instructions to the incoming procurador of 1616 gives some notion of the scope of the office. The procurador was to "plead and procure for the good of the town and its dependencies, to present proofs and witnesses, writs and other papers, oaths, appeals, rejections, citations, requirements, and conclusions, to consent to favorable sentences and to appeal unfavorable ones, to follow up appeals, to procure decrees and royal orders and other papers, and to contradict those that are detrimental to the town." To this effect he was granted "free and general administration" and the propios and rents of the town were committed to the purpose.[44]

It is no accident that these instructions resemble the general formula for the power of attorney used at the time. The procurador general was in fact something like an attorney representing clients. The office entailed a variety of not necessarily compatible duties. Ideally, the procurador was a kind of *defensor civitatis,* watching over the interests of the poor. In addition he saw to it that the cabildo performed its specific duties, met regularly, and kept buildings and roads in good repair. He also acted as the inhabitants' advocate to the cabildo, and he furthered their interests as well by joining in seeking concessions and privileges from the crown. In a different capacity, the procurador could make himself the spokesman for a particular group, whether miners, merchants, the poor, or the corporation of the cabildo. His right to act as such a spokesman was derived from the assumptions that the office represented the commonweal and that the particular interest espoused contributed to, or was at least not detrimental to, the commonweal.[45]

The alcaldes de la hermandad represented the town's jurisdiction in the countryside. There they shared control with the corregidor de naturales and the alcaldes mayores de minas, who were appointed by the governor. The two alcaldes de la hermandad were elected annually from among the younger and more sprightly vecinos. Their duty was to apprehend criminals in the countryside; cattle rustling was one of their main concerns. The corregidor's jurisdiction applied only to Indians; it included disputes with Spaniards. In Chisquío, the Patía valley, and the mines of Gelima, the governors frequently appointed alcaldes mayores de minas. Their function was to remedy the deficiencies of justice in the mining districts. Their authority was not infrequently annexed to that of the corregidor de naturales, who thus held jurisdiction over Spaniards and Indians, certainly a convenient solution.[46]

Did the cabildo represent the town? The answer may be found by looking at the concept of citizenship, at the cabildo abierto as a special kind of local assembly, and at the ways in which revenue was raised and spent.

How did one acquire citizenship? How did it operate and what did it mean? Francisco de Anaya applied for citizenship (vecindad) in 1613, one week after he had been elected alcalde ordinario. Lope de Labayen and Juan de Aranda applied for citizenship in 1614; the former had lived in the town for six years, owned some cattle, and planned to become a cattleman (in fact he remained an itinerant merchant, as may have been his intention all along); the latter had been in Popayán for sixteen years and had a house, weapons, and a horse. When Juan Díaz applied for citizenship in 1616, he also asked for a town lot and was given one at the Río Molino. For Jacobo Guaycochea, in 1625, a bill of sale for a house was sufficient proof of good intentions. His request was granted and testimony was entered in the libro del cabildo, with the condition that he was to pay the alcabala for everything up to that day. In 1672 the alférez don Francisco Torijano was admitted to citizenship; he had lived in the town for five years, was trying to buy a house, and had recently been elected alcalde de la hermandad. In 1673 a native of the town applied; his parents had been vecinos and had moved to Pasto. He himself had lived in Popayán for fourteen years. He lived in a relative's house but was willing to buy one of his own, should that be required. The following year Juan Nicolás presented a bill of sale for a house; the cabildo admitted him, with the condition that he bring his wife and family to the town within a year.[47]

What can we learn from these cases? There was no register of citizens; the libro del cabildo apparently served to record matters. Admission was not hedged by excessive formalism. A certain length of residence in town, evidence of a livelihood and of seriousness of intent—both evinced by possession of a house—sufficed. Holding office was possible without previous admission. The term *vecino* was used loosely. When used to indicate the quality of an individual, it often meant simply a long-term resident. Between usage and legal significance a distinction remained but it grew smaller as the practical meaning of *vecindad* shrank.

Only limited benefits derived from citizenship. Theoretically it assured eligibility for office. It also carried with it de facto exemption from the sales tax. The vecinos might have to contribute through an assessment only if the amount collected from noncitizens (commonly nonresident merchants) proved insufficient. This was the original meaning of *encabezamiento,* the term used for the cabildo's contract with the treasury officials. The fear 'that a relaxed practice of admissions might create too many vecinos—who then would escape payment—led to demands in 1633 to lengthen the period of residence required for admission to citizenship. Evidently no action was taken to change the customary five years. How assessments were handled can be determined only indirectly, since no registers were kept. Listings were compiled for specific occasions, such as the contribution to the cathedral's construction, the "gift" (donativo gracioso) to the crown, or the fine imposed on all who had profited from evading the mining tax.[48]

The meetings of the cabildo abierto should provide an idea of who the city's notables were. But practice was as loose here as it was for citizenship. Cabildos abiertos were assemblies of the more important of the town's citizens. In Popayán such meetings were held only rarely. Only six were recorded in the libros; for one of the meetings there is only indirect evidence.[49]

In 1630, Governor Bermúdez de Castro called a meeting. He announced a reduction in the mining tax and discussed the arrangements for festivities to honor the birth of an heir to the throne. For the governor, the cabildo abierto was a part of his way of running things. He used "local opinion" to create a favorable image at court, supported by extensive reports. Participants in the meeting were the cabildo proper and most of the local encomenderos. The purpose of another meeting called in 1659 was to parcel out a collective fine among all the miners of the region. This meeting was held in public, and all citizens and residents (vecinos, moradores, estantes, and habitantes) were to attend. No transcript of this meeting exists, but the assessment agreed upon became a matter of record through the treasury officials. It was signed by the leading mine owners of the district.[50] Wide participation also characterized a cabildo abierto called in 1681 to consult about the defense of the province against the English, who had reportedly invaded the Chocó.

An onerous decision might call for a cabildo abierto. In 1682 the cabildo could not arrange for the meat supply at customary prices. The town's notables, among them the clergy, met to discuss the common welfare. Over the objections of the alférez real, who argued that an increase of one-half real for an arroba of meat was excessive, the new price was approved. When the nunnery needed more space and asked for a whole block for expansion, the procurador general found the request reasonable but advised that a cabildo abierto should be called. The superiors of the orders and other ecclesiastical dignitaries and all the other noble and republican citizens of the town were to be invited.

The political significance of the meetings was that they marshaled agreement on controversial matters. Consultation and a formal polling of opinion beyond the cabildo were possible. The cabildo abierto served as a forum to co-opt larger segments of the town. The inclusion of the churchmen meant that meetings could promote solidarity between Church and lay institutions, associate them in common endeavors, or paper over differences.

The cabildo's property was small and its revenue insignificant. The term *propios* indicates that the cabildo had to live on its own income. Its mainstay was an annual fee of 275 silver pesos paid by the contractor for the town's meat supply. The only property in land controlled by the town was the ejido (commons). Its main use was to pasture temporarily the herds that supplied the town. At an earlier stage of settlement, cabildos had made land grants and distributed town lots. The governors took over this prerogative, hedged soon by the Council of the Indies.[51] In the town itself there were lots for the town hall (casa del cabildo), jail, and slaughterhouse, which were owned outright by the town. Squatting in the ejido was tolerated at times. The younger Anaya, a regidor's son, had a house and cattle there.[52] Yet things could easily get out of hand. In 1698 a profusion of ditches and even of estancias called attention to what had been going on. The occupants included Fernando Chaborro, who produced a title from Governor Juan de Borja; Andrés Ladrón de Guevara; María de Roja, who claimed she had permission; and the dean of the cathedral chapter, who claimed ecclesiastical privilege.[53] How these disputes were resolved is unclear. Vigilance was needed to protect the propios: that much is clear.

Keeping track of the town's finances was not difficult, since funds were so limited. The mayordomo was to keep the accounts of collections and disbursements entrusted to him. Appropriations at the beginning of the year were largely routine.[54] The alcabala did not yield any surplus to the town. Apparently the collector (alcabalero) simply gathered this tax until the amount needed for the year was reached, keeping a fraction for himself. The treasury officials at the end of the century were of a mind to take over the alcabala, and they did so for a while. But they also were unable—or unwilling—to devise a satisfactory system of collection.[55] Since the mayordomo had little authority, delinquency in collections was frequent, especially when there were several meat contractors. In this situation, members of the cabildo would be appointed collectors, to go after laggard debtors, as in 1671. Shortfalls were perennial. By 1696, only 887 pesos of a total of 1,650 pesos due between 1690 and 1695 had been collected.[56]

The cabildo's authority in financial matters was extremely limited. All levies had to be authorized by the governor, beyond an annual limit of 3,000 maravedis (about 10 pesos). In 1597 the cabildo petitioned the crown for the right to impose occasional levies. The Council agreed but limited the right to 6,000 maravedis for four years. When informed of the utter insufficiency of the sum—it would not buy even a load of bricks—it was raised to 20,000 maravedis.[57] Assessments commonly had specific purposes.[58] What was the prevailing attitude toward "public" funds? In 1672 the English threatened Buenaventura. To raise and equip soldiers against this invasion, 2,205 pesos were collected locally. Seventeen encomenderos and forty-two vecinos, mostly merchants, contributed about equally. When the danger had passed, it was found that 600 pesos were left. What to do with it? The alcaldes won the day. They argued that the sum should be returned to the contributors pro rata, since it was specifically earmarked for the defense of the province and not for other purposes. Also, future generosity would thus be assured.[59]

The cabildo was not a representative institution in the strict sense of the word. It did not represent the vecinos or, certainly, the inhabitants. Its taxing power was derisory. It was simply a corporation with a set of functions and responsibilities in the "public" sphere, relating to the república de españoles. The cabildo abierto was a closer approximation of that republic than the cabildo proper. Yet the services performed by the cabildo were indispensable to the town, particularly to its leading citizens. In this sense the cabildo "represented" important local interests.

5. Settler Affairs

Cheap labor, the town jail, burial fees, bull fights and the price of bread—these were the daily concerns of the cabildo. In general terms, the cabildo acted on behalf of the Spanish settlers vis-à-vis the crown and the Church. It also performed a variety of local services. Previously I have discussed its role as a part of government. Here I will describe what the cabildo did and how it performed.

The most pressing problem the Spanish settlers faced was the lack of labor. Projects and proposals abounded. The oidor Anuncibay, sent to Popayán in 1592 to take the residencia of Governor Tuesta y Salazar, suggested one remedy. If the province was not to become a desert, he wrote to the crown, it had to import large numbers of slaves. Stability of settlement and supervision could be assured if the slaves lived in compact villages close to the mining areas. As a safeguard, these places were to be isolated from one another. Slaves were to be kept illiterate, and they should have neither horses nor weapons. Their status was to be similar to that of serfs, since their owners could not move them or sell them without official permission. The prospective proprietors, the oidor wrote, were willing to pay up to four hundred pesos per slave, in eight installments. Payments should not be difficult to meet, since one slave could easily produce two hundred pesos of gold annually. The oidor made himself the spokesman for the local miners, whom the cabildo also supported.[1]

In 1598, Juan de Rada, the town's procurador, presented a long shopping list to the Council of the Indies. It included a plea to dispatch eight hundred slaves to the province. In 1603, Governor Mendoza y Silva and the cabildo joined in appealing to the Council for two hundred slaves. In 1615, the treasurer don Gerónimo Pérez de Ubillus associated himself with another of these petitions, reiterating the need for slaves to work the mines. The petitions and schemes are the political counterpart of the crisis in mining that befell the region around the turn of the century.[2] The Council responded to such petitions in general terms. In 1595 it organized the asiento, the contract for the importation of slaves; one of its purposes was to increase supply. But these general measures did not affect individual cities or provinces. The petition of 1615 received the curt answer that the vecinos could travel to Cartagena and haul their slaves from there. By that time the policy of using contractors to assure a stable supply of slaves had become firmly established. From then on the issue was not how to obtain slaves, but how to pay for them.[3]

The mining tax (quinto) came to be seen as an increasing burden, and efforts turned to reducing it. The implicit argument was that the miners could not afford to buy slaves, because their profits were too small. Ultimately the inability to generate capital translated into a net decline of royal revenue. Capital formation had to be encouraged rather than impeded. Originally the royal share of the bullion produced in the province had been one-fifth (quinto), but by 1596 the tax was reduced to one-tenth. Such a reduction of the tax—which continued to be called the quinto—was limited to a number of years, usually four or six. The renewal of the grant and a further reduction of the tax became recurring preoccupations of the cabildo, the governor, and the treasury officials.[4] The identification of officials with local interests is not surprising when we consider that the contador Palacios Alvarado developed and operated mines, that clerics were mine owners, and that a governor's position depended on his success in associating himself with local interests.[5]

Vigorous action was needed to procure extensions of the grant. Either emissaries had to be sent or the cabildo had to entrust the matter to someone at court. In 1611, for instance, an Augustinian friar and a vecino of Santa Fé, en route to Spain, were empowered to negotiate a renewal. In 1618, two residents at court were authorized to plead for an extension. In 1620 their petition was granted. In the following decade, the efforts of the cabildo, the governor, and the treasury officials obtained a further reduction to one-fifteenth. The success was due to the skillful arguments of the cabildo's agent at court, the licenciado Pedro Sánchez Pérez, to whom the cabildo voted two hundred pesos for his expenses (the sum was not to be taken from current income; rather the members should contribute as they saw fit). By the 1660s the tax had been reduced to one-twentieth, where it was to remain for the future.[6]

The cabildo also supported the estate owners' control over Indian labor. It sought to preserve the status quo by opposing offensive aspects of Indian legislation. The cabildo's reactions to the ordinances regulating native labor indicate the place and extent of political activity. The ordinances of 1607 had not run into major opposition, although the encomenderos resented the excessive salary of the corregidor; they also lobbied against the ordinance prohibiting payment of Indian miners in cloth. This grievance was removed when Governor Bermúdez, in response to the cabildo's petition, lifted the prohibition. The audiencia confirmed this action.[7] The ordinances were seen in a more positive light when a cédula real arrived in 1633. This ordered the governor to convene a junta of informed and disinterested persons, such as the bishop, the heads of the religious orders, and the treasury officials, to discuss the abolition of personal service. The junta recommended that matters be left as they stood. The cabildo used this decision to support its plea for a confirmation of the ordinances of 1607. To nail matters down, it empowered three people at court to represent its case. To pay the agents, the cabildo appropriated one hundred pesos. The effort was in vain. Although the fiscal of the Council favored confirmation of the ordinances, the full Council of the Indies did not.[8]

The Council's refusal to confirm existing arrangements made an inspection inevitable. In 1637 the oidor Juan Rodríguez de San Isidro Manrique arrived with a dual commission, as juez visitador and as juez de composición de tierras.[9] As juez de composición, his function was to legitimize possession of land in return for a fee (composición). As visitador, he inquired into the encomenderos' actions, depriving some of them of their encomiendas for not fulfilling their obligations. But mainly he promulgated a new set of ordinances. Despite their hectoring tone, he proved a reasonable man in regard to their substance. Nevertheless, the cabildo vented its sentiments against certain innovations, in particular the insistence on cash payments. It also voiced doubts about the realism of the tribute schedule, in the manner of all colonists. It stated, "Experience has shown that its implementation is useful neither for the república, whether encomenderos or townspeople, nor for the natives of the province, because each of its items carries with it many inconveniences, as for instance in the payments that it orders made to Indians who work either in mines or the fields and gardens, or at other tasks as disposed in the schedule. If one should need to compel the Indians to comply with their obligations, it can in no way be done, because of their poverty, and it will lead to the depopulation of the province." The routine arrangements—which did not worry about tribute payments but exacted labor instead—were preferable, from the settlers' point of view, to a complicated system of cash payments and accounting, unenforceable against peasants.[10]

Despite the protest, the encomenderos could apparently live with the ordinances. Labor service for them stayed on the books, despite some restrictions. And these were evidently not vigorously enforced. In the absence of such enforcement, the situation would soon revert to its former convenience for the encomenderos and also for the caciques.

When the next round of ordinances, remonstrations, petitions, and allegations came in 1668, the caciques testified that labor for the encomenderos was the only workable arrangement to satisfy tribute obligations, and their testimony proved important and revealing.[11] The cabildo also enlisted the bishop and the governor in its campaign on behalf of the encomenderos against the ordinances of 1668. A veritable avalanche of communications descended upon the Council, skillfully coordinated by the town's agent at court, Diego Ignacio de Córdoba. In a first action taken in May 1671, the Council suspended the new ordinances and ordered that the previous ones remain in force for the time being. It also instructed the audiencia of Quito to forward a copy with its comments. Nearly ten years elapsed before the Council decided to leave the earlier ordinances in force. If the audiencia considered changes desirable, it was to send detailed and appropriate information to Spain.[12] Local practice was saved, if not vindicated.

In another sphere—building a town hall and maintaining the jail and the slaughterhouse—the cabildo was much less successful. It did not obtain decent quarters of its own until into the eighteenth century, though not for lack of effort. In 1618 the procurador general pointed out "that this town is without a city hall decent and dignified enough for the capital of the province; the one there is, is thatched only and far from the plaza." The solution, the procurador said, was to combine efforts with the cathedral chapter, which had just come into possession of an endowment. The chapter planned to build a row of stores on the plaza, and the cabildo could benefit from the undertaking by building its meeting place above the stores. A formal contract was concluded. Yet nothing was accomplished. In 1627 the chapter asked the cabildo to withdraw from the contract, after the debate in the cabildo on whether to persevere proved inconclusive.[13]

In the face of inaction, the town hall and jail deteriorated. In 1627 a store was leased for thirty pesos to serve as a temporary jail, until the corregidor had had the roof of town hall and jail thatched. At the end of the rainy season, the two buildings collapsed. Funds and draft labor (mitayos) were allotted to make the necessary repairs under the supervision of the alcaldes ordinarios. Three years later, at the end of the dry season, the two buildings burned down. The cabildo now leased two stores to serve as meeting room and jail. Eventually the accommodations were rebuilt, although without lasting effect.[14] A generation later the town was without buildings again. After the wall of the town hall disintegrated, the building was stripped of its useful parts: the roof tiles were used for the slaughterhouse, and the alguacil mayor gave away the doors. One night, the last room, which served as the jail, was stripped of its roof. According to the regidor Lorenzo de Anaya, who made these depositions in a residencia, nobody investigated or bothered to find the culprits.[15]

Attempts to build facilities in the 1660s and 1670s were remarkable mainly for the inability of those entrusted with the job to carry it through. In 1661 the deputy don Joseph Hurtado undertook the building of the town hall and jail, and funds were allotted for the purpose. Yet the residencia two years later revealed that he had accomplished nothing except to divert some of the funds. One might assume that the corregidor Huegonaga, because of his control over Indian labor, was better suited for the job. But in 1679 nothing but a few walls testified to his unfinished effort. Perhaps the *genius loci* was to blame? The old location had never been very satisfactory, so a search for a better one was instituted. The deal for the new lot fell through when the cabildo could not raise sufficient funds to pay the difference in price between the old and the new lot.[16]

Lack of funds was a more serious shortcoming of these efforts than lack of perseverance. Without money nothing could be carried through with dispatch. Instead of living from hand to mouth, why did the cabildo not raise funds locally on the security of its annual income? A rudimentary capital market existed locally, and the Jesuits, for instance, used it to construct their church. One obstacle to its use was that the cabildo could not offer the required security in real estate, cattle, or slaves.

In the provision of local services there existed an ideal state of affairs seldom encountered in reality. A series of regulations enacted in 1697 by the fiscal Sarmiento y Huesterlin outlined this ideal of service. In their attention to detail, the provisions concerning the meat supply were especially interesting. Meat was a basic item of food; the cabildo had an obligation to assure its supply at low prices. Only well-fattened animals were acceptable for slaughter; lean ones were to be rejected. Slaughtering was to begin at midnight, to assure that the meat aged somewhat before being sold. Weights had to be supervised closely; the contractor was under no circumstances to have them in his possession. The fiel ejecutor and, in particular, the inspector of weights had to check them once a fortnight. Private butchering was not permitted even with the contractor's assent, because it could not be supervised effectively. The prevailing sense of social hierarchy found expression in the sequence in which buyers were to be served. Bishop and governor came first, the religious houses and the officials next, and other citizens followed according to the antiquity and nobility of their families. The populace was served last. The poor were to get "preferred treatment," however, when buying such lesser parts as heads and entrails. Those who could not buy a whole arroba at once were to be accommodated.[17]

Reality was a far cry from this perfect state, as every connoisseur of markets, stockyards, and slaughterhouses knows. Yet the cabildo did try to maintain some order. Each November a proclamation was issued in Popayán and in towns like Cali and Buga. Bids were solicited from cattle suppliers. Bids had to include the price at which the arroba of meat was to be sold, the price of other items such as tongue and tallow, and the fee the contractor was ready to pay. In addition, suppliers noted a series of such conditions as the right to pasture cattle on the commons and a prohibition against private slaughtering.

A major problem was the condition of the slaughterhouse. The buildings and other structures collapsed with regularity, since nobody —neither the cabildo nor the respective contractor—assumed responsibility for their maintenance. Every time this happened, the contractor would demand an assignment of Indian labor from the corregidor to do the repairs. The cost of materials would be assumed by the contractor. These repairs were provisional, hardly sufficient to keep the buildings together for more than a year. During a season of heavy rains they would disintegrate, creating a recurring emergency for which there appeared to be no remedy.[18]

A stable meat supply was not assured, since the town's district included no major cattle-raising area. The Patía valley, otherwise suitable, was subject to recurring droughts and invasions of locusts. Supplies usually came from Cali and Buga. At the turn of the eighteenth century, the region of Neiva developed as another source of supply. Major competitors for cattle were the towns of Pasto, Quito, and Bogotá. Until the 1660s the price of meat remained low, usually under two reales the arroba. In 1662, for instance, two competing cattlemen lowered their initial offer from two reales to one-and-a-half reales per arroba. At the same time they raised their offer to the cabildo from 220 pesos to 260 pesos. Statements praising the quality of their herds, while denigrating the competitor's, accompanied the bids. One offer would even have permitted private slaughtering. The deputy opposed this proviso, since it would introduce an insecurity into the supply that the monopoly contract was designed to avoid. The procurador spoke in its favor, because it would stimulate the trade in cloth (presumably because the cattle dealers would carry back cloth received for cattle).[19]

After 1670 the supply situation deteriorated, as reflected in rising prices. Earlier difficulties had been temporary. In 1634 the cabildo asked the governor for a proclamation, advertising the town's needs in Cali and Buga, after the customary announcements had brought no bids. In 1652 the cabildo seized the cattle of Martín de Albornoz as they were being sent to Pasto, until he agreed to keep them in Popayán.[20] When prices began moving up in the 1670s—with shortages developing if the suppliers' demands were not met—the cabildo at first reacted by apportioning the supply on a monthly basis to various contractors. In the long run this provided no solution. By 1681 the situation had become so critical that the deputy of Popayán threatened to confiscate cattle sent from Cali and Buga to Quito, unless suitable offers from these towns were made to supply the region.

The ultimatum produced one bid, from don Pedro de Salazar Betancur, vecino of Buga and Popayán. He offered to supply the town at a price of two-and-a-half reales the arroba. His justification for this price, higher than what was paid in Quito, was that the town's pastures were poor and each animal brought little. In Quito, with its good pastures, animals gave up to two arrobas of tallow and fourteen pesos worth of meat. Private slaughtering, usually countenanced by the alcaldes, was to be prohibited. He also needed a usable slaughterhouse; if given workmen and compensation for his outlay, don Pedro was ready to undertake construction himself. The offer was finally accepted, since no alternative appeared. In subsequent years, the cabildo was unable to check rising prices, which at the turn of the century had reached three reales the arroba.[21] The causes of this secular increase are unclear. Supply may have declined. It is more likely that demand increased, in particular from the newly opened mining areas in the north.

Other services besides the meat supply demanded attention. A lengthy memorandum by the fiscal Sarmiento y Huesterlin gives perhaps the best idea of the quality of these services. Prices were not set by the town; rather, merchants set their own, according to the fiscal. Unmarked stones served as weights. Encomenderos and Indians used no weights at all. The "pound" of bread or candles bore no relation to the weights prescribed by law.[22]

The cabildo's response to this catalogue of sins amounted to an admission of many of the fiscal's charges. No price schedule existed, because many supplies were not available locally. Instead they had to be imported at high cost over long distances. Weights and measures did not conform to the legal norm, because they were periodically altered, in response to changing supply; it was customary to change the weight rather than the price. The sellers could not afford iron weights. Indians did not have to use the customary weights, because that would drive them away and hence diminish supplies. The same explanation—by implication—seems to have applied to the encomenderos as the town's suppliers. The cabildo's overall justification for its inaction was that it made no sense to tighten the laws in such a way that they served to punish rather than relieve.

The fiscal had little difficulty in taking apart these arguments. In a veritable dissertation of four parts he reached the conclusion that it was indeed necessary to make adjustments in response to changing circumstances, that is, changes in supply. Prices might have to be lowered or raised in response to supply, but such action was to be taken by officials, persons in responsible positions. It was not to be left to individual whim or judgment.[23]

The fiscal's final pronouncement arrived in the form of a decree. It amounted to a set of general ordinances, but it also referred to specific matters that claimed immediate attention.[24] The fiscal stated that his study of the files of past residencias had shown that their provisions were usually disregarded. He therefore elaborated a series of regulations to be observed henceforth in the town. They were to apply in the whole province, except for Caloto, Almaguer, and Arma, omitted because of their poverty. The decrees were proclaimed in the plaza to the sound of drums and transcribed in the books of the cabildo.

Of particular interest were the fiscal's efforts to set minimum standards in the administration of justice. Henceforth the alcaldes had to meet the public daily in a specific place, giving equal treatment to rich and poor. No official was permitted to operate a retail store or engage in selling to the public while holding office. If he had to sell his crops, he should do so through others. The fiscal noted that, since the officials were doing all kinds of business, they had little interest in setting prices or regulating retail operations. The escribanos were to be present at the same time as the alcaldes, so that business could be dispatched. Because the poor were often unable to obtain stamped paper, sufficient supplies were to be kept at hand (when scarce, it was apparently sold at a premium). The escribanos should hand over documents only on written request, to curb the judges' habit of removing papers without returning them. Justice in Popayán suffered from the complete absence of trained lawyers (letrados), the fiscal noted. At least the governor's deputy in the capital should be a letrado. The Council of the Indies and the audiencia in Quito were to be advised of this necessity. But the policy was difficult to enforce. Only the year before, the audiencia of Quito had confirmed the appointment of don Diego Joseph de Velasco as the town's deputy. The fiscal of the audiencia, in an explicit comment, noted that Velasco was not a letrado but that this was not an obstacle since there were none in the province.[25]

Supplies at reasonable prices also engaged the fiscal's attention. In periods of scarcity the cabildo was to entrust one member with the task of obtaining supplies, if necessary by commandeering what was needed. A price list should be published and posted at a conspicuous spot in each store. Storekeepers were to register with the cabildo and post bond. Only "trustworthy" storekeepers were exempted. It remained unclear who was to establish that distinction. Actually the cabildo rarely intervened in matters of supply and prices. This is not surprising when one considers the laissez-faire notions espoused by the cabildo in response to the fiscal's strictures. Only in an emergency did the cabildo bestir itself to set prices. Bread, for instance, became scarce in the spring of 1612, because, it was said, of the strong demand from the adjacent mining areas. At first the cabildo set a uniform maximum price and prohibited the "export" of bread to the mines. When this proved ineffective, the cabildo resorted to a price differential, doubling the price in town while leaving it at the previous level in the mines (one might note here that bread was apparently baked where wheat was grown and then peddled by itinerant vendors). After a bumper crop in 1618, the cabildo moved to lower the price of bread, which had remained at a high level for several years.[26] The price of grain again became a matter for debate at the end of the century. This time the escribano was delegated to investigate how much flour went into a loaf of bread. After some debate—but without this crucial evidence—it was decided to set a price for bread but leave the consideration of corn until after the harvest.[27]

Salt and wine were the objects of sporadic attention; both items were brought over long distances. To prevent the cornering of supplies, a standing rule stipulated that all goods entering town had to be "manifested" for nine days, with no particular buyer engrossing the whole shipment. On one occasion the cabildo lowered what was considered an excessively high price of salt and had an inventory of the town's supply made.[28] The regular making of price schedules, beyond the cabildo's occasional intervention, was the fiel ejecutor's special responsibility. This responsibility and the need for it were stressed in one residencia (only one), when the fiel ejecutor was accused of permitting bread to be sold at a price higher than that stated in the price schedule.[29] The effective demise of the fiel ejecutor's office bears witness to the absence of actual control and supervision in matters of supply.[30]

What conclusions about the cabildo's performance can we make on the basis of this evidence? The cabildo's reluctance to regulate prices did not create a free market. Rather it tended to favor those who already controlled the production of foodstuffs in the province, in particular the encomenderos, with their easy access to native labor. Aside from using the services of middlemen, encomenderos also directly operated retail outlets in town. The problem of monopoly control was raised most clearly at the time of the oidor Ynclán y Valdés's inspection in 1667. In appealing the ordinances, the cabildo associated itself with the encomenderos in favor of a narrow definition of who were the labradores, that is, the farmers to whom Indian labor was to be assigned.[31] Inaction in some matters was accompanied by activity in others that concerned the interests of the encomenderos, miners, and merchants. The cabildo's efforts on behalf of importing slaves, reducing the mining tax, and maintaining servicio personal were cases in point. The cabildo's administration of the sales tax was a measure clearly beneficial to local merchants, since the tax fell as a rule only on nonresident merchants.

Was the cabildo the spokesman for particular groups and interests? In a general sense this is certainly true and hardly surprising. But groups and interests were not very well defined, if one looks for them in terms of economic or social criteria. No separate groups of encomenderos or merchants, food producers or miners existed. Individuals could fit more than one description, at one moment or over a time span. Also, espousing particular interests at a given moment was not perceived as detracting from the general welfare, for which the república de españoles provided a first point of orientation and the interdependence of the two "republics"—of Spaniards and Indians—a second point of reference. The crown, of course, thought otherwise. By separating the two republics and controlling their relations, it sought to minimize conflict.[32] But this was not the settlers' way of looking at things. Within the Spanish "republic" conflicts also existed, as we will see. But as far as the cabildo was concerned, they existed largely on the level of individuals and of families.

We therefore have to turn to an analysis of the cabildo's membership in order to understand the functioning of the institution. But local politics was not the cabildo's monopoly. Authority was dispersed among several agencies, and power could exist outside them. A look at office-holding may show the relations between formal authority and power; it will also provide insight into the local configuration of politics.

6. Offices and Officeholders

Spanish settlers shaped local affairs through the cabildos. Their power was countered by the authority of the governor. The separate realm of the Church further restrained the settlers. How did these competing sources of authority operate? Who controlled them? The questions are not the same, but answering the latter question may also give clues about the former. Hence this chapter examines recruitment to an array of local positions. Recruitment needs to be viewed broadly, since the cabildo was only one of various routes to advancement. The development of the cabildo of Popayán shows how interest in office fluctuated during much of the century.

Offices in Popayán reflected imperial goals and local aspirations. Spanish settlers sought influence and income, prestige and control. The crown's goals—to control local affairs, assure impartial and competent administration, and maximize revenue—contained contradictory elements. Sale of office illustrates the gap between imperial prescription and local outcome. The practice began because it seemed a facile device for raising revenue. Elaborate procedures were established to minimize abuses. The Council of the Indies had to confirm each sale, the audiencias checked qualifications, and sporadic inspections (visitas and residencias) were carried out. Judicial office was altogether excluded from sale, although practice increasingly contradicted legal prescription. How successful was the crown in reconciling the sale of office with control over administration? Success depended on consistency on the crown's part—it declined noticeably—and on local reactions. By following appointments we can chart how the crown's policies were implemented. A detailed study of officeholders, individually and as a group, reveals the responses of the settlers and may show us some of the interests in play.

A comprehensive series of decrees regulated the purchase and transfer of municipal and notarial offices.[1] These decrees spanned the period from 1589 to 1606. First the purchase procedure was placed on a formal footing; later the transfer of office from one proprietor to another was legalized by the establishing of the procedure of renunciation. This procedure turned what had been in effect private sales into an accepted and legal practice, stipulating a share of the proceeds for the crown. This share amounted to one-half of the sale price at the first transfer through renunciation and to one-third at each further transfer. Until then, municipal offices had been treated as grants (mercedes) in the gift of the crown, sometimes in rather offhand fashion. In 1574, doña María de Montoya was granted four regimientos on the cabildo of Pasto, to dispose of as she saw fit, in lieu of a cash grant. When it was discovered that the regimientos were still subject to annual election, the audiencia of Quito was instructed to suppress election.[2]

During the first decades of the seventeenth century the sale of offices attached to the cabildo was a thriving operation. Yet this market soon collapsed and never quite recovered. In commenting on the situation, the audiencia of Quito stated in 1600 that "nobody is content with his situation, especially in the Indies where everybody is so restless and is always changing his situation . . . many desire an office and after acquiring it turn discontented in a few days and desire another one and would like to get rid of the one they hold (even at some cost)."[3] The record of the cabildo of Popayán bears out these contentions. In 1612 it had eight members, yet only five of them participated regularly in meetings. In 1630 there were ten proprietary members, who attended sessions with some regularity. By 1661 only two remained, with one in regular attendance. In 1662 purchasers were found for the office of alférez real and the new office of alcalde provincial de la Santa Hermandad. A year later the alguacil mayor, habitually absent, was deprived of his office. For the next decade the membership of the cabildo stood at three. In 1671, five regimientos and the office of depositario general, vacant for nearly two decades or more, were briefly filled. A few years later the alguacilazgo also found a buyer. The only office not sold at all was that of fiel ejecutor, which did not find a buyer until the 1730s. Interest was short-lived. In 1693 the governor's deputy reported to the audiencia that five regimientos and the offices of alguacil mayor, fiel ejecutor, and escribano mayor de la gobernación were vacant. Between 1696 and 1699 the cabildo had only three proprietary members; between 1702 and 1707 the proprietary membership stood at four or five.[4]

How can we explain the fluctuations in the cabildo's membership and the trend of declining interest in holding office? One reason was the inadequate arrangements for selling offices. But, more important, expectations changed. Investing in local offices no longer yielded the economic advantages or the prestige initially envisioned. Competing pressures surrounded the sale of local office. The crown tried to raise revenue, the governors sought to obtain control, and purchasers strove to keep prices low. A series of trends emerges rather clearly, based on scattered observations rather than statistics: the crown got less rather than more money, the governors did not take control, and the settlers got their way as prices fell to a realistic level.

The crown's efforts took a variety of forms. Existing administrative functions were turned into offices, then to be sold. An example is the function of fiel ejecutor. The office of alcalde provincial de la hermandad was newly created and sold in 1663 for the first time. The audiencia served as a supervisory agency, to assure competitive bidding and the observation of all applicable rules. Since all sales had to be confirmed in Spain, the Council was kept informed of matters, and, as interest declined rather than rose, the Council informed the audiencia that prices were to be maintained. Hence the audiencia did not accept lower bids, and offices often stayed vacant for want of acceptable offers. In the long run the loss of revenue became serious, but only in 1670 was the audiencia authorized to accept offers substantially lower than the prices previously established.[5] In Popayán the reduction had the desired effect. Six seats were soon sold, many of them vacant for a generation. The change of policy simply confirmed the tendency for prices to fall in line with local possibilities.

Facing a continued decline in revenue from the sale of offices, the crown looked for alternatives.[6] To draw at least some revenue from interim appointments made by the governors, the crown in 1675 ordered that such offices should be rented for a yearly fee. Hence, during the election of 1677, two citizens appeared before the cabildo of Popayán bearing dispatches from the treasury officials and demanded to take part in the proceedings. One of them had leased the office of fiel ejecutor for one year for thirty-one pesos, while the other one had leased a regimiento. The cabildo received them under protest. In its appeal it pointed out that a simple electoral maneuver had caused this transitory interest. The crown revoked the edict in 1678, after the fiscal of the audiencia of Lima had pointed out its possible consequences: the devaluation of all permanent property in office and a considerable enhancement in the powers of viceroys, governors, and treasury officials, who henceforth could expedite appointments.[7] This about-face restored the status quo, with the proviso that efforts should still be made to obtain some compensation for interim appointments. In the following years there were several instances of such appointments made by the governor, but none of them were transcribed and it appears that the appointees did not hold voting rights in the cabildo.

The governor's role in the sale of offices arose because existing arrangements were inadequate, given the distances involved. In decrees of 1615, 1616, and 1626 the crown tried to improve local procedures. Because prices paid for offices were allegedly too low, it ordered that vacancies should be advertised both in the province and in Quito, as the seat of the audiencia. If a higher price resulted in Quito, the bidding was to return to the province, while the right to dispatch the title to office was to remain with the audiencia.[8] In spite of this regulation, no clear-cut jurisdiction concerning the dispatch of title to office and the handling of the transfer of office developed. In some cases the audiencia ascertained the value of renounced offices; in others the governor had testimony taken locally and dispatched the title as well. The Council, in granting confirmation to offices acquired in this way, did not object to the extension of the governor's power.[9]

Yet such an extension did not become the rule, since local offices were still sold by the audiencia. In 1661, Governor Guzmán y Toledo presented the disadvantages of this arrangement to the Council of the Indies. He pointed out that buyers were scarce because proceeding to the audiencia cost more than the office. Hence, he said, "Popayán and other towns do not have anything like a cabildo, as there are no regidores nor anybody else who wants to hold office; in this town, the capital of the province, there are only two ancient regidores and an alguacil mayor . . . with the consequence that there is nobody with experience and routine to whom to entrust anything." Matters would be better, the governor concluded, if the disposition of local offices were handled by the governor. The Council turned him down and did the same a generation later, when Governor Gerónimo de Berrío complained that there was no interest in buying municipal office in spite of all his efforts. Again he blamed the cumbersome procedure of going through the audiencia. The Council nevertheless rejected the governor's temporary appointment of a depositario general who had agreed to lease the office for forty pesos annually. It argued that, were the office needed as much as the governor claimed, buyers for it would have presented themselves.[10]

The Council had good reasons for refusing to empower the governor to sell offices. Offices filled by the governor had cost the treasury revenue. Their value was not properly assessed, witnesses were not called for testimony, and neither the fiscal nor the treasury officials were informed of the vacancy. The vagaries of one particular appointment may illustrate the problem. In 1645, Captain Juan de Angulo renounced his regimiento in favor of don Juan Domingo de Gaviría. Its value was declared to be 150 pesos, although a generation earlier it was sold for 550 pesos. The discrepancy did not prevent the governor from approving the sale. The Council refused to confirm the sale, because it considered the price too low. The matter dragged on for years, until the purchaser's agent stopped appealing the Council's decision.[11]

The governors never gained definite control over awarding proprietary offices. It was only natural that they would strive to do so, since such control was consistent with other powers they exercised. For example, they awarded encomiendas that fell vacant—a prerogative that could yield a sizeable illicit income; they appointed deputies and corregidores and named interim treasury officials. The patronage these appointments implied provided them with considerable local leverage that compensated somewhat for their failure to gain direct control over the cabildo.

The emergence of the deputy (lugarteniente) as the governor's alter ego in the town's affairs illustrates rather clearly the divergence between legislative intent and the practice of government in Popayán. The governor needed local collaborators. He was empowered to appoint deputies who were letrados, that is, who possessed legal training. These appointees were to be neither "citizens nor natives of the district" where they served, a rule consistently reiterated in a governor's title to office. Appointments made in Spain were to be approved by the Council of the Indies; if made in the Indies they were to be confirmed by the audiencia of Santa Fé de Bogotá, in order to check qualifications. The governors of Popayán did, in fact, appoint deputies for most of the towns in the province. The audiencia's approval was sought and was generally forthcoming. But these deputies were neither trained lawyers nor foreigners to the district where they served. Lawyers were a rarity in the province, as were notaries. Even the post of teniente general, with the not ungenerous salary of five hundred ducats, was not filled after 1631.[12]

What happened was that the governors discovered that the surest way to achieve local rapport was to appoint a local citizen as deputy. Several deputies in the second decade of the century were still outsiders, but most of their successors were prominent citizens of Popayán. The same observation applies to the post of corregidor de naturales. It was usually held by a citizen of the town, often an encomendero, the explicit prohibition notwithstanding. Both deputy and corregidor were, in a sense, extensions of the governor's office, since they served at the governor's pleasure.[13] Neither the audiencias nor the Council of the Indies interfered with the practice during the period under consideration. However, in 1726 a decree suppressed the governor's authority to appoint deputies altogether, with the exception of one in the capital of the province who was to serve as lieutenant governor (teniente letrado).[14]

Some other innovations on the governor's part did not become permanent features. In 1621 the governor appointed the accountant (contador) Juan de Palacios Alvarado to the post of superintendente en su gobierno en las cosas del y de justicia y guerra (superintendent in matters of government, justice, and war), but the cabildo of Popayán refused to accept the nominee. Forty years later a similar appointment was made, when the deputy of Popayán was appointed juez superintendente y de apelaciones. This time the cabildo raised no objections. In substance the position was analogous to the defunct office of teniente letrado, but no salary was stipulated nor was confirmation obtained from the audiencia.[15]

Who were the men who held local office? The record is mixed. On the one hand we see considerable turnover, yet on the other there is a certain continuity, in particular when one looks at the post of alcalde or deputy. The Creoles of Popayán did not form a closed society. Mobility and a degree of openness were evident, for instance, in the considerable turnover of regimientos. Even when one considers all the vagaries of officeholding, its analysis provides one yardstick to gauge continuity and mobility within the town's governing stratum and, by extension, the upper reaches of Creole society. This society was open to newcomers. Commonly they were co-opted through marriage, not necessarily on their own terms. In its upper reaches Creole society renewed itself through continued acceptance of immigrants. This pattern, discussed here for the space of one century, continued into the eighteenth century and, indeed, was one of the fundamental social patterns in the Indies.[16] What this analysis cannot quite do is give an idea of how Creole society renewed itself in its lower reaches, how much mobility there was in both directions, and what mechanisms of mobility existed at that level.

Alcaldes ordinarios and deputies were always persons of some weight in the community. Their actual power was limited by other jurisdictions. The recruitment to these positions indicates the consolidation of a local upper stratum renewed by a continuing flow of newcomers co-opted through marriage. The senior alcalde (alcalde del primer voto) usually was an encomendero, though this fact in itself does not tell us everything about his social or economic status. The junior alcalde was also quite often recruited from the encomenderos, at least when the election was uncontested. Yet the difference in recruitment between the two alcaldes is worth noting. In approximately half of the fifty-six elections recorded between 1612 and 1682, the junior alcalde did not belong to the established group of encomenderos and their immediate relatives. Instead he was often a merchant or an even less well defined newcomer whose election as an alcalde might signify local acceptance and occasionally a governor's wishes. Acceptance had its limits. According to the cabildo's petition of 1632, no transient or retail merchant, especially if he lived in his store, could hold the alcalde's office. Such people might use their office to promote private deals.[17] But why should only retail merchants use offices to promote deals? In fact, such merchants were elected occasionally as alcaldes. One should also note that, since much litigation dealt with mercantile matters, alcaldes of necessity had to be acquainted with them. Also encomenderos who had arrived as merchants might serve as alcalde. Altogether, bona-fide merchants were elected alcalde at least ten times between 1612 and 1642 and seven times between 1657 and 1682.[18]

Besides the merchants, other, less easily categorized newcomers served as alcaldes. Captain Juan de Mera came to Popayán after military service in Chile and New Granada. He married a daughter of Captain Lorenzo Paz Maldonado who was heiress and claimant to the encomienda of Guambía.[19] Don Lorenzo de Águila, a native of the province of Toledo, saw military service in Italy.[20] His marriage to doña Francisca de Arévalo, daughter of the prosperous miner Andrés Martín Rayo and granddaughter of Captain Juan de Berganzo, encomendero of Tunia and for two generations a power in local affairs as alcalde, deputy, and guarantor of governors, served to give him a pied-à-terre in the town. Don Fernando de Salazar Betancur originally came to Popayán in 1633 as treasurer of the cathedral, after pursuing studies a the colegio San Bartolomé in Bogotá.[21] He soon resigned this sinecure and married doña Elena de Mosquera, a sister of Christóbal de Mosquera. He served both as junior and senior alcalde in Popayán and as deputy under Governor Valenzuela. In Buga he acquired an encomienda and the estates that complemented it, where he produced sugar and raised cattle to supply the town's market. He acquired another encomienda in Caloto (Páez) in 1660. As comisario de la Santa Cruzada, he controlled the sale of indulgences for the bishopric. Of his numerous progeny—he had twelve children—he managed to put six under the church's wings: three became nuns in the convent of La Encarnación, one son joined the Augustinian order, and two became secular priests who rose to be members of the cathedral chapter of Popayán. It is worth noting that two ostensible outsiders elected as alcaldes actually had local ties: Captain Diego Rengifo Salazar of Buga was a brother-in-law of the town's alférez real, don Yñigo de Velasco, and don Francisco de Montoya y Mendoza was the bishop's nephew.

Most newcomers in later generations joined the town's governing stratum through marriage.[22] Joseph de Morales Fravega, a merchant

from Genua, married a daughter of don Ýñigo de Velasco; the brothers
Arboleda were miners with ties to the Delgado-Victoria clan, as was
Juan Nieto Polo, a newcomer from Santa Marta. The brothers in turn
sponsored Martín Prieto de Tovar from Tunja, who married a daughter of don Francisco de Arboleda. Melchor Jacinto de Saa from Cali
and don Diego Tamáris de Góngora, who came from Spain in Governor
Valenzuela's entourage, married daughters of Alonso Hurtado del
Águila. The importance of a local match for securing entry into the
town's governing stratum becomes still more evident when one analyzes
the background of the thirty-seven men deemed eligible for the function of alcalde, as stated in the listing of names in 1706.[23] Twenty-one
were descendants of families established in Popayán for a generation
or more. Sixteen were newcomers, although some had lived in the
town for a considerable time. Of these, fourteen married into the town's
established families. The remaining two may have also, although no
positive evidence was found concerning them.

The protracted discussion around Juan de Berganzo's appointment as
deputy in 1616 shows that selecting a local encomendero for the post
did not always meet with unanimous approval in the cabildo.[24] But
opposition at the time seems to have been motivated mainly by personal objections. As a rule the town's deputies were either native sons
or men with strong local connections. Of the twenty-seven deputies
known to have served in Popayán between 1601 and 1705, only five
were outsiders, twelve were vecinos, and ten were born in the region (see
Appendix C). Don Ýñigo de Velasco, who served between 1628 and
1633, was the first native-born deputy. Although no hereditary claims
existed, a clustering of the deputyship in a few families is in evidence.
Some deputies served twice under different governors. The clearest
example of multiple service is provided by the Hurtados, who held the
office eight times in three succeeding generations. This includes don
Diego Tamáris de Góngora and don Francisco de Arboleda, who were
sons-in-law of Alonso Hurtado and don Joseph Hurtado respectively.
The Velascos, Aguinagas, and Mosqueras were families with similar
claims to the office maintained over several generations. This picture
of relative dominance by a few families might be reinforced or modified
if it were possible to take full account of all relatives in important
positions and of connections beyond Popayán. Two newcomers tied
to the Mosquera family (don Fernando de Salazar Betancur, Melchor
López de Celada) held the office of deputy in the 1640s and 1650s. The
Aguinaga family held a prominent position in Almaguer, the Mosqueras and Victorias in Caloto, while the Campo Salazars divided their
attention between Popayán and Timaná.

The posts of deputy and alcalde required a mastery of affairs, whereas the possession of a regimiento was more a matter of honor. Membership in the cabildo externalized such honor, making it visible. To whom honor was due was not always a settled matter, as we will see. To judge by the cabildo's composition early in the century, it would seem that encomenderos with a claim to lineage occupied themselves elsewhere and left purchase of proprietary office to humbler citizens. Yet by the 1670s the cabildo's membership was more prominent. It consisted entirely of local notables and their relatives. The comparative inconsequence of most members earlier in the century emerges clearly from a list of seventy-six men who in 1624 made a voluntary gift to the crown.[25] Each one of the town's twenty-two encomenderos contributed ten pesos or more; of the cabildo's nine members, two of them encomenderos, only four gave ten pesos or more, three gave less, and two nothing. Judging by their contributions, most members of the cabildo did not occupy positions of economic and social prominence. A few years later the picture had already changed and a closely knit group of members with patrician pretensions was in control.

The cabildo's most prominent member during much of the century

TABLE 2
THE CABILDO'S MEMBERSHIP BETWEEN 1610 AND 1640

Alférez real
Don Yñigo de Velasco
Alguacil mayor
Melchor de Cabrera, who renounces in (i.e., transfers property claim in office to) Joan de la Puente (1617), who renounces in Antonio Ruiz de Alegría (1619), who renounces in Lorenzo de Anaya (1635, not effective) and in Alonso de Cañizares (1637)
Depositario general
Juan Ortíz, who renounces in Pedro de Salazar (1623)
Fiel ejecutor
Exercised by turns until 1624; Diego de Victoria (1624)
Regidores
Juan de Angulo
Antonio de Salazar (declared vacant for lack of confirmation, 1624), Antonio Rodríguez de Migolla (1624), who renounces in Diego Delgado Salazar (1631)
Cristóbal de Cayzedo (vacant, 1614), Lorenzo de Anaya (vacant for lack of confirmation, 1625, bought back, 1626)
Francisco de Cayzedo, who renounces in Miguel Rojo (1619), who renounces in Francisco de Figueroa (1631)
Antonio Ruiz de Alegría, who renounces in brother Francisco Ruiz de Alegría (1619)
Bartolomé de la Peña, who renounces in Gonzalo López Prieto (1626)

was the alférez real don Ýñigo de Velasco.[26] In 1598 his father bought the alferazgo with the stipulation that he himself could occupy it during his son's minority. Don Ýñigo's grandfather was a comrade in arms of the mariscal Jorge de Robledo, the founder of Cartago and Antioquia. The father, governor of Timaná at the turn of the century and henceforth known locally as the governor, married a granddaughter of the adelantado Belalcázar. Don Ýñigo himself married the daughter of a former governor of Popayán, doña Beatriz de Noguera. His standing was further enhanced by his ownership of Popayán's two largest encomiendas, Coconuco and Cajibío, with more than twelve hundred inhabitants in 1607. In addition he owned wheat and maize estancias, a series of large cattle ranches, and mines worked by Indian miners from his encomiendas. After don Ýñigo's death in 1660, the alferazgo continued in the family, held by his son and grandson. The family estates remained largely intact for over a century. They passed to the Jesuit order in 1737, after the death of doña Dionisia Pérez de Manrique, widow of the last Velasco in Popayán. The family thus furnishes the most pronounced example of continuity in Popayán. Its lateral connections as well were far-reaching. For example, two members of the cathedral chapter of Popayán, don Francisco Vélez de Zúñiga and don Antonio de Zúñiga, were don Ýñigo's cousins, apparently the first members of the town's upper stratum to attain such a position. Don Ýñigo's elevated rank was not always accompanied by a commensurate position of influence on the cabildo. During much of the 1610s and 1620s he was in a distinct minority, as was evident in his frequent objections to the selection of alcaldes ordinarios. When he became deputy in 1628 this situation was already changing, since by the 1630s the Zúñigas, as the descendants of Catalina de Zúñiga, his great-grandmother, were called, held a commanding position in the cabildo.

Yet in earlier decades such one-sided domination of the cabildo by one kin-group or parentela was an unlikely event. There were, for instance, the brothers Cayzedo, whose stepfather Juan de Berganzo bought them two regimientos.[27] Christóbal, the profligate son of the family, returned penniless to Popayán, where he died in 1614. He squandered his inheritance "studying" in Spain. Francisco was set up with a regimiento in Popayán and an encomienda in Almaguer that his stepfather "bought" for him for three thousand pesos. He finally settled in Almaguer and gave up the regimiento in Popayán, having attended seldom enough. The only other encomendero on the cabildo before 1626 was Captain Juan de Angulo, regidor from 1609 to 1645. He fought with distinction in the campaigns against the Pijaos, thus establishing a claim to consideration. He did not find a successor; his daughter Ana married Diego Hurtado de Aguilar, a local merchant, and his encomienda was granted to a newcomer after his death.[28]

Alegrías and Anayas formed another powerful combination on the cabildo, bound together by kinship and a common Andalusian background.[29] Three were proprietary members: Antonio Ruiz de Alegría, alguacil mayor starting in 1619, regidor before; Francisco Ruiz de Alegría, brother of Antonio and his successor as regidor; Lorenzo de Anaya, brother-in-law of the Alegrías and a regidor since 1615. These three men—together with Captain Antonio de Alegría (father of the two brothers), encomendero of Jolomito, and Francisco de Anaya (brother of Lorenzo), encomendero of Cajete—formed an extensive kin network with common interests from politics to trade. Their major money-making enterprise was conveying cattle to the Quito market. The linchpin of this and other operations was the older Alegría, a man of great experience who served numerous times as alcalde ordinario. When already an encomendero and serving as alcalde, he kept a store in town. He also was accused of collusion with local meat suppliers. After his death, his older son took over the direction of the family's enterprises, apparently with less success. At his death in 1635 the estate was burdened with debts, and creditors pressed for payment.[30] As a result, Lorenzo de Anaya was unable to claim the alguacilazgo that Antonio Ruiz had renounced in his favor. The creditors, among them his brother-in-law Francisco de Anaya, were unwilling to defer their claims to the principal sum he owed to the estate for the alguacilazgo. In fact, the crown offered better terms for payment of the transfer tax (a third of the office's price) than did the creditors. The episode shows what might be evident anyhow. Kinship did not always serve as an element of cohesion or as a basis for cooperation. In the heyday of the combination Lorenzo had been a simple hanger-on, notable only for his quarrelsomeness. The extent of his dependence showed in that he was even accused of sharing a house with the brothers Alegría rather than being his own man. While the connection lasted he was on the fringe of their various enterprises. He acted as deputy for the alguacil mayor, collected debts for both of them, and generally voted with them on all issues.

Bartolomé de la Peña, an alderman until 1626, was also a hanger-on, voting regularly with don Ýñigo de Velasco and picking up odd chores, such as collecting the tithe in the district of Caloto. Along with Lorenzo de Anaya and Miguel Rojo, he showed an inordinate interest in taking turns at being fiel ejecutor. Among the members of the cabildo he alone was so impecunious that he was exempted from paying for mourning clothes when King Philip III died.[31]

Miguel Rojo, a regidor from 1619 to 1631, was not quite in the same category. He was a retired storekeeper who also ran the inn.[32] His fitness for office was called into doubt when he presented his title. But, in spite of the initial objections raised against him, he became a member in good standing. A vendetta between him and Lorenzo de Anaya seems to have heightened Anaya's reputation for quarrelsomeness. Anaya had insulted Rojo's wife, and the matter was even taken to the Council of the Indies. When not yet a regidor, Miguel Rojo, together with Melchor de Cabrera, alguacil mayor at the time, and Juan Ortiz, depositario general, was in the forefront of the disputes with Bishop González de Mendoza that rocked the town in the 1610s. Cabrera's sole source of income was the fees he collected. He did not even own the gun he used.[33] In the cabildo's discussions, Cabrera and Ortiz usually opposed don Ýñigo de Velasco, whose family upheld the bishop's cause. Little more is known about the two, except that Cabrera, a native of the Canary Islands, left his estate to Governor Lasso. It consisted mainly of debts owed for services he had performed as alguacil. Juan Ortiz renounced his office in 1625 in favor of Pedro de Salazar and moved to Pasto, where he obtained the encomienda vacated by Diego Delgado, an uncle of the beneficiary of the renunciation.[34]

Three members who acquired office after 1620 represented the successful self-made man. Diego de Victoria, from Zamora in Castile, participated in the campaigns against the Pijaos in New Granada and obtained an encomienda in Anserma, in the northern part of the province of Popayán. By 1624 he decided to make Popayán his main residence. After marrying doña Luisa de Salazar, widow of the merchant Luis de Olea and daughter of Diego Delgado and doña Mariana del Campo Salazar, he bought the office of fiel ejecutor for three thousand pesos. He thus allied himself with the Delgados and the Campo Salazars, two of the most prominent families of Popayán. At the same time he acquired an advantageous position in the commerce of the region. In a later residencia he was accused of having operated two stores, one for foodstuffs and one for general merchandise. In 1627 he offered security for the new governor and became corregidor de naturales for one year, until he resigned the post under the pressure of other duties. At the same time he was granted nine estancias in Anserma by the governor, as well as an encomienda and large parcels of land in Caloto. At his death in 1660 he held two encomiendas in the province. He owned a sugar plantation and a mine in the district of Caloto—both worked by gangs of Negro slaves—grew corn and wheat in Popayán, and owned large herds of cattle there. In Victoria's case office does not appear as a necessary ingredient of success. He had asked for the right to appoint a deputy during his frequent absences, who would even have voice and vote on the cabildo. When this was not accepted he asked to have the purchase price returned. He finally relented after the audiencia notified him that he could use the office with all the conditions attached to the original bid. There is in fact no record that he ever tried to appoint a deputy to take his seat on the cabildo.[35]

Another successful merchant and relative newcomer, Antonio Rodríguez de Migolla, invested in a regimiento as a favor to his brother-in-law. The latter purchased the office in 1609 but subsequently ceased to attend meetings (he probably moved away from the town). Moreover, he never validated his title. When the audiencia, after an investigation, declared the office forfeited in 1624, Antonio Rodríguez bought it. One-third of the purchase price went to the treasury and two-thirds to the former proprietor, his brother-in-law. Officeholding allegedly went to his head. Instead of continuing his mercantile interests, he turned to other pursuits, becoming corregidor de naturales in Popayán and later even obtaining an encomienda in Cali. He acquired these positions by paying large sums to the governor, if a series of hostile witnesses is to be believed.[36] One may also assume that commerce acquainted him with other local opportunities, and as a result he extended his operations.

By comparison with these two, Gonzalo López Prieto, corregidor de naturales under three governors, was in Popayán for a long time before he became a regidor in 1627.[37] His advancement was due chiefly to his own exertions. The ingredients of success—trade and office—were the same as in Diego de Victoria's case. Residencia records show him accused of dealing in cloth, building houses with Indian labor as his predecessors had done, using conscript labor in his brickyard, and generally underpaying the Indians who worked for him. Under Governor don Pedro Lasso de la Guerra, he obtained the encomienda of Timbío but continued as corregidor. He was administrator for the nuns' convent of Encarnación, surely not an unprofitable occupation. A series of transactions shows the extent of his good fortune. In 1627 he married doña Agustina de Figueroa, whose dowry was some 2,000 pesos. At the time of his marriage, López Prieto declared a capital of 15,500 pesos in cash, cattle, farm land, mining and grazing rights, slaves, houses, and household belongings. In 1629 it was López Prieto's turn to give a dowry of 4,000 pesos to a daughter from an earlier marriage. She married Diego Gerónimo Delgado Salazar, another regidor. In 1637 he became deputy of Governor Juan de Borja. Ultimately the fortune he assembled passed to his daughter Juana, who married her uncle Garcilaso de la Vega, son of Francisco de Figueroa and encomendero of Puracé. The only child of that union married don Joseph Hurtado, son of Alonso Hurtado del Águila. The combination of these fortunes formed the basis for the Hurtados' strong position in the region. In López Prieto's case, office, with its attendant opportunities for enrichment, was an indispensable part of success, not the mere adornment it was for Diego de Victoria.

Victoria and López Prieto were distant relatives of don Ýñigo de Velasco, while Pedro de Salazar, depositario general since 1623, and Diego Gerónimo Delgado and Francisco de Figueroa, regidores since 1631, were somewhat closer relatives. All three claimed descent from conquistadors and early settlers. Their fathers and grandfathers had held encomiendas. Their entry as members must have changed the makeup of the cabildo considerably. Diego Gerónimo Delgado was nephew to both don Ýñigo de Velasco and Diego de Victoria, and he was the son-in-law of Gonzalo López Prieto. Francisco de Figueroa was don Ýñigo's cousin, Gonzalo López Prieto's father-in-law, and Pedro de Salazar's uncle. The genealogical chart (table 3) shows the extent of consanguinity among cabildo members at the time. The result of these changes in the cabildo's composition was clearly evident in the elections of 1631 and 1632, when a majority of closely related members voted for one set of alcaldes and a minority of three for another set of candidates. The governor twice annulled the elections, alleging the candidates' unfitness for holding office and their close relationship with those who had elected them.[38]

After a generation, the cabildo was reconstituted in the 1670s. What distinguished this new group from the cabildo of the 1620s was a certain quasi-aristocratic homogeneity in status and background. Of the twelve who held proprietary office in the 1670s, eight laid claim to the title of don and nine were encomenderos.[39] Although an encomienda by then meant relatively little in economic terms, it still denoted considerable social prestige. At least ten were also mine operators and slave owners. Perhaps the most important fact connecting them was that, with one exception, they were all related to one another either directly or by marriage. It also seems that certain well-defined claims to particular offices existed, besides the Velascos' regular claim to the alferazgo. When four vecinos moved in 1671 to acquire membership in the cabildo, each one insisted on buying a specific seat held earlier by a relative or at least having some family link; they also agreed that none was to have precedence.[40]

Despite considerable homogeneity, differences in service, origin, and status remained strong. The cabildo included Lorenzo de Anaya as a survival from a former age. He was still participating in an election

TABLE 3
THE ZUÑIGAS IN POPAYAN IN THE 1630s

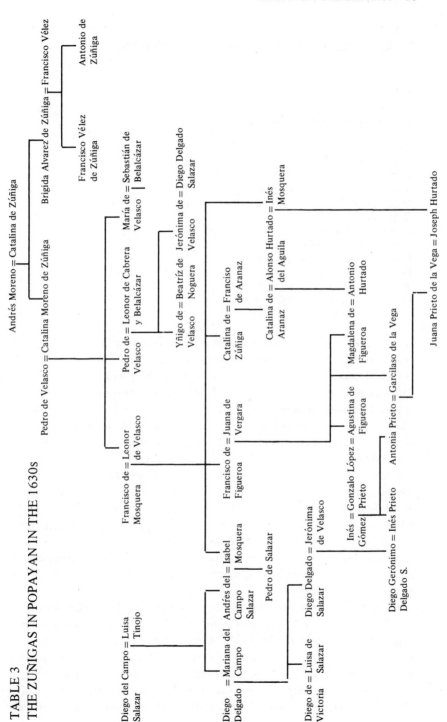

TABLE 4
THE CABILDO'S MEMBERSHIP IN THE 1670s

Alférez real
Don Diego de Velasco Noguera
Alguacil mayor
Juan de Huegonaga Salazar (1676)
Depositario general
Joseph de Morales Fravega (1672)
Fiel ejecutor
Vacant
Alcalde provincial de la hermandad
Don Blas de Aguinaga, don Lorenzo del Campo Salazar (1676)
Regidores
Lorenzo de Anaya
Don Joseph Hurtado del Águila (1672)
Don Christóbal de Mosquera (1672)
Don Nicolás de Gaviría (1672)
Melchor López de Celada (1672)
Don Francisco de Arboleda Salazar (1672)
Don Gregorio de Bonilla (1674)

in 1677, when he must have been far beyond eighty years, and he still took turns at the chore of being fiel ejecutor. A junior member in terms of service was don Diego de Velasco Noguera, alférez general. He was the son of don Ýñigo and held substantial encomiendas and mines. His sisters married respectively don Bernardino Pérez de Ubillus, the treasurer, and don Lorenzo del Campo Salazar, alcalde provincial since 1673 and concessionaire of the road over the Guanacas pass route.[41] Another of don Diego's brothers-in-law was the depositario general Joseph de Morales Fravega, an immigrant from Veri near Genoa, who arrived in the Indies around 1650 and was soon engaged in trade between Cartagena and Quito. In 1664 he married doña Gerónima de Velasco. His business took in everything from dealing in clothing imported from Spain to selling cattle and slaves on commission. Toward the end of his career he built up an extensive mining operation as well. In 1680 he was naturalized, after paying four hundred pesos to the treasury.[42]

Other newcomers became members of the cabildo in the decade of the 1670s. Melchor López de Celada came in Governor Valenzuela y Fajardo's entourage in the 1650s. After serving as deputy and interim contador, he obtained the encomienda of Totoró with sixteen Indians in 1657, on the basis of his marriage to doña Isabel de Figueroa (or Mosquera). This marriage allied him to the powerful Mosquera clan.[43] Don Francisco de Arboleda was another relative newcomer.[44] His father, the bachiller Jacinto de Arboleda, was a miner in the region of Anserma who had shifted his operations southward to Popayán, in conjunction with Diego de Victoria. Two of his sons, don Francisco and don Jacinto, took over the management while he devoted himself to an ecclesiastical career, rising to vicar general and ultimately becoming archdeacon of the cathedral chapter. Don Francisco married a daughter of don Joseph Hurtado and his brother a niece. Indeed, by this time the Hurtados were the major force in the town's affairs, through officeholding, encomienda grants, and judicious marriages.[45] Don Joseph, for instance, had served as deputy under two governors and also became a regidor in 1671. He controlled four encomiendas during much of the 1650s and 1660s, one through his wife (Puracé) and three that he managed to obtain from pliable governors for his son Lucas López del Águila (Pinguata or Pandiguando, Cajete, Chapa). Although confirmation for two of the encomiendas was finally denied in 1667, the family still controlled Puracé and Pandiguando. Only the office of contador eluded don Joseph. He bid for it in vain in the 1650s. His son García Hurtado finally acquired it in the 1680s. Alonso, who had joined the Church, became the local representative of the Inquisition, and Francisco, another son, known as el Gordo, served twice as deputy during the turbulent years at the turn of the century.

It would be tedious to pursue further these details concerning the cabildo's members. Given the absence of membership data for many years of the century, they do not lend themselves to precise statistical tabulation. Nevertheless, it is possible to draw some conclusions. The cabildo of the 1670s strongly represented the leading elements of Popayán, the "personas principales y beneméritas" who formed a kind of town patriciate. This contrasted with its composition during the first decades of the century, when self-made types (not all of them successful) and ambitious merchants prevailed—men who were described in petitions as upstarts who bought favors and encomiendas from the governors. By the second half of the century, some descendants of these upstarts, such as don Joseph Hurtado, were members of the town's ruling group. By then, they regarded their claims as hallowed by tradition. This was possible because the town's leading families had a flexible attitude toward adopting new members. Marriage not only sealed success, it also opened the door to further advance, because it translated economic achievement into social acceptance. Since by the end of the century everybody of importance was related to everybody else in Popayán, kinship supplied a common social basis. By the same token, the very generality of the fact makes it a less useful tool for tracking down alignments and groupings.

The appearance of a cohesive upper stratum interested in local office, in particular the cabildo, was only a passing phenomenon. Cabildo meetings became less frequent within a few years after 1680. When the minute books became available again in 1696, after a hiatus of fourteen years, the cabildo had dwindled to its former numerical weakness and relative insignificance. Three explanations of this feeble record and lack of permanence are plausible enough to bear discussion in some detail.

The social consolidation of an upper stratum, in which sets of families held the levers of local power, with their claims recognized and with a working mechanism for integrating newcomers, did not necessarily strengthen formal political institutions. Informal bonds reinforced by family connections tended to make an institutional platform redundant. The amount of business conducted in public decreased as private negotiation took the place of public transaction. It is no accident that the office of fiel ejecutor went unfilled after 1660. What limited supervision the cabildo had over prices and commerce ceased, and contracts became an affair between buyer and seller, without public intervention.[46] Family ties and marriage alliances were bound to play a role as offices endowed with jurisdiction or carrying local responsibility came within reach of local citizens. Even if local appointments did not lead to corruption, shortcuts to information and decisions were bound to occur, as they do in any political system. Cohesion and loyalty, it seems clear, remained tied to the family and kin group, which provided a set of primary social relations for which there was no substitute. There was, however, no guarantee that cohesion and harmony would last. Conflict was always a possibility—between old-timers and newcomers, crown officials and local citizens, and one local clan and another. The ties that bound them were not permanent: they had to be maintained and renewed. Also, there always might be ambitions that the existing arrangement could not contain.

One not so paradoxical byproduct of social consolidation was the fact that leading citizens began taking wives from outside the area. Don Diego Joseph de Velasco married an oidor's daughter from Santa Fé. Don García Hurtado, the contador, married the niece of a contador mayor of the tribunal in Santa Fé.[47] One may assume that consolidation increased the need to differentiate among families, through marriages if need be. Rivalry had many facets, of which membership in the cabildo was only one. A shared stake in the deputyship—as was evident in the alternation between don Diego Ignacio de Aguinaga, don Francisco Hurtado, and don Diego Joseph de Velasco during the 1690s—provided an alternative. It proved insufficient to prevent the outbreak of local altercations between supporters of the Hurtado and Velasco clans in 1700 that continued in various forms until 1706. Local rivalry served to revive interest in the cabildo, at first chiefly as an instrument for partisan purposes. This was the case in the four purchase bids for regimientos made in 1701 by supporters of the Hurtado cause, whose reception a partisan cabildo first delayed. Later they were imposed by force.[48]

Membership in the cabildo carried risks and liabilities. The four who applied for regimientos in 1701 stressed the pressures governors could bring against members. They alluded to the governor's ability to apply laws in discretionary fashion—for instance, in enforcing regulations against miners and encomenderos. Officeholders, they alleged, had preferred to write off their investment in office by resigning, rather than expose themselves further to these tactics.[49] Another negative aspect of office was that it placed obstacles in the way of conducting business. Conflict of interest was not really a consideration, but availability was. Office confined a conscientious incumbent to the town and the district. Alcaldes, in particular, had to be present and available at definite times. It is hence not surprising that some individuals asked to be excused from serving. In one petition a group of peninsular merchants opposed the introduction of the alternativa (rotation of office between Creoles and Spaniards) put forward by some immigrants. They alleged that there were plenty of vecinos patricios in town with time on their hands. They, at any rate, had to attend to their business, with no time to spare. The audiencia granted their petition, exempting them from the obligation of holding office.[50]

Access to local positions with more scope was a third reason why the cabildo at times proved unattractive or even irrelevant to those who were interested in the realities of power. The deputyship was the most important of these positions. The two treasury offices came within reach of native sons in the second half of the century and may have constituted equivalent positions. The treasury officials' responsibility extended over a whole region, but they played the largest role in the town where the treasury was located. Before 1642 the treasury officials resided in Cali. There the accountant (contador) Juan de Palacios Alvarado was an important figure during his long tenure (from 1592 to 1631). He also served several times as the governor's deputy. He became active in mining and agriculture; for instance, he brought a mining specialist from Quito to Almaguer. After the wars of the Pijaos had ended, he took a leading role in opening up mining in the district of Caloto.[51] The men who succeeded this remarkable entrepreneur moved the treasury to Popayán and married into local society there.

Palacios Alvarado's colleague as treasurer had been don Gerónimo Pérez de Ubillus, a Basque from Guipúzcoa, who before his appointment in 1613 worked twelve years for the Council of the Indies. When he died in 1633, Governor Villaquirán appointed his son don Bernardino to the job, and the Council confirmed the appointment. Don Bernardino married one of don Ýñigo de Velasco's sisters. Two of his sons chose ecclesiastical careers; one rose to be archdeacon in Popayán, the other became a canon of the cathedral of Quito. Besides its ecclesiastical extension, the family had a mercantile and fiscal side. Two daughters married immigrants from Spain, don Sebastián Torijano from La Mancha and don Sebastián Correa, a Catalan. Both of these men were merchants of means in Popayán, and they were active in purchasing unregistered gold that they delivered to the treasury. Early in the eighteenth century, one of don Sebastián Torijano's daughters married don Felipe de Luzuriaga, who was treasurer of Popayán. A niece married don Joseph de la Cuesta, the actual successor to Pérez de Ubillus in the treasurer's post.[52] Juan Leandro de Bonilla, appointed contador in 1631, had served the crown faithfully for twenty-one years in Europe, seven of them in the Netherlands. In Popayán he married doña Mariana de Velasco y Salazar, a daughter of Diego Delgado Salazar. His son, don Gregorio de Bonilla Salazar, married a descendant of the adelantado Belalcázar. He became a local mine owner and encomendero and bought a seat on the cabildo in the 1670s.[53] The first native son to acquire a treasury post was don Juan de Larrainzar, who purchased the office of contador in 1657 from the audiencia for seven thousand pesos. Don Juan was closely related to the Aguinagas, and his father, Captain Martín de Larrainzar, served several times as alcalde ordinario in Popayán. Nonetheless, his reception by the cabildo was delayed for three years, ostensibly because the quality of bond offered was insufficient. In fact, the cabildo was acting to protect the interests of don Fernando de Salazar Betancur (who had married doña Elena de Mosquera) and don Joseph Hurtado. Both men had served as governor's deputies, and don Joseph at the time served as interim contador.[54]

After don Juan de Larrainzar's death in 1668, continuity in the treasury's operation was preserved by the treasurer don Bernardino Pérez de Ubillus, who served in that capacity until 1694. No proprietor for the office of contador appeared for nearly twenty years. The prolonged vacancy may have suited the governors, who made interim appointments, and it may have been welcome to the local notables who might expect such nominations. Yet it remains incomprehensible that no permanent appointment was made until 1687, when the Council of the Indies and the audiencia of Quito "awarded" the office to different applicants, the former to don Juan de Sobrecasas y Palomares in consideration of a contribution of 2,500 pesos, the latter to don García Hurtado, son of don Joseph Hurtado del Águila, for the sum of 12,500 pesos. Don García was ultimately confirmed. The Hurtados thus obtained a stake in the treasury similar to that obtained earlier by the Velascos.[55]

The discussion of officeholding demonstrates that government in the province was the domain of a cohesive local group during much of the seventeenth century. The presence of the governor as the crown's representative made little difference, since he depended on local cooperation. The governing stratum was not closed to newcomers. As the conquest economy gave way to new arrangements that demanded entrepreneurial ability and mercantile acumen, newcomers possessing these talents were accepted as local leaders. Through marriage they could share in the aura and the tangible rewards derived from the conquest. Social mobility, though never totally absent, was most pronounced in the first half of the seventeenth century, while the pattern of officeholding in the later decades of the century indicates a degree of local homogeneity and cohesion that had not existed earlier.

Officeholding within the cabildo serves as one indicator of local control over affairs. Yet it mirrors such control only imperfectly. Around the turn of the century, municipal office may have been bought largely as an investment in expectation of a return. Before long, offices had ceased to be sought for monetary reward. Instead they served to enhance and support the position of the local upper stratum. Office was not necessarily sought as an ornament. Rather, interest in officeholding was maintained as long as there was competition within the ruling group. When such competition ceased, interest waned. The ruling group tended to become a network of families. It was this network that assured the cohesion and continuity of the settlers' society. There was mobility. Discord might break out and things would fall apart for a time, to be put together again. The politics of officeholding reflects these phenomena only partially. Yet neither office nor benefice was a simple extension of the settlers' society. State and Church existed as separate institutions, manifestations of another world that continued to command allegiance, perhaps because its demands were limited.

Neither the crown, when it introduced the sale of office, nor the governors undermined local government in the Indies. Its vitality was a reflex of the society it represented, of the clash of interests and groups during the conquest, and of the relatively unformed state of that society during its aftermath. The formation of lateral ties, mainly through marriage among the conquerors, their descendants, and successive waves of immigrants, was the most important avenue of consolidating that society. Yet vertical ties—to the land, its native inhabitants, and its resources—also played a role. Where they proved unstable, as in Popayán, the formation of a cohesive upper stratum could be delayed or interrupted for generations. Once it had been achieved on the basis of the extended family, the society's forum proved to be the family reunion rather than the council chamber.

7. The Governorship and the Treasury

The governor was the crown's representative in the province. The importance of the office rested on its capacity to transcend—at least potentially—local ties. The governor was in a position not only to implement crown policy but also to supervise local bodies and office-holders. Governors were appointed by the crown from a slate of nominees submitted by the Council of the Indies, usually for a term of five years, though longer service was not uncommon. The annual salary was two thousand ducats, paid by the local treasury from general funds. This not inconsiderable salary and the fact that the governors were mostly recruited from the peninsula should have freed the office of the more obvious local pressures. Yet the governorship was a weak institution. This weakness derived from the organization of the office itself, the local constellation of politics, and the expectations of the appointees. Governors and treasury officials, however, were not the only agents of empire in Popayán. In a different sense the Church also served to control, and so did the administrative and judicial inquests of the residencia and visita. In the conjunction of these controls, weak as they individually were, one has to seek the explanation for the crown's continuing influence over local affairs and also for the continuing tie between metropolis and colony.

What were the powers of an incoming governor and what degree of local cooperation did he need to be effective? To what extent could a governor bend local arrangements to his purposes? Before discussing the activities of particular governors, we must first assess the potential of the office. The corregidor of Castile provided the model for the office of governor. The capítulos de corregidores, a set of ordinances promulgated in 1500, applied to the corregidors in Castile and to their counterparts in the Indies, among them the governors. Indeed, governors and viceroys were essentially in the same category, although prestige, range, and attributes of office were different.

The governor's powers were extensive, as he had jurisdiction in temporal matters and possessed patronage and supervisory rights in ecclesiastical affairs.[1] As vice-patron of the Church, the governor appointed clerics to benefices from a list of candidates drawn up by the bishop. In the temporal sphere, his official powers related to administration, justice, finance, and war. He was a judge of the first instance, and he also heard appeals from both his deputies in the towns and the alcaldes ordinarios. He could grant the right to make appeals to the audiencia of Quito or of Santa Fé. Periodic visitation of prisons was another responsibility. Although finance was not properly the governor's sphere, he was expected to watch the treasury officials' performance. Occasionally he was delegated to take accounts or to tighten methods of collection. In military matters the governor was subordinate to the president of the Audiencia of New Granada as captain general, but he could make military appointments up to the rank of captain. In practice, governors regularly usurped the title of captain general.

The governor's legislative powers became attenuated in the seventeenth century. In the 1580s, for instance, Governor Sancho García de Espinar promulgated ordinances concerning Indian labor in the province; later this function was routinely exercised by oidores dispatched by the two audiencias.[2] The governorship lacked a permanent staff, since the escribanía de gobernación showed little continuity. It was filled only occasionally, and its affairs were often in disorder. Indeed, governors seem to have had the habit of having somebody from their entourage perform its duties (and collect the fees). The practice jeopardized the position of the proprietor if there was one; it also must have made potential applicants reluctant to compete.[3] Since a special constable (alguacil) was not provided, the governor relied on the town constables, who often proved recalcitrant although legally obliged to cooperate and execute the governor's decrees. A governor could appoint local deputies (tenientes). If he chose his deputies in Spain, they had to be approved by the Council of the Indies. The audiencias of Santa Fé or Quito confirmed appointments made in the Indies. The governor could appoint a letrado as his lieutenant governor to assist him in judicial matters, an appointment that carried a salary of five hundred ducats.

The governor's title contained a general injunction to observe all antecedent legislation, decrees, provisions, and orders. But he did not receive specific instructions tailored to local problems, nor did he get copies of "antecedent legislation." The only laws alluded to in the documentation were the capítulos de corregidores of 1500. A governor might by chance have a copy of Castillo de Bobadilla's *Política para corregidores y señores de vasallos* . . . (Policy for corregidors and lords of vassals . . .), a manual of government widely used in Castile. But it seems unlikely. Governors in the Indies were not usually lawyers, as were many of the corregidors of Castile. They were drawn from the ranks of the lesser nobility who had served at court or in the armies of Spain (hombres de capa y espada).[4] In short, the governorship was not a bureaucratic "office" in the way we understand it today, with a staff, settled procedure, and a basis in administrative law, nor was the governor a trained civil servant with definite career expectations. As we will see, private considerations not only tinged the public functions of the office but practically deformed and redirected them. This situation was not peculiar to the Indies. It simply corresponded to the arrangements prevailing in Europe, where there was no clear demarcation between the public and private sphere as yet and where social and pecuniary considerations frequently determined not only the performance of incumbents but also the character of offices.[5]

The greatest obstacles to effective government were lack of expertise and the related difficulty of obtaining relevant information about the province. The disarray in the records of the escribanía de gobernación is a case in point. In a residencia of 1633, the escribano de gobernación, Juan de Espiñosa, was found to be without any of the prescribed books.[6] At other times, there was not even an escribano de gobernación, and the governor had to rely on the cabildo and its escribano for information on legislation and precedent. The governors themselves contributed to this unsettled situation. Governor Lasso, for instance, dispensed with the services of the regular escribano and used a notary he brought along for the residencia, in spite of the escribano's complaints.[7] A governor could enhance his knowledge of the province by handling his predecessor's residencia, conducting inspections, or reading reports. The residencia could acquaint a new governor not only with his predecessor's frailties but also with the opportunities of the office awaiting him.[8] Inspection trips declined in importance during the seventeenth century, because the audiencia had limited the governors to one each year, in response to the inhabitants' complaints. To them these trips did not confer benefits but rather seemed like biblical plagues. Governors did not usually make reports on the state of their province, as was the wont of viceroys at the end of a term of office. Information about the province was therefore sparse and no procedures existed for making it easily available.

A governor's powers were limited, despite their apparent latitude. Some restraints were of deliberate design. Others, perhaps more effective, were imposed by provincial realities. Governors presented their credentials before the cabildos of the province, either in person or through a representative. They also presented a list of guarantors who were willing to vouch for the governor's compliance with the residencia and ready to bear the consequences. The cabildo of the capital therefore had to approve this list, ascertaining the credit-worthiness of these bondsmen who might have to pay the governor's fines in a residencia.[9] The residencia was an ex-post-facto check on the governor, though its effectiveness is debatable. Many of the governor's appointments were subject to confirmation, as were his encomienda grants. Just as a governor's judicial decisions were subject to appeal, so were many of his other actions of a quasi-judicial character. Hamstrung at every turn, governors could do relatively little harm, but neither could they do very much good.

In these circumstances it is not surprising if a governor's record was unspectacular. It was rarely characterized by initiative and was even deficient in routine activity. The formal description of the office provides only a limited measure of the governor's performance. The agencies that a governor dealt with routinely—principally the cabildo and the treasury officials, but the bishop and the clergy as well—have to be considered in their relations with the governorship. Furthermore, the background of the governors and their expectations should be noted. By way of illustration, let us take up some individual cases.

The governorship of Captain Juan Bermúdez de Castro (1628–1633) offers the most evidence. There are the governor's communications to the Council of the Indies—more frequent than any other governor's. We have an extensive report by Bishop Ambrosio de Vallejo on the state of the province, and we can examine the results of the governor's residencia. Finally, there is the record of the governor's participation in municipal affairs.

Bermúdez received his appointment in April 1626 and took up duties in Popayán in February 1628. His credentials were impressive. After ten years of service in the royal household he was appointed treasurer of Vera Cruz and corregidor of Micantla in New Spain, offices he held for six years because his term was extended several times by the viceroy Marquis de Guadalcázar. During this entire time his performance met with approval, as his residencias attest. Also, royal revenues increased during his tenure as treasurer.[10]

In Popayán, Bermúdez displayed considerable initiative. He moved the governor's residence to Popayán—theoretically capital of the province since its establishment—and proposed to transfer the treasury there as well. In numerous communications to the Council of the Indies the governor pursued his pet project, the pacification of the Chocó. While advocating diverse schemes to that end, he did not neglect his own interests, and in doing so he aroused opposition, principally on the part of the bishop. The governor was able to maintain control through judicious appointments and by intervening in the cabildo's affairs, but his residencia with its evidence of irregularities and corruption confirmed earlier accusations and at least temporarily halted his career.

A change in the governor's residence from Cali to Popayán was considered for many years. In 1609 the Council left the ultimate decision to the audiencia of Quito. In 1620 and again in 1621 the tribunal ordered the governors to reside in Popayán. Governors Lasso and Menéndez Márquez demurred, insisting on Cali's favorable central location and the need for their presence near the critical regions of Buenaventura and the Chocó. Despite his continuing concern with the Chocó, Bermúdez finally made the move, and in fact he never left Popayán except for a two-month visit of inspection to the southern towns of Pasto and Almaguer.[11]

In these circumstances the governor's insistence on schemes for the pacification of the Chocó may appear slightly suspect. The crown's interest in the "rich mines of Toro" never vanished, even though they were abandoned after 1580. An ambitious governor in search of a reputation and perhaps a fortune could easily rekindle this interest. In his first letter to the Council after his arrival, Bermúdez reported on meetings held in the northern towns of the province to discuss the best tactics for manning armed expeditions into the Chocó. One such expedition was made under the leadership of Captain Martín Bueno. In his letter of the next year, the governor went one step further. He proposed a set of agreements to the Council to counter the alternate proposals promoted by don Antonio Maldonado de Mendoza, a vecino of Anserma with considerable experience in Indian warfare. Bermúdez's proposal included a demand for the title of adelantado, the right to found towns and appoint their officials, and six thousand ducats as compensation. If successful, he wanted a marquisate. Apparently the Council did not respond to these overtures, which explains the plaintive note in the governor's dispatches of 1632. He now asked simply for an extension of his term or at least a delay in appointing his successor so that the task of pacification could be finished. He mentioned that three hundred slaves were already at work and that the Indians were already at peace. He also pointed to his outlays—thirty thousand ducats for arms, gunpowder, and other supplies.[12]

While promoting these projects with their air of fancifulness, the governor did not neglect affairs closer to home. In a memorial of 1630 addressed to the Council, he summarized his accomplishments and noted continuing problems. Besides the Chocó proper, there were other critical areas. The fort guarding the port of Buenaventura was burnt several times by the Noanamá Indians. In Popayán proper, the Indians of Páez were still not pacified effectively or settled in compact pueblos. In the capital itself the governor repaired the roads to Quito and Santa Fé. Work on the roads and repairs on many houses in town were carried out by Indians assigned for the purpose by the governor. A water main was laid to supply the nunnery and the principal residences. A well-built store was used as the new prison. Members of the cabildo and local encomenderos endorsed this report in a series of depositions made before the alcalde ordinario Juan de Mera and then added to the governor's letters.[13]

Governor Bermúdez needed the endorsement because Bishop Vallejo had been collecting evidence against him for months. The falling out between bishop and governor resulted from Bermúdez's refusal to punish one of his slaves for breaking into the bishop's residence at night in pursuit of female companionship. According to testimony presented at the residencia, the governor not only refused the bishop's demand for justice but even insulted him and members of the clergy in public.[14] The potential rivalry between the two "heads" of the province was thus transformed into actual antagonism.

A reason for sending derogatory information about the governor to Spain was not hard to find. In reply to a cédula of 1629 that had inquired about the treatment of the Indian population, the bishop sent a report to the Council that included detailed testimony by the local clergy, both secular and regular.[15] The report argued that in a kind of chain reaction the governor's exploitation of the Spanish population led to more exploitation of the Indian population. It charged that the governor traded in cloth and other merchandise through intermediaries who monopolized trade to such an extent that other merchants now bypassed the town and prices had risen. The report further accused him of selling deputyships, corregimientos, and encomiendas in outright fashion. Witnesses mentioned sums between fifteen hundred and two thousand pesos. All the witnesses claimed that the governor maintained a gambling setup in his house that brought him at least fifty thousand pesos and that several prominent citizens had vowed—after heavy losses —never to enter his house again. The clerics accused the governor of simony in awarding a doctrina for money. Another serious accusation bolstered by detailed evidence charged him with selling Indian captives as slaves in the guise of entrusting them in encomienda.

In their testimony the clerics emphasized the governor's arrangements with local merchants and encomenderos. One of his servants, Antonio de Aguilar, ran a store in town. Another part of the governor's business was handled by Gerónimo de Patiño, procurador de número and collector of the alcabala. The two brothers Muñoz and Juan de Aranda were other citizens named by the clergy as merchants serving the governor's interests. Most important was the cooperation of Alonso Hurtado del Águila, who was alcalde three times during Bermúdez's tenure. The clergy named him as one of the principal collaborators. At least initially, Bermúdez gained the support of a local majority by appointing don Ýñigo de Velasco to two offices at the same time: deputy and corregidor de naturales. After more than two years of apparent cooperation, local opposition appeared when the governor twice vetoed the cabildo's nominees for the office of alcalde ordinario, thus keeping the same alcaldes in office for more than two years.[16]

In his correspondence the governor did his best to neutralize the clergy's accusations. The bishop turned against him, he wrote, because of some difference concerning the royal patronage. The audiencia was kept informed of these matters, but, knowing the bishop well, the judges did not lend much credence to his complaints. As for the treatment of Indians, the governor wrote, "it is public and notorious that it is the doctrineros who do the most harm to the Indians and who in particular want to be the heirs whenever an Indian dies though there be rightful claimants." [17]

The governor's residencia administered by his successor, Lorenzo de Villaquirán, substantiated many of the earlier accusations and in fact added a few more. It confirmed the charges of running a gambling establishment, trading through intermediaries, and selling Indians. It further convicted the governor of partial administration of justice. No proof concerning the sale of appointments and encomiendas was produced. In the revision of the sentence by the Council of the Indies, the governor was fined 4,700 ducats and excluded from holding judicial office for four years.[18]

The case of Governor Bermúdez illustrates two related phenomena: the governor's dependence on local support and the incidence of corruption. The latter phenomenon is difficult to discuss because of the elusive nature of the evidence and the problem of arriving at a definition of what constituted corruption in seventeenth-century Spain and America. Although it may be difficult to arrive at a definition, the evidence does help to establish the line that divided permissible from illicit behaviour.

The most common accusation leveled against a governor in the residencias was that he neglected his duties, whether in road maintenance, upholding morality, or protecting the Indians. Beyond such sins of omission there were infractions of a more direct nature. Governors Lasso and Guzmán y Toledo, for instance, were fined for accepting presents from the local encomenderos. Governor Sarmiento was fined for giving encomiendas to his friends while neglecting the claims of more meritorious contenders. Governors Guzmán de Toledo and Valenzuela actually sold encomiendas and had to pay heavy fines. Governors Sarmiento, Lasso, and Bermúdez all engaged in mining and trading through intermediaries.[19]

A series of charges against Governor Rodrigo Roque de Mañozca drawn up in 1695 by the fiscal of the Council of the Indies illustrates some of the possibilities for enrichment and at the same time indicates the residencia's failure to keep rapacious officials in check.[20] The fiscal, for example, took it for granted that a decline in the yield of the quinto meant that the governor had pocketed the difference. Mañozca was further charged with retaining considerable sums from the license fee for stores, the sales tax collected from nonresidents, and the statutory fine for immigrants without license. Another sum he was accused of using for his own purposes was 10,000 pesos collected from the encomenderos of the province as media anata (the half-year income from a grant or office). Yet another item charged Mañozca with extortion, abusing his position as residencia judge by claiming the payment of fees in advance, and asking for 2,500 pesos in order to disqualify an adjunct judge of the residencia.

Since residencias evidently ceased to serve as a corrective, the fiscal recommended dispatching a commissary judge armed with detailed instructions and extraordinary powers to investigate Governor Mañozca's conduct and at the same time finish the accumulated residencias. The Council accepted the fiscal's recommendations. Concurrently, the Council issued a severe reprimand to the audiencia, informing it that in extraordinary situations—with accusations of fraud and extortion against a governor supported by incontrovertible evidence—it had a duty to intervene and to suspend the governor if necessary. The new fiscal, Pedro Sarmiento y Huesterlin of the audiencia of Santa Fé, was commissioned for the task. His mission, however, proved a complete failure.[21]

The foregoing discussion shows that exploiting office for private gain was common enough but that standards did exist, though they were less well enforced as the century wore on. One might ask, however, to what extent legal norms can exist independent of the opportunity for enforcing them. At a certain point they become mere ethical injunctions that can in practice be contradicted with impunity. Venality became virtually institutionalized when the crown resorted to what amounted to a covert sale of the governorship during the last decades of the seventeenth century.[22]

The crown started selling reversions to the governorship of Popayán from 1677 on, when don Gerónimo de Berrío offered two thousand doblones for the privilege. He obliged himself to equip one hundred men for an expedition into the Chocó and agreed to draw only one-half of his salary. The other half was to come from the increased mining taxes he promised. The only favor he asked was to be given a cédula permitting him to visit his jurisdiction as often as necessary, especially the mining area of Barbacoas. This permission was to supersede the prohibition on frequent visits imposed by the audiencia of Quito in response to complaints of vecinos vexed by too much attention from their governors.[23] In effect, the applicant was asking for a free hand in the collection of taxes.

Sums changing hands at the time of appointment to office were nothing new. For more than forty years the media anata, one-half of the first year's income from an office, was a required payment. Don Fernando Martínez de Fresneda paid three thousand doblones as a gracia in 1674.[24] It was a fairly easy transition from the media anata, in reality a kind of tax on certain types of income, to the gracia or the servicio. The servicio was defined as a donation but was really a purchase price, though it was never designated as such nor were the procedures devised for the sale of office applied to the transaction. Martínez de Fresneda and de Berrío, whose payments initiated the practice, were both well acquainted with the region. De Berrío was a vecino of Santa Fé de Bogotá and Martínez de Fresneda was a longtime resident of New Granada. Hence they both knew what they were investing in.

Once started, the practice of granting reversions continued without fail. A future appointment was secured in 1683 by don Juan Camargo de Flores for ten thousand pesos; in 1686 two reversions were granted, one to don Rodrigo Roque de Mañozca for six thousand pesos and another to don Gerónimo José de la Vega y Caviedes for fourteen thousand pesos. Other reversions were granted, in 1690 to don Tomás Ponce de León and in 1692 to don Gregorio de Miera Ceballos for six thousand escudos. In 1695 don Gregorio's reversion was renewed on behalf of his nephew and heir, against an additional payment of one thousand pesos.[25]

Was the granting of reversions a good business for the crown? It seems most unlikely that it was, though it did bring in some revenue when and where it was needed, exemplifying the hand-to-mouth style of the last Hapsburg's reign. It seems unlikely, too, that such grants were made in ignorance of what was involved. They departed from a legal tradition that prohibited the sale of judicial office and constituted an open invitation to "buyers" to reimburse themselves. A salary of ten thousand ducats over five years less the media anata of one thousand ducats did not warrant the investment made, unless there were additional compensations. The case of don Gerónimo José de la Vega y Caviedes (later the Marqués de Nevares), alderman of Seville, is typical. He offered twelve thousand pesos for the corregimiento of Cajamarca (in this case equivalent to a governorship) but changed his mind and offered fourteen thousand pesos for Popayán instead.[26] Word of Governor de Berrío's successful acquisition of visitation rights and his permission to deduct part of his salary from an increase in taxes had reached Seville, making the governorship of Popayán more attractive.

One can envisage a situation in which officials, miners, and merchants of the province cooperated to defraud the crown, though there is no conclusive evidence. The lack of evidence is not surprising, since successive investigations made little progress in clearing up apparent frauds. In 1705, Licenciado Pedrosa, inspector (visitador) of the treasury in Popayán (where the last such inspection had taken place in 1659), stated that the town of Popayán was in continuous conspiracy against the royal treasury. This conspiracy was facilitated by the fact that ultimate jurisdiction in fiscal matters belonged to the distant audiencia of Quito. The jurisdiction of the tribunal of accounts in Santa Fé applied only to liquidating accounts. Any litigation arising therefrom pertained to Quito, giving rise to obfuscation and endless delays. The visitador therefore decided to suspend the visita for the time being. For the mission to be successful, he needed to be armed with greater plenary powers, and the province would have to be in a less agitated state. In view of the great potential revenue to be gained, in particular by reorganizing the provincial treasuries, he even toyed with the idea of going immediately to Spain to present his plans at court.[27] His representations may have had the desired effect, because twelve years later he returned as the first viceroy of New Granada. One of his reforms was the separation of the Chocó from Popayán. As a separate province it could be more easily supervised.[28]

Three main factors created the situation that prompted the visitador's assessment: the governor's investment in his office, a weak and disorganized provincial treasury, and the frontierlike conditions in the new gold-bearing areas of Barbacoas and the Chocó. A branch of the treasury of Popayán was not established in Barbacoas until 1709, when it became clear that collection of the quinto and the supervision this entailed had to be closer to the areas of production. Similarly, registers of the slave population—indispensable for keeping a check on the mine owners—were instituted only that same year. Previously either the governor's deputy or an alcalde of Santa María del Puerto, the only town in the area, acted as collector of revenue. These reforms were achieved by the Marqués de San Miguel de la Vega, governor after 1707, who put the administration of Barbacoas and the Chocó on a firm footing.[29]

The treasury officials needed the governor's cooperation for procedural reform as well as for the simpler job of collection. Such cooperation—along with a modicum of mutual supervision—was institutionalized in the meetings of the junta de real hacienda, which comprised the two treasury officials and the governor. Such meetings, to judge by the absence of evidence, may have been scarce. Governor and treasury officials had not necessarily the same interests. Governor Guzmán y Toledo, for instance, simply evaded paying a fine imposed on him by the Council of the Indies for making a land grant without authorization. In the end the grantee and the treasurer paid the fine. The treasurer, don Bernardino Pérez de Ubillus, noted that there were no other officials to lend force to his directives.[30] During most of the century the officials were not conspicuous for their zeal, except perhaps in supporting the miners' requests for a reduction in the tax they paid. Don Bernardino Pérez de Ubillus succeeded his father to the office of treasurer in 1633. He did not retire until 1694, at the age of more than eighty. The office of contador was vacant for over twenty years before it was bought in the 1680s by don García Hurtado, brother of don Francisco Hurtado del Águila, who was then the governor's deputy.[31] Making interim appointments to the post of contador provided the governors with an additional source of patronage, although in theory such interim vacancies were to be filled by the alcaldes ordinarios.[32]

Although it is not my purpose here to discuss the functioning of the provincial treasury in detail, some indication of its scope and the problems it faced is useful. These problems, in short, were lack of personnel, lack of competent supervision, and ignorance of revenue potential.[33] The treasury was understaffed. In 1687 the treasury officials requested that a scribe (escribiente) be hired at two hundred pesos annually, half of what a scribe received in Quito.[34] We do not know whether the request was granted. The officials did use clerical help, but there was no position for it among the allowable expenditures. There were no functioning branch offices; rather, the collection of taxes, like the quinto, was entrusted to alcaldes ordinarios or governors' deputies. The treasury officials maintained some control by making occasional inspection and collection trips or by dispatching collectors (jueces de cobranzas), who reimbursed themselves for their pains by tacking on fees. Inspections gave information about tax liability only if they were thorough and painstaking, checking all mining settlements, reviewing the miners' accounts, and counting the slave population.[35] Only then could the officials make a rough calculation of the gold mined and the tax owed. Generally, however, the officials had to rely on merchants' or miners' declarations, a method analogous to the handling of the United States income tax but without its bureaucratic backup.[36] Some taxes were farmed out, for instance, the alcabala (sales tax) to the cabildos. Monopolies were farmed out (playing cards) or handled by the officials (stamped paper). Crown encomiendas, if large enough, were managed by administrators. The tribute of vacant encomiendas was the corregidor's responsibility. In all these cases and more the officials had to collect the taxes themselves, aided by the posting of appropriate bond, in some situations, and by the threat of imprisonment in others.

The treasury officials in turn were liable to render accounts to the superior tribunal at Santa Fé, which also had general supervisory powers. Summary accounts were forwarded every year to Bogotá. If they were not sent within a stipulated term, the officials' salaries would be embargoed. Nevertheless, accounting frequently fell into arrears. By 1700 the treasury of Popayán was four years behind. The tribunal itself did not improve matters by leaving accounts unprocessed. This failure was not surprising, since there were only two contadores mayores then, one of whom was advanced in years and the other kin to everybody in the region, as the president of the audiencia of Santa Fé complained.[37] The arrears prompted the investigatory mission of Licenciado Antonio de la Pedrosa y Guerrero, with its acute assessment of problems but no immediate remedy. The licenciado in fact witnessed the turbulence in the province that grew out of an argument between governor and contador.

The altercation started with a dispute between the two about the supervision of the treasury. Material for conflict was ample, and in the end the treasury figured as only one element in the drawn-out sequence of events that was later called the War between the Tripitenorios and the Pambazos.[38] Treasury and governorship had become increasingly valuable prizes, given expanding gold production, the absence of supervision, and official ignorance of the province's revenue potential. Local groupings, if they could not control these prizes, could at least retain influence over them. Influence could be shared or contested. Also, the audiencia of Quito was more willing to interfere then, while the crown was less able to intervene, with Spain in the throes of the War of the Spanish Succession (1701–1714). Hence the conflict expanded into a contest over the governorship, a little "war" that lasted from 1701 until

1707. It involved the principal families of Popayán and drew into its vortex the audiencias of Quito and Santa Fé and the viceroy of Peru.

Events began unfolding after Governor Nevares started to audit the accounts of the contador García Hurtado, doing a spot check and cash revision in response to a royal cédula. Such an audit inevitably revealed shortages and irregularities, since treasury funds, instead of lying idle, were used in trading and other ventures. Delays in forwarding accounts, if tolerated, increased the profits of such undertakings and could turn the treasury into a veritable local bank, serving a select clientele. The contador refused to cooperate, accusing the governor of blackmail, and the governor then suspended him, appointing in his stead his own man. This action polarized the locality into supporters and antagonists of the governor. Don Diego Joseph de Velasco, the alférez real who then served as deputy, and his adherents joined the governor's side; the Hurtados, Mosqueras, and their clients went into opposition. The issue turned into a trial of wits and strength. The contador, for instance, obtained his reinstatement from the tribunal of accounts in Santa Fé, but the governor replied by deposing him altogether, alleging his close relationship to one of the members of the tribunal (García Hurtado had married a cousin of one of the contadores mayores). When a successor to the governor appeared, the cabildo of Popayán, dominated as it was by Nevares, refused to recognize him, thus keeping Nevares in power. The contest did not end until February of 1702, when the successor, don Juan de Miera Ceballos, reappeared with an armed expedition, headed by Licenciado Juan de Ricaurte, an oidor of the audiencia of Quito. Miera was duly acclaimed by a new cabildo installed by the oidor. Those partisans of Nevares who had not fled with him were imprisoned.

The second stage of the contest began when don Juan de Miera was in turn suspended by the audiencia of Quito in December 1703, because of an accusation that he was tampering with the mails. As his temporary successor, the audiencia confirmed Captain don Pedro de Bolaños, appointed to the governorship the year before by the new Bourbon king, Felipe V. Miera's removal upset his local supporters and a distant one, the viceroy of Peru. He pressured the audiencia not only to clear Miera as quickly as possible but to reinstate him as well. The audiencia finally complied after the viceroy had appointed a commissioner who embargoed the oidores' salaries. The suspended governor was cleared of all accusations. Oidor Ricaurte for the second time headed an armed force willing to do battle for Miera. This time Miera did not even get beyond Pasto. After a battle in the vicinity of Tulcán, south of Pasto, that claimed two dead and seven wounded,

Bolaños fled and the forces of Ricaurte and Miera occupied Pasto. But Miera's success was short-lived. The audiencia withdrew its support from him and suspended both contenders, undoubtedly aided in its decision by news of the viceroy's death. Miera returned to Quito to continue arguing his case, but he died a few months later. Bolaños maintained himself in the northern towns of the province while keeping away from its southern half. Upon instructions from Quito, the southern towns refused to recognize him and administered themselves until an interim governor appointed by the president of the audiencia of Santa Fé arrived in March 1707.

The governorship became an object of intense local factionalism by the turn of the century. The danger always existed, of course, but the granting of reversions, with their expectation of a quick return, undoubtedly increased it. Governor Berrío, for example, became the object of near universal vilification during his residencia. His successor, Roque de Mañozca, managed to focus local antagonism on the fiscal Sarmiento y Huesterlin, who was taking the accumulated residencias. Under Nevares and his successor, however, the governor came to be identified with local factions. The cabildo contained only his partisans, all others having either resigned or left. Under Miera it held only the adherents of the Hurtados and Mosqueras, who, it can be said, had put him into office to ward off the threat to their position posed by Nevares. The contest that originated with Governor Nevares's audit of the contador led to attempts to replace him with a more pliable official. This struggle soon transcended its original objective and became a contest for power in which the governors and the audiencia contended, oblivious to their main responsibilities: guaranteeing the legal order rather than subverting it, dampening conflict rather than fanning or creating it.

A governor was supposed to remain a disinterested outsider in the province. But, to be effective, governors had to become insiders, typically by aligning themselves with local intermediaries. Whether they pursued their own interests or the crown's, the governors needed the support of the local aristocracy. The governors' dilemmas, if they faced any, may be ascribed as much to the way the office was designed as to the incumbents. There was no permanent bureaucratic staff to serve them. In the absence of such an apparatus the governors could, in theory, turn to the cabildos. The cabildo of Popayán, however, was at best an indifferent agent for a governor's designs. It certainly did not see itself in such an agent's role, nor was it the kind of permanent institution that could implement a governor's decisions with any consistency.[39] Ultimately governors either were reduced to impotence or became local politicians who looked for cooperation wherever they could find it. In either case they were unable to fulfill the roles assigned to them, even if they were disinterested and energetic.

In a more fundamental sense the shortcomings of the governors' performances were neither their fault nor the consequence of the particular office they served. Rather they reflected the failure of a judicial and administrative system designed to meet the demands of the Spanish monarchy concerned with its global responsibilities, not the demands of the settlers caught up in local affairs. Mediation between these conflicting demands was entrusted to a "bureaucratic" apparatus that could only react, hardly ever taking action in a positive sense. This failure to act is nowhere more evident than in the mechanisms of residencia and visita that exemplified the thrust of Spanish imperial control.

8. Imperial Control

Spain's rule in America endured. Its presence was pervasive. Beyond mere presence and endurance, what kind of authority did the Spanish monarchy possess in America? Was it an effective power to command, preserve justice, establish order, and introduce efficiency in the appropriation of wealth? Many empires appear deficient when measured against such standards. But here these standards were not imposed by a later observer. Rather they derive from a theory of empire that found its ultimate expression in the Recopilación de Leyes de Indias (Code of laws of the Indies). The crown in America followed a design that translated this theory into a practical edifice of government, however unsystematic or incomplete by our lights.[1] The strength of the empire and the authority of the crown depended on the quality of this design and on the practice of government. In this chapter I will discuss a crucial part of the design of government: the residencia and the visita as institutions of imperial control.

The relative modernity of the Spanish monarchy in the sixteenth century resided not only in its central institutions but also in the novel ways it confronted local and regional power. In many ways this monarchy was simply the Castilian state writ large. In Castile the corregidors represented the king's justice in the major cities, and the two chancillerías of Valladolid and Granada served as capstones of the system of royal justice. These institutions were transferred to the Indies, with modifications as required. Functional equivalence was therefore not always complete: audiencias in America exercised administrative functions that Castilian chancillerías did not possess. Under the circumstances of the New World, periodic reviews of performance, as established in Castile, became quite important, in particular since the crown assumed a protective attitude vis-à-vis the native population that it did not show to the peasants of Castile. Supervision was also aided by the fact that the settlers' political formation did not have the strength of tradition and custom it possessed in Spain. Yet the crown's task was not therefore easier in America—it was simply different. It is the purpose of this chapter to describe the particular problems the crown faced in its attempt to maintain control.

The main function of government was the preservation of justice, a part of the traditional conception of kingship. How could the crown make sure that justice was done? The establishment of appeals tribunals was a first step. Ultimately a whole network of audiencias emerged. Another device used was inquiries by commissary judges who were invested with broad investigative, judicial, and regulatory powers. The establishment of a permanent mechanism to supervise judicial and administrative performance, the residencia, constituted another vital step. These institutions and procedures emanated from the crown only at one remove. Actually they were the work of university-trained lawyers whose efforts had gone far in establishing legal training as a requisite for service in the higher reaches of government.[2] A precondition of this pretension—and a consequence—was the growth of codified law that applied in Castile and in the Indies. A reasonably consistent legal order existed, then, upheld by an apparatus of courts and by judges trained in the law, with the will and the ability to enforce it. This organization of apparatus and of trained functionaries resembled in some ways a modern bureaucracy. But did it really function like a bureaucracy? Its functioning is best understood in terms of its origins and of contemporary circumstances. Only after examining this context might one use standards of judgment not necessarily pertaining to the period.

The residencia was formally introduced into Castile with the ordenanzas de corregidores of 1500.[3] The installation of the corregidor as a judge and administrator was accompanied by a set of rules and procedures designed to keep the new office in check. The corregidors became the representatives of a legal order emanating from the crown. Their installation, unsystematic at first, was formalized under Ferdinand and Isabella, and with the promulgation of the ordenanzas or capítulos de corregidores in 1500 the corregidors changed from being ad hoc commissioners of the crown to more permanent officials whose responsibilities had to be strictly defined. The residencia served this purpose. As a device to curb arbitrary judges it had been known in Castile since the fourteenth century. Its formal combination with the office of corregidor in the ordinances of 1500 was a means of bringing this new type of official, who performed both judicial and administrative functions, under supervision. The residencia was a mandatory review of a magistrate's performance, taken at the end of his term; the official was required to remain in "residencia" during the investigation. Besides providing information about an official's conduct, the residencia offered the inhabitants an opportunity to air grievances, lodge formal complaints, and seek remedies against arbitrary actions. It was designed to overcome a major limitation of ordinary judicial process—its lack of publicity. Residencias and visitas included the publication of edicts and an invitation to testify. The visita was a tour of inspection, usually by an outsider, with either a specific task, such as the regulation of Indian tribute, or the more general purpose of investigating the workings of government. There were also specific investigations (pesquisas) responding to particular complaints or suspicions. In practice these differences were often blurred. A juez de residencia, for instance, might also carry a whole set of commissions as a juez perquisidor and visitador. Also, each residencia included a secret proceeding, pesquisa secreta, designed to collect testimony from witnesses. A residencia was no different from a visita in this respect.[4] Most important as an element common to all of them was probably the formalism of justice that pervaded the procedures.

In Popayán the residencia was administered by a judge appointed directly by the crown. Typically, the incoming governor was chosen to take his predecessor's residencia. In other cases, for instance in 1621, the crown delegated the authority to appoint a residencia judge to the president of the audiencia of Quito.[5] The papers and sentences accumulated in the course of the inquiry were sent to the audiencia in Quito, which in turn forwarded them to the Council of the Indies for confirmation.[6] The final verdict was handed down by an executive order of the Council, which stipulated whatever fines and penalties were to apply. It was not unusual for many years to elapse between the actual residencia and the Council's final verdict.

In Popayán, practices did not always conform to these regulations. In the course of his investigations in 1697 the fiscal, Sarmiento y Huesterlin, complained that the laws and ordinances established as a result of past residencias were never observed.[7] The fiscal's task in Popayán was to finish three residencias, one of them dating back to 1679 and for various reasons never completed. The fiscal's efforts to reduce the backlog were unsuccessful despite the tomes of testimony he accumulated. Nor does it appear that any of these residencias was ever finished. The final sentences have never been found, and the papers of the local treasury officials contain no record of fines or of the claims for payment so frequent in the aftermath of residencias. By the turn of the eighteenth century the residencia as a check on provincial government had broken down, at least temporarily. Not until 1714, nearly twenty years later, was a governor, the Marqués de San Miguel de la Vega, again subjected to a residencia; none of the men who held the office after 1696 faced a residencia judge. Yet during most of the seventeenth century residencias were held regularly, sanctions imposed, and fines paid, even if tardily.[8]

What was a residencia like? Before attempting to evaluate it and the reasons for its breakdown, let us discuss a specific case. The residencia of Governor Antonio de Guzmán y Toledo (1659–1667) was originally entrusted to his successor, Gabriel Díaz de la Cuesta.[9] Guzmán y Toledo complained that Díaz delayed taking the residencia for more than one-and-a-half years on the grounds that there was no qualified escribano, when his real purpose was to extract a bribe of twenty thousand pesos; the audiencia of Quito accepted the recusation.[10] By 1670 the Council authorized the president of the audiencia to appoint a more qualified judge. An oidor of the audiencia, Licenciado Carlos de Cohorcos, was appointed on June 6, 1671, and within a month had set out on his way to the province. At three o'clock in the afternoon of August 5, the oidor made his entry into the town. Two days later his commission was exhibited before the alcaldes ordinarios.

In the following days a series of preliminaries took place preparing the ground for the inquiry that was to begin officially on September 25. Testimony detailed the governor's term, the officials who had served him, his guarantors, and the cabildo members who had approved bond. Jueces receptores (collectors of evidence) were appointed in each of the province's towns with detailed instructions for taking depositions. The oidor brought most of these assistants from Quito. Their outside recruitment insured impartiality. But there was an additional motive for selecting the judges from the audiencia's and the oidor's clientele: it provided a nice source of patronage, especially since salaries were not unattractive—four hundred patacones, to judge by other residencias.

The governor objected to having to appoint agents in each town to defend him against accusations brought before the receptor. This procedure, he charged, put the burden of proof and disproof on some ignorant agent, instead of forcing accusers to bring their proof to the residencia judge. In his support he cited a decree from the audiencia of Santa Fé stating that jueces receptores were not to take cognizance of any local complaints and claims but were to send them on to the judge of the residencia. The oidor rejected this contention. He noted that distances in the province were too great for the inquiry to be held solely in Popayán and that, at any rate, charges would have to be substantiated before the judge of the residencia in Popayán.

After dealing with the governor, the oidor turned to municipal affairs. He ordered the escribano de gobernación to compile a list of all officeholders for the period under investigation, exercising particular care to note any financial transactions. One case in particular demonstrates the oidor's meticulous attention to financial affairs. The records examined by the escribano had mentioned a local assessment for which no accounts could be found. Escribanos and officials searched for weeks, harassed by threats from the oidor. But, beyond a note in the estimates for 1654, discovered by the contador don Juan de Larrainzar, no clues were found. The note included the signatures of the deputy, the alcaldes ordinarios, two regidores, and the procurador general, as well as those of captains don Joseph Hurtado del Águila, don Diego del Campo Salazar, and Francisco López Guerrero, who as "vecinos republicanos" vouched for the town's contribution of four thousand pesos to make up for frauds in paying the mining tax. In the oidor's disposition of the case, governor and cabildo were fined for allowing such an assessment without proper authority. It was not until sentence was already passed and both the governor and local officials were fined for neglecting the accounts that the records were discovered. The records were then included in the residencia report and forwarded to Spain. Ultimately the governor and the cabildo were cleared of the charge of negligence.[11]

The inquiry went smoothly after the initial difficulties were surmounted. Twenty-nine witnesses were cited to testify about the governor's performance. The governor objected to two witnesses who were his proven enemies, and they were removed from the list. Nineteen witnesses gave testimony about the cabildo and other officials. Evidence was given by a balanced number of clerics, encomenderos, and merchants, and even by some inhabitants who were not vecinos. After they stated their age and identity, the witnesses were asked a set of uniform questions, many nominal in character. Forty-two questions concerned the governor's performance; on the average only ten elicited more than a *pro-forma* response. Another questionnaire contained forty-three questions about the ministros (officials) and the cabildo, twenty of them related to the alcaldes, five to the regidores, four to the alguacil mayor; two each concerned the performance of the depositario general, procurador general, and the mayordomo; and eight finally scrutinized the escribano's activities.

Some characteristic questions about the cabildo and, in particular, the alcaldes were: How had the alcaldes ordinarios administered justice, in impartial or partial fashion? Had they punished public scandal and kept nuisances in check, whether concubinage, gambling, usurers, thieves, or sorcerers? Had they used their office to exploit women or to solicit cases? Had they kept regular hours to receive the public and posted the fee schedule?

Questions about the regidores were limited in scope, dealing primarily with their official duties. Had they participated twice weekly in the sessions? Did they elect fit candidates to fill offices? Had the regidores dressed decently and behaved correctly in the assembly of the cabildo? When they dealt in items of supply did they set moderate and convenient prices? The whole questionnaire was prefaced by a general question: Did witnesses know anything about the cabildo, its members, and the other officials? The clerics gave testimony only about the deputy and the corregidor de naturales. They accused them of exploiting the Indian population because they continued to tolerate the practice of servicio personal. The testimony revealed very little about the regidores; the witnesses allowed that they held their elections, met occasionally, and sometimes even inspected the slaughterhouse.

Although often perfunctory, testimony could be quite frank. The clerics, for example, charged that the governor failed to act against public scandals. For example, he tolerated the practice of concubinage by several well-known citizens. The alférez real, don Diego Velasco Noguera, went even further with his accusations, despite the fact that the governor had served as godfather at his wedding. He charged that the governor interfered in the cabildo's elections and kept most of its papers in his house. According to him, the members were unable to vote freely. If the governor was absent, he sent letters with instructions on how to vote; one such letter was included as proof among the papers of the residencia. According to the alférez real, the elections of 1664 were an especially flagrant example of the governor's intervention. The governor, displeased with the vote, rose from his seat, proclaimed his own preference in a loud voice and asked the deputy to follow suit. It made no difference when he was told that the deputy actually had no vote. In the end the governor's proposals were accepted after friends of the alférez asked him not to cause a commotion, though it was customary to draw lots when there were dissenting votes. In the course of later testimony the alférez's story was confirmed by the other cabildo members.

Once the rounds of testimony were completed, the oidor proceeded to consolidate the accusations into a set of twenty-three charges against the governor and a more limited number against the other officials. Each official under investigation was then permitted to offer a defense on his behalf. In his defense the governor drew up his own questionnaire and presented it to appropriate witnesses. In addition, he included decrees from his libro de gobierno and other papers. He was, for example, accused of neglecting the settlement and protection of the Indian population, a charge already made earlier in an exhortation sent to him by Bishop Contreras. In his defense he produced the exhortation, together with his reply. The governor was absolved of the charge, the documents demonstrating his concern: the governor's argument was that the Indians should look to their own encomenderos for basic protection, since neither corregidor nor protector de naturales could do much for them. The governor's modesty as to the capacity of officials to perform their duty appeared plausible to the oidor.

Not all accusations against the governor were disposed of in such fashion. For seventeen charges the oidor found sufficient evidence to impose a total fine of 7,550 pesos. Penalties ranged from 50 pesos for not paying his bills to 5,200 pesos for selling encomiendas to the highest bidder.

Other local officials and the members of the cabildo did not merit the same degree of attention as the governor. The deputy was fined 440 pesos in total. He was fined 150 pesos because he never built either the casa del cabildo or the prison he had promised, even though he received an advance. He was ordered to complete construction within eight months. Fines were imposed for neglecting to punish public scandal, not keeping the roads in good repair, and not watching over municipal accounts—common enough offenses. These charges show that the deputy and the alcaldes ordinarios shared responsibility with the governor for watching public order and morality, providing certain services and amenities, and, of course, administering justice. On the other hand, the nominal amount of the fines indicates that primary responsibility rested with the governor.

The Council of the Indies reduced most fines with its revision.[12] The deputy's fine was reduced to thirty-five pesos, and the alcaldes' from between thirty and forty pesos to six pesos on the average. In most matters the deputy and the alcaldes were either absolved altogether or simply exhorted to watch matters in the future and to observe the laws. The only charge left standing against the regidores was their failure to appoint a mayordomo of the cabildo. All three charges against the procuradores of the cabildo were upheld—indicating, perhaps, the importance attached to the office—for not insisting on cabildo meetings once a week, employment of a mayordomo, and the construction of a prison and a casa del cabildo.

The Council reduced the governor's fine from 7,550 to 2,700 pesos. It revoked some sentences, assessing only nominal fines in others. The fine for selling encomiendas, for instance, was reduced to 1,500 pesos. An important feature of the revision was the instructions and inquiries accompanying it. While the Council revoked the 200-peso fine for tolerating servicio personal, it dispatched a cédula that ordered future governors to supervise closely the commutation of tribute by labor and to obtain the Indians' consent in each case.[13] Another cédula pertaining to the mismanagement of the archive and the papers of the cabildo reminded the governor to keep documents in a strong box with three keys and to keep an inventory of official papers. Such procedures were routine, but obviously a reminder was deemed necessary. The governor's practice of collecting a fee for inspecting stores was condemned by the Council—countermanding the oidor's verdict—and a cédula was dispatched instructing governors not to collect such fees in the future. Even the town's need for a casa del cabildo caught the Council's attention. The governor was told to send a report on the matter.

The Council's revisions were based on the documents it received. These records included the oidor's investigation and final verdict. They contained a wide range of information obtained only partially from witnesses' testimony. Much of the evidence derived from a scrutiny of records and from special inquiries the oidor made, where such records were missing. The whole of this separate investigatory effort constituted the pesquisa secreta, the closed inquiry, in contrast to the public or open part of the residencia in which individuals could voice complaints and bring charges of malfeasance in office against any official.

Governor Díaz de la Cuesta's residencia sheds some light on its public or accusatory aspect.[14] His successor, Miguel García, compelled Díaz to restore 3,575 pesos with 5 percent interest to the heirs of Antonio Enes de Acosta, who accused him of exacting that amount as a forced loan. Díaz apparently accepted this verdict, but he did appeal another of García's decisions. He was ordered to pay 5,000 pesos in "damages" for systematically harassing a former escribano de gobernación. The appeal was granted with the condition that the sum of the judgment be put in deposit. García rejected, because of insufficient evidence, a charge that Díaz did not repay the 10,000 pesos loaned to him by his predecessor, though he allowed an appeal.

The capítulos were another type of charge brought against officials. They were made at the accuser's expense, with bond posted to indemnify the accused in case the charges could not be proved. For example, Governor Sarmiento's residencia, sent to the Council in 1621, included more than 2,200 folios of testimony, the capítulos brought against him by Licenciado Diego González de Mendoza, Bishop Juan González de Mendoza's nephew.[15] Beyond this single case no reference to the practice has been encountered.

A residencia did not come cheaply. In 1672, oidor Cohorcos collected 3,308 pesos in salaries for himself and 1,241 pesos each for the services of the alguacil and the escribano of the residencia, calculated on the basis of 191 days for the investigation and necessary travel. There were additional expenses of 1,099 pesos for paper and copies of documents, and 614 pesos for such other items as messengers. These sums still did not include the per diem allowances for the jueces receptores. In its revision the Council reduced salaries considerably. The oidor was allowed only 1,680 pesos, computed on the basis of a per diem allowance of twelve patacones instead of eight-and-a-half gold pesos. A cédula of 1660 had settled salaries for jueces togados anew. Only 140 days were allowed for the residencia.[16] These salaries must have been collected at the time they fell due, in contrast to fines, which were not collected until sentences were confirmed or revised. How these salaries were in fact assessed remains unclear.

In its outline the residencia conducted in Popayán conformed to the pattern established in the earlier part of the sixteenth century. The procedure followed was essentially standardized, and much of it could be applied by persons with little or no legal knowledge. The residencia purported to check an official's judicial as well as administrative performance. In its judicial aspect it was designed to maintain standards of justice and to remedy some of the shortcomings imposed by the distance between provinces and the audiencia. Its administrative purpose was not very clearly delineated in practice. Governor Guzmán's residencia suggests that no effective framework for enforcing and maintaining administrative norms existed. This can be seen in the continued sanctioning of the practice of servicio personal, the indifference shown to municipal affairs by judges and the Council, and the slowness with which sanctions, especially fines, could become effective.[17] In effect, the residencia was at best a monitoring device. It could not assure standards of performance. Governor Guzmán's residencia shows a divergence between purpose and design, between intention and execution. The origin of the residencia as a quasi-judicial procedure is partially responsible for this state of affairs. It is also explained by the residencia's thoroughly formalistic application.

The divergence between intention and execution stands out in some of the other residencias of the period. The choice of a juez de residencia constituted one major problem. The most frequent practice was to appoint the incoming governor; eight of fifteen governors received such an appointment, although two were ultimately disqualified. Of the other men appointed to the job, four came from outside the province; three were members of the audiencia of Santa Fé; and one was an advocate with the audiencia of Quito. The identity of the three remaining judges remains unknown. Choosing the governor's successor as residencia judge found local favor. When the cabildo of Popayán learned in 1675 that the crown had decided to discontinue the practice, it vigorously defended the old custom. The principal argument was that outside judges were more costly. The recent residencia conducted by the oidor Cohorcos was still fresh in people's minds.[18] In the end a judge from Santa Fé de Bogotá was appointed to conduct the next residencia, but later on governors again were appointed to the task.

Choosing the governor's successor as residencia judge was favored by the cabildo as a cheap solution; the crown preferred the practice because it was convenient, or so it appeared. But the deficiencies were glaring by the century's last decades, when successors were often disqualified or recused and accusations of bribery became frequent. As accusations were traded rather indiscriminately and legal proceedings were rarely terminated, it is nearly impossible to separate fact from fancy in many instances. Matters took a downward turn when Governor Antonio de Guzmán y Toledo accused his successor, Díaz de la Cuesta, of trying to blackmail him. Ultimately Díaz de la Cuesta was prevented from holding Guzmán's residencia. When he in turn underwent his own residencia, Guzmán's allegation that Díaz extracted a "forced" loan of ten thousand pesos from him was rejected as unproven by the judge, Governor García. García, however, was later convicted of accepting a bribe from Díaz to assure smooth sailing in the residencia.[19] Nonetheless, the case against García is not completely clear. The former governor maintained his innocence until death overtook him, penniless, in Honda on his way to Spain. A group of local citizens had enough faith in his probity—or his connections—to guarantee his appeal to the tune of fifteen thousand pesos. In addition, the bishop of Popayán, Bernaldo de Quirós, who conducted a running feud with García during most of the latter's term, begged forgiveness on his deathbed for the unjust accusations he had brought against him.[20] García's residencia itself was never formally terminated despite various attempts to bring it to a close.

Governor García's case dramatically posed the problem of how to select a suitable residencia judge, but no permanent solution was found. The Council originally nominated a judge of the audiencia of Santa Fé, but the oidor Mier y Salinas fell ill after he had begun García's residencia and returned to Bogotá despite García's entreaties to continue. Complications increased when García belatedly rejected the next judge appointed to the task, Governor Berrío, after most of the depositions were taken. Berrío nevertheless concluded the residencia. His proceedings were not countenanced by the Council. Instead it entrusted the next governor, Roque de Mañozca, with finishing the residencias of both García and Berrío. In the meantime García died and Berrío refused to accept Roque de Mañozca as judge, repeating the now familiar charge that the latter attempted to blackmail him into paying twenty thousand pesos; the audiencia upheld his refusal. Since Roque de Mañozca was supposed to recoup the costs of García's residencia from the assessment of costs to be collected in Berrío's, he did not proceed with the former either. At least this was the excuse he gave when fined one thousand escudos by the Council for neglect. At this juncture the Council became so exasperated over the situation that it sent a special judge to finish the two pending residencias and also to undertake that of Roque de Mañozca. It directed the new judge to investigate carefully Roque de Mañozca and his local collaborators, because it suspected frauds in collecting the mining tax.[21]

The Council's choice of a judge to clear away the obfuscations of two decades was unfortunate. The newly appointed fiscal of the audiencia of Santa Fé, Doctor Sarmiento y Huesterlin, an untried jurist from the Canary Islands, was dispatched to Popayán even before he had entered upon his duties in Bogotá. He finished the three accumulated residencias between September 1696 and August 1697, but he was unable to carry out the second part of his assignment. After he had spent another year and a half in the province, the audiencia of Quito relieved him of his duties, spurred into action this time by a recent reprimand for inaction in an emergency.[22] The audiencia responded to a chorus of complaints from the province, headed by the governor, the cathedral chapter, and the cabildos of Popayán and Pasto. This local opposition was exacerbated by the recent sack of Cartagena, in which the merchants of Popayán allegedly lost 350,000 pesos, a loss that made the inhabitants rather less willing to put up with fees and fines resulting from the residencia and pesquisa. The fiscal's shortcomings contributed to his fall: arbitrariness, greed, and dishonesty, combined with excessive notions of the respect due a judge. Such, at least, were the inhabitants' complaints.

The fiscal had announced the special investigation more than two months after he had finished the residencias. He ran into immediate resistance, heightened not a little by the manner in which the announcement was made: a proclamation in the plaza made to the sound of drums, in the governor's absence, and without any advance notification to the cabildo. After he refused to show the cabildo his commission to undertake the investigation, it fired off a series of complaints to the audiencia of Quito that related in detail the highhanded manner in which the fiscal had conducted the residencias: his way of intimidating and soliciting witnesses, his use of an unqualified escribano, and the excessive salaries he had collected. The members added that they had endured his presence and his excesses for so long only in hopes that an end was in sight. Now, with the prospect of further investigations at hand, they were asking the audiencia for his recusation. Two emissaries, don Francisco Hurtado del Águila and don Diego Ignacio de Aguinaga, were empowered to represent the cabildo before the audiencia. In a conference including the fiscal himself, who had traveled to Quito, the oidores, and the cabildo's emissaries, the president of the audiencia managed to compose matters: the emissaries agreed to retire their complaints, the fiscal assented to being accompanied henceforth by another judge, and the audiencia expedited a supporting decree after it examined the fiscal's commissions and found them in order.[23] Yet less than a year later the fiscal was dismissed and had to give up the task.

The immediate cause of the fiscal's dismissal was that he had the governor's deputy in Barbacoas executed without even granting an appeal to the audiencia. The deputy, don Bartolomé de Estupiñán, a member of the town's most eminent family, was accused of complicity in the murder of Captain Diego García de Real, who had acted as the fiscal's juez receptor in the residencias in Barbacoas. One day in September 1698, while the fiscal was still in Pasto, the captain had been found brutally slain in his bed. A slave belonging to the deputy's son was accused of the deed, while the deputy himself was named the instigator.[24] For the fiscal, the incident was the last of a series of pinpricks and humiliations. His actions in Popayán met with ridicule and disrespect. On the way to Quito his mules had been stolen twice —hardly an accident—and while he was in Pasto the audiencia had asked him peremptorily to speed up his proceedings. Now his representative was murdered. It is not surprising that he decided to act rigorously, although his defiance of the law in not granting the appeal remains inexplicable. It also proved his undoing, since the cabildos of the province in feigned or genuine fear hastened to repeat the old accusations against him and obtained his dismissal on February 18, 1699.[25] The fiscal's end would seem to support the cabildo's interpretation that he was not only inept and conceited but also dishonest and arbitrary. In 1706 he was jailed in Tunja on orders of the president of the audiencia of Santa Fé; he was accused of various crimes, including the precipitate execution of Estupiñán in Barbacoas. He fled from prison and disappeared from sight. The Council did not get around to his case until 1726. It condemned him to death in absentia and ordered his property confiscated.[26]

This episode reflects not only the fiscal's personal shortcomings but also the deficiencies of an imperial system of administration in which the absence of continuous and expert supervision was inadequately compensated for by sporadic checks. These checks easily degenerated into formal exercises or self-defeating enterprises that only served to gratify a judge's purse and vanity. A suitable appointee not only had to be found: he had to be supervised. The mechanism of control had itself to be kept under control. Revision of a residencia's sentences by the Council implied a certain degree of supervision. Governor García in his capacity as residencia judge, for instance, was fined three hundred pesos for not examining enough witnesses before absolving Governor Díaz de la Cuesta, who was charged with neglecting the defense of the province. The oidor Cohorcos's mission to investigate the charge of bribery against Governor García demonstrates both the Council's concern and the speed that it could muster at times.[27] Speedy action, however, remained an exception.

The residencia as a device for maintaining control and monitoring performance had numerous shortcomings. The fact that governors "bought" reversion to the office, at least from 1677 on, certainly changed the incumbents' expectations as to the character of the office. The residencia became a prelude to the governorship rather than a postmortem. It offered a successor leverage that could be turned into blackmail. Only an outside appointment or an independent investigation could break this vicious circle. But quick intervention was difficult and the exception in this slow-moving system. The initiative had to come from the Council itself, whose fiscal severely reprimanded the audiencia of Quito for not acting in a scandalous situation. The fiscal considered such intervention in an emergency an absolute necessity. Still, while the audiencia could remove judges, it could not replace them if they were crown appointees. Developments in Popayán were not unique. By the 1690s, fifty-five corregidors in Peru alone were waiting to have their residencia taken, some with their term of office already twenty years past.[28]

The failure of the residencia to uphold standards effectively was no accident. Sale of office, reaching in the end to all levels of the state, led to an ever-widening circle of corruption that not only neutralized the residencia but also turned it into the opposite of what had been intended. This explanation also connects what happened in Popayán to the general financial crisis of the Spanish monarchy. It is convincing —as far as it goes—but still not quite satisfactory. The shortcomings of the residencia and the consequences of venality were known to contemporaries—how otherwise would we know about them?—yet no changes were made. There was nothing, in fact, to take the place of these devices. Only in the second half of the eighteenth century was an attempt made to substitute another system of controls, more modern and more "bureaucratic" in character, although not necessarily more successful in creating a durable order.

The crown's main problem in America was how to create a political order on a scale different from Spain's. The ingredients of such an order were there in Castile, in Aragon, but not in America. There the crown chose to disregard Indian political formations. In America the Castilian state had the chance to impose an order impossible to achieve in Europe. America as a tabula rasa in political terms encouraged this attempt, while the enormity of its space defeated it at the same time. Concurrently a more modest and more appropriate tendency manifested itself: to keep matters under control by negative rather than constructive action. This tendency, at any rate, was in line with the prevailing judicial character of Castilian administration. The residencia, then, despite the ideal of order and good government enshrined in its substantive provisions, constituted an intervention after the event, characteristic of judicial procedure. In this it corresponded to a variety of other procedures, such as composición and pardons, all of which demonstrated the inability of the "bureaucratic" apparatus to control affairs. What they accomplished was more akin to closing the gate after the horses are gone, a proceeding congenial to the judicial temper. Government thus was largely static and reactive, willing to codify reality but not likely to reorganize it. Only in the eighteenth century, when a new group of administrators, the intendants, appeared on the scene was this to change. The intendants pursued the idea of order and good government, albeit in narrow fashion. They tried to reconstruct the cabildos as local bodies in order to find collaborators, resurrecting a problem the crown had buried two hundred years earlier.[29] Then the crown saw little profit in granting authority to the cabildos sufficient to handle local affairs, in the absence of bureaucrats to keep them under control. Now the lack of such bodies was a liability. Yet the question remained: how could local power effectively be built into an imperial system of government?

9. The Church and the Settlers

The Church in Popayán appears to us in a dual perspective. It was an extension of the Church universal, representing the religious traditions of the Spanish world in America. Yet the Church was also bound to the daily concerns of local people. Its strength as an institution resided precisely in the ways in which it combined these two aspects of its existence. The dimensions of the Church's presence were not only spiritual, they were also material in the literal sense, as expressed in sumptuous or simple buildings, in sights and sound. They were also social and economic in character, deriving their shape from the ways in which people made a living but also, conversely, affecting that shape. The Church was, of necessity, a political institution, one that profoundly touched peoples' daily lives. The Church was a complex institution, not easily subsumed under its proselytizing mission or under its role as an agent of colonial domination. Two tendencies existed within the Church, sometimes in balance, sometimes at odds: justification of an existing social order and criticism of that order. My concern is to describe the Church as a part of a social and political order, rather than to stress its role as an antagonist. Such a description entails a look at the Church as an institution of government and as a beneficiary of the inhabitants' social energies and economic resources.[1]

The bishop embodied the authority of the Church. The governor and the bishop were the two heads (cabezas) of the town, the cabildo noted in one of its petitions.[2] Within the Church the bishop's power was checked by that of the cathedral chapter and tempered by the rules that defined his position. The clergy was divided into seculars and regulars and, also, into those holding a benefice and those not. The Church was far from a monolithic institution. Its very divisions were a source of strength rather than of weakness, enabling it to appeal to differing constituencies and varied loyalties.

A bishop's position rested both on the powers explicitly vested in his office and on his control over the apparatus of ecclesiastical government. Among the bishop's powers were ordination (conferring holy orders) and the right to nominate candidates for ecclesiastical

137

benefices. Bishops usually reserved certain powers for themselves: imposing and lifting ecclesiastical penalties like excommunication and censure. Bishops possessed limited ecclesiastical patronage. They made appointments to the positions of provisor and vicario general, promotor fiscal, and examinador synodal. The provisor, in his capacity as vicario general, served as the chief judicial officer of the diocese and the bishop's alter ego. He also did duty as administrator and troubleshooter.

Bishops acted as judges in addition to performing their apostolic duties, delegating jurisdiction or exercising it themselves. As judges they presided over a court that included the vicario general, the promotor fiscal, who was a kind of ecclesiastical attorney (he had to be a cleric), and a notary, who was supposed to be a layman. Priests in their parishes were often entrusted with judicial duties. As vicarios they had to gather evidence, hear affected parties, and forward evidence for adjudication to the bishop's court. Appeals from the bishop's court went to the archbishop of Santa Fé as juez metropolitano.

A bishop's hold over his diocese was directly reinforced through the visita pastoral (pastoral inspection). Most bishops made only one such inspection—understandably so when one considers the mountainous nature of the region. Usually surveillance was exercised indirectly, through visitadores, who received detailed instructions. Their duties were specified in the constituciones synodales of 1717, along with the fees that they and the notary they employed could collect.[3] Their duties were varied. They were to inquire into public morals—but not to pry into private ones (as long as there was no scandal). They checked the state of church buildings and took their inventories, investigated the accounts of sodalities, inquired into the curate's performance, and even made sure that midwives knew how to perform baptism. Altogether, a visitador's fee schedule contained thirty different rates ranging from twenty-four patacones for processing a parish priest's title to one patacón for a simple petition.

Next in importance to the bishop in the local hierarchy was the cathedral chapter, which governed a diocese in the bishop's absence. By the end of the seventeenth century, its membership (dean, archdeacon, chantre, maestro escuela, and tesorero) had become the domain of Creoles born in the region.[4] The advantage of employing Creoles was stressed by the cabildo in 1677, when it extolled the virtues of don Pedro de Arboleda, who was provisor and vicario general of the diocese. Don Pedro's father, the bachiller don Jacinto de Arboleda, had also served as vicario general and had been a member of the cathedral chapter as archdeacon. He became a cleric after a successful career as a mining entrepreneur. He never abandoned his worldly concerns; with a large family to provide for, this was only natural. The cabildo in its memorial to the crown also noted that the newly appointed dean, a canon from Campeche in Yucatán, had not yet arrived after six years had elapsed, and that the post of tesorero had been vacant for three years. Native sons, the cabildo added, were preferable to strangers who did not see the needs of the town and the diocese.[5] Whatever the merits of the argument, the crown in future appointments seemed to heed it. Before that time the chapter's only Creoles from the region were don Francisco Vélez de Zúñiga, don Antonio de Zúñiga (both of them cousins of don Ýñigo de Velasco), and don Agustín de Olea, who later became a canon in Bogotá (he was a stepson of Diego de Victoria and brother-in-law of don Jacinto de Arboleda). Canons, like bishops, were selected by the Council of the Indies. The governor, as vice-patron, made appointments to lesser benefices from a list of candidates presented by the bishop, after the candidates had been examined for their fitness by the diocesan examiner and a competition for the vacant benefice had been opened.

Until early in the eighteenth century, five of the town's ten rural parishes (doctrinas) were administered by friars; after 1706 the Franciscans lost the two they held, and by the 1720s the Dominicans lost theirs as well.[6] Neither the Franciscans nor the Dominicans found local recruits, although the Jesuits did. The Jesuits abandoned their rural missionary enterprise in Tierradentro earlier, and the two parishes there, Tálaga and Toboyma, were taken over by secular clergy.[7] The limited opportunities for employment did not keep pace with the increasing number of secular clergy. In 1701, 19 priests in Popayán were without benefice; in 1706 there were 25. Altogether there were 117 ordained priests in the diocese in 1706, and at least 33 resided in Popayán.[8] This increase in the number of clergy was in some respects a burden, but it was also an opportunity. More personnel could put the Church on a sound local footing because it could staff an expanded network of parishes, improve priestly performance by frequent inspections, and raise revenue by permitting reforms of tithe collection. These were matters tackled by the synod held in Popayán in 1717, the third synod since the bishopric was founded.

The rules for the Church in Popayán were supplied mostly from outside the bishopric. These rules included canon law, the enactments of the Council of Trent, and crown legislation concerning patronage. Yet the Church in Popayán could also make its own rules to meet the needs of its particular situation. The constituciones synodales (synodic articles) of 1617 and 1717 reflect in their character a body of American-made ecclesiastical law, consisting principally of the enactments of the Councils of Mexico and Lima.[9] Since the conciliar legislation of the archbishopric of Santa Fé de Bogotá was never approved, the rules of the third Council of Lima (1583) applied there as well, at first provisionally and later permanently.[10] This conciliar legislation did not preclude the making of diocesan rules. In theory, as stipulated by the Council of Trent, each diocese was to hold a yearly synod. In practice this proved impossible, and a blurring of the distinctions between synods and councils was the consequence. Whereas the task of councils was to enact fundamental norms, that of synods was to confront current problems within the framework of these norms. The two synods of Popayán provided a framework and spelled out how general norms applied locally.

A synod was a convocation of the diocesan clergy, who had to attend in person; monasteries (conventos) were to be represented by their procuradores. The towns could present petitions when appropriate, as, for instance, in the matter of fees. The work of the synods reveals how the Church responded to local conditions. The papal bull that erected the cathedral and Bishop Juan del Valle's decrees represented the first constitution of the diocese[11] They spelled out who the cathedral's dignitaries were to be and set their salaries. They provided for the allocation of the tithe among bishop, cathedral chapter, and parish clergy. The cathedral was the nucleus of the diocese, and upon its establishment hinged everything else. Yet the detailed regulations concerning the liturgy and the numerous personnel they mention, following the custom of the cathedral of Seville, have a curiously unreal air when one considers the actual state of the diocese. They constituted a blueprint for a future that was never quite to be. The Church could be moved to America, as a cathedral on paper, but it could survive there only if it confronted the new environment realistically. In Popayán this environment meant poverty—exemplified by the straw-roofed cathedral, the search for wealth by the settlers, and the exploitation of the non-Spanish population by these settlers in search of gold.

The synods of 1555 (of which we know only little), 1617, and 1717 represented confrontations between the Church and its American environment. The legislation of 1555 contained sixty constituciones, or articles, dealing with the internal organization of the Church and forty constituciones that dealt with the native population.[12] Concern with the affairs of the Indians continued in the constituciones of 1617. They spelled out the obligations of the doctrineros and encomenderos, providing appropriate penalties for offenders. Another typical feature of these constituciones was a host of practical regulations concerning marriage, thus indicating the laxness that characterized the region. A third emphasis of the regulations was their attempt to suppress particular abuses, superstitions, and bad customs.[13] The constituciones of 1717, arranged in three books with eight, fourteen, and six chapters (títulos) respectively, had a more general character as diocesan legislation than the earlier rules. They also indicated the state of the diocese. Indians, for example, became a mere afterthought. One chapter in book 3 was headed "De Indios," yet only two of its eleven constituciones dealt in fact with Indians, the rest pertaining to funerals, court procedure, and tithe collection.[14] This synod of 1717, with its detailed attention to procedures and fees, feast days and funerals, presents to us a mature colonial Church that had taken hold of its setting but in turn was beholden to it. The bishops were perhaps the strongest force able to shape that environment. How well did they do?

The government of the Church was not only a government of rules exercised through an impersonal apparatus; it was also a government of men. Personal attributes no doubt played a role at all levels, the parish as well as the cathedral chapter. But they are more visible to us in the case of a bishop than in that of a simple cleric. A bishop's performance reflected his personality and the particular situation he encountered. Yet one should not forget that a bishop could rely on a degree of institutional backing that a governor could not expect. A necessary corollary of such backing was institutional resistance. A bishop's success as the head of an organization lay in his ability to marshal this support without provoking the opposition.

For most of the bishops the see of Popayán was the end of a career, not its beginning.[15] Nevertheless, a few made notable contributions. Maestro Juan del Valle (1548–1561), the first bishop, made the Indians' plight his special concern. Fray Juan González de Mendoza (1609–1618) took the questionable morals of the inhabitants as his special target. Don Christóbal Bernaldo de Quirós (1672–1684) devoted his considerable energies to completing the cathedral, after work on it had languished for two generations. Only one of the incumbents of the seventeenth century made a notable career beyond the diocese: Bishop Melchor de Liñán y Cisneros advanced to be archbishop of Las Charcas and later served as interim viceroy of Peru and archbishop of Lima.

I have chosen to treat in some detail Bishop González de Mendoza's tenure because it offers episodes worth describing in their own right and because it shows the difficulties a bishop with an elevated sense of

his office might have with his flock.[16] Bishop Juan González de Mendoza's tenure of office was among the stormiest in the history of Popayán.
In his nine years as bishop he managed to antagonize virtually every
important group and institution with which he had to deal. A bishop's
task in Popayán was very difficult; the region in many ways was still a
frontier area. In the abstract the settlers respected the Church, but they
had little patience with its representatives.

Bishop González de Mendoza was a man of wide experience who had
made a remarkable career for himself. Born in Castile in 1545, he joined
his uncle in Mexico at the age of seventeen and soon afterward entered
the Augustinian order. His great opportunity came when he was selected
to go to Spain with Padre Diego de Herrera, who was on his way there
from the Philippines to obtain more missionaries and arrange for an
embassy to China. While returning to the Philippines, Herrera and
his ship were lost at sea. His companion stayed in Spain, became prior
of a monastery, and prepared himself for the mission to China. Though
he was named ambassador to China in 1581, he never got farther than
Mexico, where difficulties held up the mission and forced him to return
to Spain. But his efforts were not quite fruitless. In 1585 he published
a book on China entitled *Historia de las cosas más notables, ritos y costumbres del gran reino de la China* (History of the most notable things,
rites, and customs of the great kingdom of China), which was quite a
success, though its author had never reached China. Between 1586 and
1590 González de Mendoza was in New Granada as a preacher. After
his return to Spain, he presented an extensive memorial on the state
of the New Kingdom of Granada that led to an interview with the
Council of the Indies. The memorial was a veritable catalogue of complaints stressing the ignorance of the friars and the corruption of the
judges. After 1590 he occupied a variety of different positions. He spent
some time in Rome as a delegate of his order and then became assistant
(visitador general) first to the archbishop of Seville and later to the
archbishop of Toledo; at the same time he was made a titular bishop.
In November 1608 he was nominated to the see of Popayán.[17]

The new bishop created apprehensions in his future flock before his
actual arrival in Popayán. He first passed through Antioquia, a part
of the diocese never before visited by a bishop, where he liberally distributed censures and fines. On his arrival in Popayán he asked that the
cabildo receive and escort him into town on foot while he himself was
enthroned on a white horse and covered by a canopy. The cabildo,
acquainted with the custom of Lima that conceded such an honor only
to a viceroy, refused the request. The bishop, in his turn, refused to

receive the members, excommunicated them, and entered the town on foot, accompanied only by his clerics. The excommunications were not lifted until the audiencia interceded with the bishop.[18]

A host of minor incidents followed, mainly, it seems, related to the pastoral inspection (visita) and the edicts published in its wake.[19] In a letter to Spain the cabildo of Popayán took the offensive and denounced the bishop's proceedings, his rashness in excommunicating the members, his designs on the property of the nunnery of La Encarnación, and his rancor manifest after the cabildo had refused to accept his nephew, don Diego González de Mendoza, as the governor's deputy.[20] The religious orders followed suit and procured a juez conservador after the prior of the Augustinian monastery was mistreated by the bishop's servants for talking about their master's superstitious practices. The juez conservador in his turn was attacked by the bishop's followers led by don Diego, the nephew, as he tried to put a notice on the cathedral door. In neither this nor the next incident were the municipal authorities very successful in asserting their authority. In order to learn the accusations the cabildo lodged against him, the bishop invaded the house of the depositario general, Juan Ortiz, under cover of night and in the latter's absence; he took away a writing cabinet with its contents, and asserted that he was after a Koran and thus could proceed as an inquisidor ordinario. Alerted after the fact, the governor's deputy threw a cordon around the bishop's residence and tried to get hold of some laymen in the bishop's employ; he succeeded in grabbing a secretary, but the bishop retrieved his man with the help of an armed crowd. As a consequence the town was put under interdict, the bishop asserting that all persons in his employ benefited from ecclesiastical privilege. Governor Sarmiento de Sotomayor, who had been absent in Cali—perhaps wisely—and had been engaged in the campaign against the Pijaos, now took the case under consideration and ordered the culprits taken prisoner, whereupon the bishop excommunicated him.[21]

At this stage the tug of war between bishop and town took on a different dimension. Potentially, most inhabitants were likely targets for a censorious bishop who took the duties of his office seriously and chose to apply rigorous standards of conduct. Even before the arrival of Bishop González de Mendoza in May 1609, the dean of Popayán, Juan Montaño, had denounced irregularities in the convent of La Encarnación to the authorities in Spain.[22] The nuns allegedly received male visitors, among them monks. Some nuns even became pregnant, and at least one child was born in the convent. The Council of the Indies reacted energetically to the news. The superiors of the orders concerned were directed to investigate the matter, and the governor of Popayán was ordered to proceed against the laymen involved in the scandal. The matter might have ended there, with some limited steps taken to correct the irregularities, if the case had not been pursued by the bishop. Urged on by his nephew, don Diego, the bishop demanded that a secular judge be dispatched with full powers to investigate the scandal. When the audiencia hesitated and imposed conditions, don Diego drew up the relevant information and posted bond to cover the costs of the investigation.[23]

Licenciado Diego de Zorrilla, the oidor sent by the audiencia of Quito, arrived in January 1611. By April he had concluded his investigation, which bore out the earlier accusations. He pronounced sentence against those involved in the sacrilege committed against the convent of La Encarnación: sixteen death sentences, of which thirteen were in absentia; three sentences to serve for varying terms in Chile; and six sentences of banishment from the province of Popayán for a varying length of years. Those sentenced included eight encomenderos —one of whom was condemned to death. Of the others sentenced to die, five claimed to be hidalgos, two were regidores of Popayán, and one was the escribano of the cabildo.[24]

The bishop was mistaken if he assumed that these drastic measures would cow his enemies and confirm his ascendancy. Even with Licenciado Zorrilla still investigating, the contador Juan de Palacios Alvarado confiscated what he called a "supply of unregistered cloth and merchandise from Castile" that was sold in the plaza of Cali on order of the bishop's nephew. The bishop insisted that the items were part of his wardrobe and retaliated by excommunicating the contador and suspending all services on Palm Sunday. But the merchandise remained embargoed and had yet to be returned to the bishop after four years.[25]

Meanwhile the battle of appeals moved to Quito, as the accused, laymen and nuns alike, attempted to have the sentences laid down by the oidor and the bishop reversed. The bishop himself went to Quito in order to mobilize support for his case. In this endeavor he was only moderately successful. The rigor of the law was chiefly applied to three unhappy merchants who had not sought their immediate salvation in flight and hence were available for questioning. One of them, a Portuguese merchant, was executed even though his case had been thrown out on procedural grounds; under torture he had confessed the sacrileges imputed to him. Another defendant broke prison and fled with the alcaide de cárcel (prison warden) after his sentence was commuted and considerably moderated. The third defendant denied all accusations, even under torture; his sentence was similarly commuted and moderated. Many of the erstwhile fugitives from justice also submitted appeals; some of them could post bond and remain at liberty, while others were imprisoned in Quito. To explain their proceedings, the president of the audiencia and the fiscal wrote that in most cases there was no conclusive proof and not enough evidence to warrant torture.[26] Licenciado Zorrilla, on the other hand, was highly critical of the leniency shown to the defendants. Most of them, he wrote, returned to Popayán after the bishop left for Quito; they could do so without any risk since the local judges were their relatives. In addition, they could get all the testimony they wanted, either through their connections or through the fear these inspired, Zorrilla asserted. The nuns, for example, revoked their confessions, insisting that they were obtained under pressure from the bishop, an accusation that "no one would believe of so Christian a man," Zorrilla added.[27]

By 1613 the center of argument and commotion had shifted back to Popayán. The bishop's enemies, if not destroyed, had been given notice and hence were on the defensive. His main effort was now to dismantle the nunnery and to distribute its inhabitants to other convents, or so his adversaries alleged. Just as the first group of twelve nuns was to be sent away, a riot, in which a cleric was injured, broke out. A temporary delay of the transfer gained by the town's procurador from the audiencia could not prevent the ultimate move of these nuns to Quito.[28] Transferring the eight or nine nuns who remained in Popayán was a far more difficult matter. They moved heaven and earth and in the end, it seems, could not be budged from Popayán. Bishop González de Mendoza did not get much support from the local authorities from the governor on down, and it seems that his support from the audiencia in Quito was not unequivocal.

The audiencia was divided in its counsels. The president, Juan Fernández de Recalde, died in 1612, and Licenciado Zorrilla was left in charge as senior oidor. Other members of the audiencia had shown less sympathy than the licenciado for the bishop's designs. This caused the latter to assert that oidor Matías de Peralta and fiscal Sancho de Múgica had been bribed.[29] When confronted by the nuns from Popayán, the audiencia accepted them, in spite of the fact that the bishop did not even put up the necessary financial security. The fiscal, Sancho de Múgica, was directed to inquire into the disorders in Popayán, an effort that was certain to lead to nothing in view of the fiscal's well-known attitude toward the bishop.[30] Licenciado Zorrilla, for his part, belittled the charges brought against the bishop before the Council of the Indies. The problem, he wrote, amounted essentially to a jurisdictional squabble between the governor and the bishop in which the governor refused to be conciliated; the original charges had been drawn up by the governor and his deputy in Popayán, Fernán Díaz de Ribadeneyra, who traveled around the province soliciting complaints from the cabildos.[31] The cabildo of Popayán, when confronted by the licenciado with this allegation, emphatically denied it.[32]

For a while the situation amounted to a standoff, with the bishop in nominal command but unable to dislodge the remaining nuns without assistance from the local authorities. This precarious balance, unsatisfactory to everybody, was broken by charges that Governor Sarmiento had engineered an attempt on the bishop's life, indeed had promised an encomienda as reward. At the same time contador Juan de Palacios Alvarado was accused of malfeasance in office. In response, the audiencia of Quito dispatched a commissary judge (juez de comisión), Licenciado Alonso de Carvajal, to investigate all these charges. Carvajal was armed with orders to convey the governor to Quito and sequester his papers.[33]

The governor managed to evade capture by escaping to that part of his province under the jurisdiction of the audiencia of Santa Fé. He refused to return even when papers were served on him in Toro by a notary from Popayán. Faced with this defiance, Licenciado Carvajal attempted to suspend the governor from office, but the cabildos of Cali and Popayán refused to implement the decree, maintaining that the judge held no explicit authority for this step.[34] Thus the curious situation existed whereby the cabildos and alcaldes of the province were empowered to take the governor prisoner but at the same time continued to acknowledge his authority and to receive orders and appointments from him.

Contador Juan de Palacios stayed with the treasury in Cali, knowing from previous experience what to expect. In his mind the investigation was simply an act of revenge by the bishop and his nephew, who were trying at all costs to recover the merchandise still in his custody. They did not retrieve the goods, but the contador was fined heavily for using treasury funds in his business enterprises rather than remitting them.[35]

At this stage, the investigations were taken over by superior tribunals. In dispatching a judge to take the contador's accounts, the audiencia of Quito overstepped its jurisdictional limits. Since 1607 the treasury in Cali had been subject solely to the tribunal of accounts in Santa Fé. The tribunal, when appealed to by the contador, first protested against the proceedings of Licenciado Carvajal and then dispatched Captain Martín Bueno de Cartago, a veteran of the wars of Pijaos, to imprison the overzealous licenciado. Governor Sarmiento from his partial exile appointed the captain to be his new deputy in Popayán. Licenciado Carvajal had to beat a hasty retreat to Pasto, there to await the outcome of the dispute between the two tribunals.[36]

The situation in Popayán became even more complicated when Licenciado Fernando de Betancor y Barreto appeared there. He was a member of the cathedral chapter of Santa Fé. This august body, which governed the archdiocese sede vacante (during a vacancy), had committed the cause of the nuns and other citizens to the canon to investigate. Their pleas had finally reached the appropriate tribunal, the archbishop's jurisdiction. The canon was empowered to investigate matters locally, since the bishop of Popayán had not forwarded the testimony against the accused to Santa Fé. The bishop still refused to hand over the evidence and remained obdurate, even after the canon had obtained an injunction from the audiencia in Quito. Instead, the canon was attacked by a mob of clerics and was hit by stones while fleeing to safe quarters.

Under these circumstances he gave up the task and repaired to Quito, there to seek the remedy and pry loose the evidence, because, as he wrote, "the suspicion is rife that he [the bishop] has not proceeded in the way he advised His Majesty." The canon never found the remedy, as he died in Quito before he could return to the task.[37] Meanwhile, don Diego, the bishop's nephew, petitioned the audiencia for the return of Licenciado Carvajal, asserting that during his presence the commotion among the inhabitants had ceased but that in his absence Captain Bueno and Canon Betancor terrorized the regidores and other citizens of Popayán.[38]

Deadlock in Popayán—described by fiscal Sancho de Múgica as a situation in which "the land is laid waste by the judges dispatched," no alcalde dares to administer justice, and the bishop is always accompanied by armed men—was relieved by the arrival of the new governor, don Pedro Lasso de la Guerra.[39] At first, the new governor and the bishop made a determined effort to get along. It helped that former governor Sarmiento was imprisoned by the alcaldes of Cali as he returned from Santa Fé to have his residencia taken. He was released only after the audiencia granted his plea that he be allowed to undergo the residencia before facing charges in Quito.[40]

Harmony reigned only a short while. Before long the usual state of discord returned, and cabildos, governor, and religious orders were ranged against the bishop. In March and April of 1617, the cabildos of Cali and Popayán and Governor Lasso reported their difficulties to the Council in Spain.[41] The cabildo of Popayán wrote that the bishop was crankier than ever, going so far as to insult people to their faces; people were even avoiding him in the street. This time the complaint was preceded by lengthy preparations. First the cabildo had empowered a procurador to plead its case before the bishop. When this step was of no avail, the cabildo decided to put its case before the Council of the Indies and the audiencia with a complete report on the bishop's "quarrels, lack of respect, and exchange of words with the governor, as well as the things that have happened to this cabildo, such that the whole province has been scandalized." [42]

The chorus of complaints could not be overlooked this time. The Council addressed a reprimand to the bishop, exhorting him to avoid scandal and rumors, to treat the king's servants well and with politeness, and in general to proceed in the future in accordance with the dignity of his office.[43] When this exhortation was dispatched, the pugnacious bishop had already died and thus was spared a last humiliation. It remained for his nephew to protect the inheritance. A few days after his uncle's death, in March 1618, he obtained an injunction from the audiencia of Quito to protect the late prelate's belongings from local officials. He offered to guarantee all salaries and costs connected with the task. On April 18, 1618, the deputy and the alcaldes of Popayán received the commissary judge dispatched from Quito and, after having examined his credentials, promised to obey and implement his commission.[44]

When, nearly two generations after these events, a headstrong bishop, don Cristóbal Bernaldo de Quirós, clashed with a strong-willed governor and the townspeople found themselves in the line of fire, the experience was quite novel to them. With the governor excommunicated and the town in danger of being put under the interdict, there was no precedent to follow. After extended discussions the cabildo resolved to send a chasquí (messenger) to Quito to ask the audiencia for instructions and assistance. At the same time it was decided to call a cabildo abierto that would include the superiors of the religious orders and the "nobles" (todo lo noble) of the town. Emissaries dispatched by this cabildo tried to intercede with both the bishop and the governor. In the end the assembled cabildo abierto appeared before the governor and the bishop in succession, pleading for a reconciliation. It seems that this intercession changed the potentially explosive situation.[45] Two years after this crisis the cabildo even managed to effect a formal—though hardly cordial—reconciliation between the two antagonists.

The confrontation between governor and bishop began, as confrontations did so often, with a jurisdictional dispute. An alcalde ordinario of Popayán, in a surfeit of energy, inquired into the ownership of a herd of 2,200 cattle and 137 horses being driven through the town. When informed that it belonged to Licenciado Antonio Ruiz Navarrete, curate and commissioner of the Inquisition in Pasto, he handed the matter over to the jurisdiction of the vicar general of the diocese. The alcalde expected swift action, since the licenciado had clearly violated the rule, only recently reiterated in a papal breve, that clerics should not engage in trade. Instead of receiving recognition for his diligence, he was fined 250 pesos and excommunicated for infringing ecclesiastical jurisdiction.[46]

The alcalde's mishap might not have stirred up much trouble if a new governor, don Miguel García, had not taken the defense of his royal master's jurisdiction seriously. His military experience—he had served twenty-two years in Flanders and Italy—perhaps had not prepared him to deal with churchmen on their terms. The bishop, a graduate of Salamanca and son of a royal chamberlain, had enjoyed satisfactory relations with the previous governor and had already received eulogies from the town for this efforts at finishing the cathedral and for his charities and good works.[47] Matters between bishop and governor, both evidently men too big for so small a town, grew heated within a short time. Relations broke down, as was common at the time, on a formality of communication. Bishops tended to appoint one of their own clerics as notary. In a specific injunctions addressed to the bishop, the governor, exasperated at the impossibility of getting ecclesiastics to testify before him without the bishop's dispensation, got the audiencia to repeat the general prohibition against clerics serving as notaries. But the bishop refused to accept even that decree, alleging lack of proper notification, since there was no notary to serve it and the alcalde could not and would not do so. At his wit's end, the governor prohibited the cabildo and the alcaldes from accepting any communications from the ecclesiastical notaries.[48] The breakdown in communications ended with a riot in front of the bishop's residence that was reportedly stirred up by the governor, who had just been excommunicated a second time and was trying to mobilize support.

By its timely and efficient attempt at mediation, the cabildo spared the town the possible consequences of a major struggle between the "two heads of the town." Later another governor was to characterize the cabildo's conduct in this situation and its reporting to the Council as two-faced and dishonest, "with letters in favor of each one without worrying about the inconsistency." When apprised of these aspersions, the cabildo reacted indignantly, since belief in its veracity was its only asset with the Council. In a letter of baroque phraseology it emphasized its obligation to give punctual account without regard to persons but with attention given to performance, whether it deserved applause or censure.[49]

That it performed a mediating function in regard to reporting and politics may have occurred to the members of the cabildo for a fleeting moment. But was it needed? Conflict between governor and bishop was the exception, not the rule. The confrontation between Governor García and Bishop Bernaldo de Quirós was only a squabble that did not engage a major interest, except the desire for peace and quiet (an opposite desire may sometimes be present). Also, the two "heads" were willing to accept mediation. A cabildo abierto representing the república was the best way to deal with the problem. Ecclesiastical dignitaries attended and were effective members. Things were resolved in this fashion, at least temporarily, because the issue was not one that engaged local partisanship—as the struggle between Governor Nevares and contador Hurtado was to do—but was simply a question of jurisdiction. The episode shows, as do earlier local conflicts between governor and bishop, that disputes easily got out of hand. Beyond a certain point no local mechanism for resolving them existed. The audiencia then had to intervene, in both secular and ecclesiastical affairs, by decree and, if need be, by dispatching a judge to take matters in hand. The rarity of this kind of intervention does not therefore make it less a part of the operation of politics and government.

The function of the Church in Popayán had, by this time, become the organization of routine. The bishop's role was largely confined to providing embellishment for that routine, such as ornaments for the cathedral, a bell tower, charities. The nature of the routine—or rather the proper function of the Church—was an issue under the first bishops of Popayán, who still tried to bring their vision of Christian life to the region in active fashion. Bishop González de Mendoza still shared in this tradition, which was established by his predecessors Juan del Valle and Agustín de la Coruña. He tried to impose his will in such matters as church attendance and public mores. He may have had mixed motives, as they were imputed to him by the local citizenry and indeed were nicely represented in the person of his nephew. Nonetheless, his reforming drive was partially effective. The synod he held in 1617 affords some proof of his efforts. He was supported by the secular clergy (although not by the cathedral chapter), perhaps out of fear, perhaps in expectation of benefices. He was also supported by one group of important families under the leadership of the alférez real, don Ýñigo de Velasco, which later came to be called the Zúñiga faction. They were willing to testify in favor of the bishop, with an undertone of aristocratic disdain for the prevailing low standards. But they abandoned the bishop when he proceeded to dismantle the convent in which they, as well as the rest of the citizenry, had a stake. A reforming bishop did have some local leverage if he used it wisely and with discretion. The Marqués de Montesclaros, viceroy of Peru, commenting on the bishop's difficulties and offering some unsolicited advice, wrote at the time that "though subjects of great gifts and prudence have to be employed in the larger places, I do not know whether small and distant ones need them of equal perfection," and added that persons of modest and impartial disposition were to be preferred.[50] Ultimately, though, it was not a prelate's character and disposition that made the difference in the local position of the Church; it was rather the strength of its organization, the services it offered, and the kind of men it recruited on all levels.

The Church, despite the impression created on previous pages, was not a source of conflict in Popayán; rather it was a force of cohesion and integration. By responding to the settlers' needs, giving them direction and shape, the Church filled a social function in the town's life as, obviously, it had done in Europe for centuries. It did so by fusing spiritual, ritual, and material elements to serve divine and human purposes. Some of these human purposes I will describe briefly, to the extent that they show the relation between settler society and Church.

First and foremost the Church was a visible institution. There were the cathedral, the other churches, and the religious houses; there were processions, devotions, and music; feast and fast days. Holy days punctuated the year, thirty-four for Spaniards. Holy Week was the most solemn of these occasions. The rhythm of day, week, and year was set by the Church, and so was that of peoples' lives. A day began at sunrise with the clanging of bells, and a life ended with the funeral rites, simple or elaborate as the occasion demanded. The Church, in short, ordered space and time, dividing them into manageable and comprehensible segments.

The building of churches and their decoration displayed the region's resources and the inhabitants' piety, especially since that part of the tithe set aside for this purpose was utterly insufficient. Donations had to make up the difference. Sodalities, for instance, could underwrite the cost of annual devotions and feasts or pay for the construction of an altar and its upkeep. Private benefactors included the "governor" Pedro de Velasco, who in 1613 agreed to rebuild the brick walls and thatched roof of a small chapel, the Ermita, at his own expense. A wealthy artisan, Juan Antonio de Velasco (no relation of the former), built the chapel of Belén in the 1680s. The Arboleda family underwrote the construction of the Dominican church.[51] Whoever could not contribute in this substantial fashion could still show devotion in smaller ways, for instance by acquiring devotional paintings mass-produced in Quito. Paintings of this sort, small and large, were owned widely, often in large numbers.[52]

In essence the Church was a sacramental institution. Good works, such as the building of churches, could contribute to salvation, but they could not guarantee it. Only sacraments as instruments of grace could accomplish that. Sacraments accompanied life, in both a single and a recurring cycle. The significance of sacraments—besides their religious meaning—lay in the regulations surrounding their administration, which touched peoples' lives in many ways. Matrimony may serve as an example.[53] The Church emphasized the freedom of individuals to contract marriage and insisted on this freedom for slaves. At the same time, marriage was surrounded by obstacles and hurdles, erected principally because of the problem of bigamy and the prohibition of consanguinity. The granting of marriage licenses was not taken lightly, precisely because so many interests could be involved and because abuses were frequent. Forced and fraudulent marriage unions, among Spaniards and among Indians (sometimes promoted by the encomenderos), were common. According to the regulations, objections to a marriage were to be treated seriously, with evidence to be forwarded by the vicario to the diocesan courts. Frivolous objections, on the other hand, were to be punished severely—if need be by excommunication—and only the bishop (except in *articulo mortis*) could lift the penalty. It is also worth noting that if the priest in charge found no impediments to a marriage, although objections were raised, he was to proceed with the ceremony, but the woman was to be put under safeguard, out of the reach of her husband, until the matter was resolved; a marriage not yet consummated could be annulled more easily. When it came to the administration of the sacraments, the Church found it difficult —yet not quite impossible—to compromise with local preferences. The doctrineros, for instance, were to take care that Indians married within their encomiendas. They were not always successful, as the frequent marriages between urban and rural Indians in Popayán attest.[54]

For salvation and spiritual sustenance the region needed the Church.

For material support the Church depended on the region. Clerics were not supposed to engage in trade, an otherwise natural occupation for them. They took no vow of poverty, mendicant friars excepted, but neither were most priests independently wealthy. How then was the clergy to make a living and maintain itself in decency without transgressing the rules? Beyond the tithe, first fruits, and a doctrinero's stipend proportionate to the number of tribute payers, the Church depended on the clergy's ingenuity in tapping good will or in fleecing their flock. Fees afford examples of the latter procedure; weddings and funerals were expensive not least because of the high charges of the clergy. No fees were to be charged for the administration of sacraments, but the repeated prohibition would seem to show that fees were indeed charged.[55] The ingenious and often time-honored ways in which Indians were exploited by the clergy need no retelling here.

Religious sentiment and the priesthood's needs were more evenly matched in the operation of cofradías, capellanías, and obras pías that generated an income through the endowment of masses. The will of Lope de Labayen, a Navarrian merchant and muleteer, shows an interesting combination of capellanía and cofradía supported by one mortgage of a thousand gold pesos.[56] In his will Labayen stipulated thirteen sung masses for the benefit of his soul, at an annual cost of twenty-five gold pesos. The capellanía was to be served by the cathedral chapter as the beneficiary. The remaining income of twenty-five pesos was to buy wax for the cofradía of the Santísimo Sacramento of the cathedral, a religious brotherhood that Labayen reinstituted on the basis of this endowment (an obra pía for the benefit of a cofradía). In his will, Labayen also stipulated a set of rules for the cofradía: membership was to be open to everyone upon the payment of one pound of wax and one silver peso; the cofradía's mayordomo could reduce the amount in line with a person's means; members had to confess and celebrate communion five times a year and were to attend the masses endowed by the founder.

The tithe and a fraction of Indian tribute were revenues that accrued ipso facto to the Church. Their collection was not automatic and was by no means an easy matter. The tribute contribution was collected and disbursed by the corregidor; in 1667 and later it was 2 silver pesos per tributary. Tribute shrank, in line with the declining native population. The increasing number of slaves could not quite make up for this decline, although the owners paid the same amount.[57] The tithe, after a secular decline, rose again after 1710. Customarily it was farmed out to the highest bidder, with its award in the hands of the treasury officials and one of the canons as juez privativo de diezmos. In the 1590s the annual amount was 1,500 to 1,600 gold pesos; in the 1690s it was 1,250 silver pesos, only half the amount collected a century earlier. The decline may at first have reflected the depressed character of rural production; eventually it ceased to bear much relation to actual production. This becomes clear when one considers that in 1720 the town's tithe farm amounted to 4,000 patacones. The increase occurred after it was reorganized by a newly formed junta de diezmos that divided the district into three different partidos (sections), farmed by different bidders.[58] At the same time the first detailed inventory of rural properties for collection purposes was made. Earlier in the century the tithe farmers had come frequently from the town's smaller merchants and dealers. Now they were drawn from among the vecinos of substance.[59] In either case, they must have had a pretty good knowledge of rural properties and their potential, although substantial men like don Nicolás de Mosquera or don Francisco de Arboleda undoubtedly entrusted collection to others. It was important, however, that their wits be matched by the men composing the junta de diezmos, a matter assured when it included don Pedro de Arboleda and don Francisco Xavier Torijano, who faced don Nicolás de Mosquera, don Bernardino de Saa, and don Francisco de Arboleda as tithe farmers.

For a long time the region's material contribution was insufficient to support the local ecclesiastical establishment; such at least was the gist of the cathedral chapter's representations to the crown in 1628.[60] This is also evident from the annual subsidies paid by the treasury to curates and sacristans whose income did not meet the stipulated amount. In this situation the clergy tried to exact as much as possible, unwilling even to say mass gratis for the sake of a good harvest, as the cabildo wrote. Most of their services had to be bought. As the cabildo complained to a synod sitting in Bogotá, marriages and burials were so expensive that many of the poor never married (burials offered no such simple solution). This petition contained a veritable litany of complaints about the clergy's exactions and shortcomings.[61]

In its representations the cabildo also noted that there was not one teacher of Latin in the whole province, that the seminary remained a mere idea, and that the town's religious houses did not fulfill their obligation to provide preachers. In fact, the inhabitants had to take up a collection to procure a preacher for the Lenten season. The coming of the Jesuits in the 1630s and their immediate success in engaging local interest was thus not an accident. They promised education and edification, which hitherto had been lacking. They also promised the discipline to tame the energies of the town's young men, who, in a previous generation, had made furtive visits to the convent. And finally they gave direction in both a spiritual and a material sense to the latent piety of the inhabitants.

The seminary was founded in 1643. Directed and staffed by the Society of Jesus, it was the basis of the Jesuit establishment in Popayán.[62] There was an initial enrollment of twenty students, including Manuel Rodríguez of Cali, the future author of *El Marañón y el Amazonas* (The Marañón and the Amazon), one of the first missionary accounts of the Amazon region (printed in 1684). An earlier local recruit of the order was Francisco de Figueroa—a son of the regidor Francisco de Figueroa. He became one of the "martyrs" of the Marañón, killed by Indians while a missionary there. His account of the missions of Maynas, written in the 1650s, was not published until 1904. On the average, six seminarians attended, as well as six more boarders who paid their own way (in one case the parents paid by deeding a mine to the order). Tithe income specifically set aside for the purpose and taken from the hospital's share paid for the seminarians' scholarships. The transformation of what was intended as no more than a simple residencia into a regular college and seminary with students, a rector, benefactors, and lay brotherhoods is the more striking when one compares this success with the Jesuits' concurrent failure to establish themselves in Pasto. The Jesuits' educational achievement was securely founded on local good will, which the order capitalized, as it were, and put on a permanent income-producing basis. The order's rigorous procedures are also evident in the congregación de Nuestra Señora de Loreto, a variant of the cofradía but with strict supervision and a definite educational function.[63] The rules of the congregación stated that, after the recital of the rosary and the litany, Christian doctrine was to be explained by the father in charge and an attempt was to be made to attract Indians, Negroes, mestizos, and servants to the occasion even if they were not members. Such teaching, not "a big fiesta with a lot of noise about town," stated the order's visitador, would ultimately draw people toward the sacraments.

The capellanía in its many functions exemplifies the fusion of spiritual and material purposes in the town's religious life.[64] Its spiritual aim was to speed the progress of its founder's soul by means of masses said in his memory. Its social function was to establish the clerical profession as a desirable career independent of the vagaries of preferment, particularly when a family as patron of a capellanía controlled the appointment of the beneficiary. To achieve this purpose, the founder would take particular care to ensure continuing control by laymen rather than the Church. The mortgages that underwrote ca-pellanías served to keep inheritances intact, since they produced an-nuities drawn on a property. Thus coherent enterprises—whether rural estates or mining operations—did not necessarily have to be broken up among heirs or sold. Castilian law stressed equal partition among heirs, with only slight improvements in favor of individual heirs. Entails could make such improvements permanent, but they were cumbersome and costly devices. A simpler and more temporary arrangement, suitable in particular for supporting ecclesiastical careers, was to mort-gage a property in favor of some heirs. The interest on the mortgage would pay for a number of masses and support the chaplain, although perhaps not in style.

The primary economic function of the capellanía was to provide a living for a cleric. The principal represented by this income could serve as a capital sum available at the low rate of 5 percent, because the mortgages were usually redeemable and could thus be retired and invested anew. The function of capellanías and other similar endow-ments in providing loan capital appears most clearly when one con-siders the town's religious houses. The convent of nuns in 1701 had an endowment of 82,627 patacones, much of which was on loan to various individuals. A part of this sum was in nuns' dowries, capitalized in name only and in fact represented by annual payments in cash or kind.[65] Dowries of nuns apparently were not usually secured by re-deemable mortgages but rather by temporary liens, if they were not paid in cash. The Jesuits were active users of cheap credit, which they obtained from other clerical lenders, among them the convent of nuns and the cofradía of Rosario. At the turn of the eighteenth century, they had taken up eight different mortgages of nearly 10,000 pata-cones.[66] Some of these supported capellanías. The Franciscans and Dominicans were, like the nuns, holders of mortgages and patrons of capellanías, but they were not active users of credit.[67]

We observe here the operation of a rudimentary capital market, in large part under ecclesiastical auspices. Clerics (and nuns) represented a class of *rentiers,* for whom future incomes were set aside and secured in specific fashion. In some cases available funds were invested, that is, turned into capital so as to produce an income stream; otherwise an income was stipulated and an appropriate property (or a part of it) was set aside to satisfy the recurring claim or serve as security in case this was not met. At the beginning of this process there were tangible assets, connected with a beneficiary through an obligation. The assets could change and so could the beneficiary, but the obligation would remain. Since the obligation was convertible into a capital sum (at 5 percent this would be twenty years' purchase), it could move from holder to holder, through a recurring process of redemption and renewed encumbrance. It never stopped, in theory, unless the assets supporting it at a given moment were consumed. Since a capellanía supported by a mortgage was a perpetual obligation, the principal was never retired. In this it was different from current mortgages. In the long run there were important consequences, in particular for capellanías established under Church supervision through canonical institution (capellanías not so instituted presumably could also fall under Church control). The mortgages that sustained them tended to become a capital stock independent of the personal and spiritual motives that had called them into being. Whether this capital stock would be real estate directly managed by the Church, rental property, or funds lent at interest depended on circumstances. At this point, then, the Church could appear as an economic actor, a boon to the "economy," or a drag as the dead hand; it was separate, at any rate, from the society that had cast it in this role.[68] Although a lively market in mortgages was in evidence in Popayán at the turn of the eighteenth century, a situation of this sort was there still in the distant future.

How capellanías served the career and estate planning of local families can be seen in the Arboledas' case. In 1659 the bachiller Jacinto de Arboleda, by then already an ecclesiastic, had set up a capellanía with a principal of 7,000 pesos and an annual return of 350 pesos, secured by fourteen slaves engaged in gold mining. The patrons—that is, administrators of the capellanía—were to be his three sons and their descendants. The chaplain—that is, beneficiary—was to be selected from among those of don Jacinto's grandsons who had chosen ecclesiastical careers. Until a qualified descendant could be appointed, the canons of the cathedral were to serve as chaplains. The income of 350 pesos was to pay for 153 masses and various other expenditures. Any surplus was to be invested in purchasing additional slaves. The family was to retain exclusive jurisdiction over the capellanía. Only the patrons and the chaplain were to have the right to sell slaves or to take accounts.[69] At the turn of the century the chaplain was Doctor don Carlos de Arboleda, the founder's grandson. He had studied in Quito, where he received his doctorate in theology in 1696. He was ordained a priest in Santa Fé. In Popayán, Bishop Villafañe appointed him diocesan examiner and recommended him warmly for preferment in a letter to the crown, as he did on behalf of four more Arboledas, all of them doctors, and two of their nephews.[70] The Arboledas were only one of the families of Popayán who linked their fortunes to the Church. The brothers don Francisco Xavier and don Fernando de Salazar Betancur held two positions on the cathedral chapter at the turn of the century. Two sons of the treasurer Pérez de Ubillus became canons in Quito and in Popayán. One could easily multiply the examples to show that by the eighteenth century the Church was a preferred career for many native sons of Popayán.

Local recruitment on a large scale became possible after the Jesuits founded the college and seminary. It became a reality as local wealth was increasingly channeled so as to make ecclesiastical careers not only possible but attractive. The Church became domesticated in Popayán when native sons (hijos patrimoniales) made up the local clergy. In this sense, community standards prevailed over those of the Church universal. It may be true that the Church ceased to criticize the social and economic reality within which it had to function. Yet it would be mistaken to assume that the Church was a mere extension of that reality, just as no necessary identity of interest had to exist between the clergy and local notables simply because the clergy was recruited from among them.

The Church, much more than the crown, could mobilize parochial interests and resources, mediating between them and a larger world conceived in spiritual and organizational terms. It was this ability to integrate personal and local affairs into a larger universe that made the Church an indispensable collaborator of the state, a potential competitor, and, ultimately, an antagonist.

Conclusion

This book does two things: it tells a story, and it analyzes that story as one version of a historical process. The story describes a town, its people, and their way of life; it tells of the settlers, their activities, and how they ran the town. Its interest as a story lies in the telling. Depending on the evidence and on inclination, one can expand it in breadth and depth, like any local history. Despite an irreducible element, it is not a unique tale. The town of Popayán represents one case among many: the growth of a Spanish colonial society within the larger process of European settlement in America. This conclusion throws some light on this process, from a local perspective.

Three features of settlement are worth particular emphasis: the settlers' struggle with the new environment in both its physical and human aspects, the internal articulation of settler society, and the nature of the tie between colony and mother country. The emphasis on general features allows us to determine what was distinctive in each regional process of settlement. Without such implicit comparison local history easily turns into chronicle. But how do local investigations help us to understand a more general process? The actions of conquest and the forms of settlement and government were often similar, but the conditions under which they occurred, or were elaborated, frequently were not. This book, then, examines the conditions under which colonial society and institutions functioned as much as it does their forms.

Spanish settlement in the New World hinged on the Indians, who mediated between the environment and the newcomers. The initial character of settlement was determined by the kind of native presence and by the opportunities it offered, in combination with other resources, mainly gold. Somehow Spaniards had to reconcile their urban tradition—reinforced by the exigencies of control over the natives— with the challenge presented by the new environment. Unlike those in Mexico or Peru, where the Aztecs or the Incas possessed an urban tradition of their own, Spanish settlements in the Cauca could not be grafted onto a native base. Towns were a Spanish innovation there.

How they fared gives important clues to the Spaniards' ability to cope with their new setting.

The founding of towns started a process of transformation. Its main tendencies were to incorporate the area's inhabitants into the Spanish world and integrate them into a settler-operated exchange economy. The speed of the transformation varied from region to region, as did the results; its ingredients also differed. In Popayán, its momentum was the lure of gold, as myth and as reality. Other elements entered, perhaps slowing down the process but not altering its direction. In Popayán the most important factors were changes in population and in the configuration of Spanish settlement, the penetration of the countryside by Spanish enterprise, and the emergence and expansion of a regional market tied to a rudimentary world market. These are not separate phenomena; their significance resides in their multiple connections.

Changes in population included the catastrophic decline in the number of native Indians, the immigration of Indians from other regions, a trickle of Spanish immigrants, and a large influx of slaves from Africa. What did these changes mean, and what were their consequences? It is clear that the settlers' ability to draw on a surplus produced by the natives fell drastically. The towns' capacity to accommodate settlers was reduced correspondingly, unless they succeeded in reorganizing production and closing the labor gap. At first, would-be settlers were spun off, either into native warfare or into peaceful pursuits in the countryside. At the fringes of the zone of settlement, the search for gold and native labor continued for a long time, exemplified by the intrusions into the Chocó and Barbacoas and by the wars of the Pijaos. Despite this turbulence, the center continued to hold, as evident in continued immigration. For those who came voluntarily, the situation cannot have been without promise of profit. Those who were forcibly imported had to be paid for—a sign of means, if not prosperity. The labor gap was closed also, because in the long run an intermediate class of people emerged between the masters and servile labor. Indian immigrants settling in or near the town were the first members of this group.

The string of towns that was the province had been founded with a view to the needs of conquest, communication, and control. In some cases they dwindled as their functions disappeared, with the decline of the natives and the emergence of Cartagena and Quito as poles of trade. Popayán became the junction point of trade, politics, and government, connecting distant points of supply with shifting centers of production, relegating other towns to a second rank. The town's regional functions increased and so did its local role. As the taproot of encomienda grew weaker, the town put down other roots. Grazing ranges and harvest land were turned into ranches and farms; some of these units ultimately became compact estates. Mines functioned in the town's immediate vicinity and in the distant rain forests. It may be a moot question whether the increasing operation of rural enterprises by settlers and their hangers-on signified a ruralization of settlement or the penetration of the countryside by the town. The settlers did not lose their urban orientation; rural expansion occurred in response to the opportunities of a market. The phenomenon of increasing rural penetration represents one stage in the development of a regional market spanning town and country. Its first stage had been described by encomienda, which served as one vehicle for mobilizing labor and procuring commodities. The regional market was in turn tied to Cartagena and Quito, as stabilizing sources of supply and demand and as points of a circulatory system through which people, manufactures, commodities, and bullion moved. Despite the thinness of settlers on the ground, the Spanish presence was durable and even capable of expansion. Its strength had to do with its design as a network of mutually supporting elements. Its costs in human terms were considerable, even appalling. Its resilience it owed to the actions of Spanish entrepreneurs, whether encomenderos, miners, or merchants. To be successful, they not only mobilized resources but also managed people and manipulated institutions.

The cycle of population whose sign was the switch from Indian to African labor had not only economic repercussions: it also affected the town's society and institutions. Changes in the town's upper stratum were inevitable, as new men and new wealth emerged. Names such as Arboleda, Hurtado del Águila, Victoria, Salazar Betancur, and Torijano were unknown in the town before the seventeenth century. The composition of the town's upper stratum was in flux during this entire period. Yet stability was not absent and the break with the past was hardly complete. Some continuity was provided by marriage, which allowed newcomers and their descendants to share in the real and the psychological benefits of being beneméritos de Indias, of participating in the distinction that accrued to conquistadors and first settlers and their descendants. Traditional sources of wealth and prestige, such as control over land and Indian labor in the town's vicinity and over the estancias that supplied Popayán with the bulk of its necessities, continued to be important. Families such as the Velascos or the Mosqueras, who combined encomienda-recruited labor in agriculture with slave labor in mining, remained at the top during the seventeenth century.

Despite radically changing conditions, the town's upper stratum maintained links with the past and established claims to the future, although not yet in the form of titles or entails. Its authority was not based only on wealth, official position, or racial distinction, but derived also from lineage, operating in bilateral fashion. Descent in the male line was preferred, but descent in the female line would do. The most notable characteristic of this aristocracy of lineage was its ability to absorb new members and infuse them with the group's ethos, despite the absence of institutionalized, corporate forms. Then—and seemingly even today—inclusion in family networks sufficed to incorporate new members and legitimize their local standing. The cohesion, continuity, and permanence exhibited by kinship ties produced an aristocracy based on families rather than an elite identified by position and career. Definition of membership rested with the group, since one could not become a member simply by acquiring an "elite" position. This was the mistake of some of those who purchased seats on the cabildo early in the seventeenth century. Membership rested on acceptance, and marriage was its surest sign. After a period of erosion, social authority based on tradition was stabilized in Popayán. What happened to political authority?

One need not assume absolute symmetry between society and institutions to relate the fitful history of the town's government to that of its upper stratum. The continuous recruitment of new members into the cabildo shows that no "clase capitular" existed—no closed oligarchy with patrimonial claims to office. While such claims were never completely absent, as the town's alferazgo demonstrated, they remained the exception. This can be seen in the neglect of renunciation of office as a device that could assure continuity. Only a few families (Velasco, Aguinaga, and Hurtado) had a record of office-holding over three generations. In all likelihood, a greater consolidation of office in the hands of a select group occurred during the eighteenth century.

Participation in government through the cabildo was a two-edged affair. No tradition of service was in evidence, in the sense of devoting time or money to "public" affairs. On the other hand, there was a sense of honor, of social standing, that could strive for expression in office. Membership in the cabildo thus gave visibility; it also could procure influence and connections. Pecuniary advantages were insignificant, so it seems. But office could also be a liability. The need for regular attendance and for availability at certain times excluded merchants more effectively than any formal obstacles. Governors could use office as a lever against incumbents, by insisting on formal compliance with all obligations. It is perhaps characteristic that the cabildo showed little interest in its regulatory functions, so important in many towns. Merchants, shopkeepers, traders, and peddlers thrived under a minimum of supervision. Artisans did not exist as cohesive groups. The town's economic structure—it was more a center of distribution than of production—contributed to the small importance of regulation. The cabildo was hardly an embodiment of community spirit. The existence of such a sentiment is more in evidence in contributions to the Church —where they could serve many purposes—than to the town, which elicited no similar identification.

The governors could make themselves the spokesmen of the community, ordering frequent meetings, inquiring into prices, and inspecting shops. Such intervention was fitful at best. Neither the governors nor the treasury officials were as a rule equipped or inclined to uphold standards or to become advocates of the community. They had their own interests, as had the cabildo.

Judged by continuity of office-holding and administrative performance, the cabildo of Popayán hardly accomplished much. Its achievement was of a different nature. The cabildo maintained a nominal claim by the vecinos to a share in government. Such a claim did not rest on a notion of direct representation. The cabildo did not represent the town: it *was* the town in a legal sense. A notion of virtual representation evidently did exist, exemplified by the office of procurador general. The town remained separate from the state and was not absorbed into it, nor was it fitted into a bureaucratic framework. Rather the cabildo formed an intermediate body between the crown and the vecinos.

The link between cabildo and vecinos was weak. Members had to possess citizenship in the town. But citizenship itself was not very clearly defined, as is evident in the haphazard way in which reception was handled and in the loose fashion in which the term was used. Frequently it simply meant, as the century wore on, an inhabitant of long standing. No separate register of citizens was kept by the cabildo, despite its role in granting citizenship. More important than vecindad was a loose category of prominence (todo lo noble) that qualified members for elective posts and that was formalized in a listing in the minutes of 1706. Also important was inclusion in a cabildo abierto's deliberations. As a consultative arrangement, it defined the town's notables.

The cabildo's share in government was symbolized by the mandatory accreditation of an official before he could enter upon his duties in the district, be he an oidor or a notary. The importance of this requirement appears repeatedly: in the protracted argument about the contador Larrainzar's bond in 1659, the cabildo's insistence that fiscal Sarmiento y Huesterlin present his commission to them, and the oidor Ricaurte's forcible imposition in 1702 of a purged cabildo that could receive Governor Miera and thus legitimize his government of the province.

The election of the alcaldes by the cabildo and the handling of appeals is further evidence for the cabildo's claim to a share in jurisdiction. The collection of the alcabala through contract with the treasury and the cabildo's role in imposing contributions, whether for the construction of the cathedral in 1608 or for the fine to make up for tax evasion, in 1658, shows its position as an intermediary between the crown and the inhabitants. In addition, the cabildo acted as a spokesman for local interests in mining and agriculture. The miners, however, acted on their own in a petition to the Council of the Indies in 1645. Also, the corporation of the cabildo and the meeting of a cabildo abierto were separate affairs. The cabildo thus had no exclusive role as a spokesman. In residencias the cabildo did not appear in its corporate capacity; rather the members testified as individuals.

Is it meaningful to speak of "local autonomy" under these circumstances? The cabildo indeed was a local factor that had to be taken into account, in particular by governors jockeying for position. It possessed no power of its own but rather depended on the energy and ability of others to mobilize it. In the crisis at the turn of the century such power rested principally with the three families of Velasco, Mosquera, and Hurtado, who could mobilize their dependents and clients in bandos (factions). Governor Miera, for instance, was alleged to govern at the pleasure of the Mosqueras. It may thus be more accurate, as far as the cabildo is concerned, to speak of potential for autonomy. Actual autonomy rested with families and family networks. They controlled slave and Indian labor and claimed positions in the Church, the town, and the province's government. Such de facto autonomy could clothe itself in the garb of the cabildo and invoke the institution against the crown's servants.

Government in Popayán existed on two levels. The institutions of government, including the cabildo, operated as formal extensions of the state, with the occupants of office or benefice subject to appointment, confirmation, and administrative inquest. On another level, government depended on the backing of local social authority; it could break down when such backing was absent, as happened, for instance, under Bishop González de Mendoza's tenure and also during the commotions at the turn of the eighteenth century. Usually, however, accommodation between the two levels prevailed. The attitudes toward accommodation were ambivalent. On the one hand, bureaucratic absolutism was prefigured in America long before it became a reality in Europe. The crown possessed more extensive claims in America than in Castile. There the towns—at least some of them—were built into a dualistic system of crown and estates, while in America a monistic system of direct relations between towns and crown existed. The crown's attempt to protect the native population was a persistent source of conflict in America, unlike Castile, where the crown took no interest in the peasants. Nevertheless, conflict was usually muffled, in part because the bureaucratic tendency was opposed by an older one, patrimonialism, and also because the monarchy's claims ceased to be backed at the center with sufficient force, although they were not abandoned in theory.

The details of how accommodation worked need no retelling here. Adjustment and trimming were as much the result of loss of direction at the center as of pressures from the periphery. Appointment to office, as we have seen with regard to the governorship, was not usually based on competence and depended only in a limited sense on merit. Largely it was a reward for services, personal or pecuniary. Between institutions, differences remained important. The Church, given its separate position and relatively independent construction, was less responsive, if not impervious, to direction from the crown. It proved more amenable in its relations with the settlers. After all, they possessed a patrimonial claim to benefice that the crown honored. But, just as the Church could be subverted by such internal takeover, it could subvert those whom it recruited. Any true institution possesses this capacity. They could become its servants rather than remain beholden to their origins. The Church commanded not only spiritual allegiance but also practical loyalty. Its recruitment tapped talent educated under its auspices and gained by financial inducements. By comparison, the state was weak. Its very weakness demanded the control over the Church exercised through the patronato real, the system of royal patronage that provided it with an additional chain of command, practical allegiance, and trained servants.

The governors were not really crown servants. They had their own interests at heart; nothing more was to be expected of them. The treasury officials, although not necessarily dishonest in any strict sense, identified with the place where they settled and married. It is thus safe to affirm that government in Popayán not only existed in a social context but also largely merged into it, appearances notwithstanding. No clear and practical distinction between public and private standards of behavior existed, as was evident in the residencia, which in effect served to affirm private considerations over public ones. It is doubtful whether this situation reflected an actual conflict between different standards. More likely it was the result of the inability of the limited apparatus to carry out rules designed for one place, at one time. This inability had to do with organization and staffing, but it also resulted from prevailing norms and values, from the "goal orientation" of officials. Practical devices of government were not the residencia and visita, as instruments of control, but the gracia, composición, disimulación, and indulto, as instruments of legitimation. These juridical figures upheld law in theory and acknowledged its inability to affect prevailing circumstances in practice.

The absorption of government into local society was not complete, because the Creoles, despite their claim to constitute a república de españoles, never managed to form a political society in the older, Aristotelian sense. There was also the república de indios, not easily absorbed by that of the Spaniards, given the special protection it enjoyed, whatever its actual situation might be. Crown and settlers were juxtaposed in an odd fashion. While the crown proved incapable of providing government in a modern, bureaucratic sense, it did not relinquish its claim to ultimate sovereignty and to control over local affairs. The Creoles were thus unable to establish unquestioned authority, let alone autonomy. Their transformation into a political society was blocked, except on the crown's terms.

The Creoles' authority was limited not simply because the crown distrusted them: their de facto power found little institutional expression, because the existing state apparatus could handle jurisdiction and defense, so it was thought. The encomienda atrophied because there was no need for it, except as a reward. It remained a limited and transitory privilege, with no jurisdiction, limited military relevance, and no corporate basis. The need for defense was either too small to be of much import or on a scale that could not be handled by local levies of armed encomenderos and vecinos. Jurisdiction was in the hands of professional judges who served as the prototype of the state's servants. For these reasons, devolution of authority was hardly considered and delegation was kept in limits. The "kingdoms" of America had a fictitious quality. There was neither a king (rey) nor a realm (reino), since the Creoles never advanced beyond the corporations of the towns. Beyond these, they had no institutions—like the Cortes of the peninsula—to represent them.

The relation between the Church and the settlers was, in a way, analogous. The Church remained a separate institution, although hardly independent of local interests. Its power as an institution affecting the *hic et nunc* was limited, yet its authority was unquestioned. Crown and Church provided an overarching framework—ideas frozen into institutions—that the settlers could not easily transcend, even had they wanted to. Yet the settlers' situation was ultimately characterized by contradictions. They were suspended between potentially conflicting identifications: one with the distant crown and the ancient fatherland, and the other with the land their ancestors had conquered but whose full masters they were not allowed to be.

The relationship between government and a partially articulated society—in which Creoles held power but authority escaped them—was appropriate for the region at the time. It represented a balance that broke down when the crown attempted to recover effective control over affairs and when the Creoles ceased to be content with definitions of the political order made by others. Until then Popayán would remain a town in the empire.

Appendices

A. GOVERNORS OF POPAYÁN, 1598–1706

Don Vasco de Mendoza y Silva (1598)
Don Francisco Sarmiento de Sotomayor (1607)
Don Pedro Lasso de la Guerra (1615)
Captain Juan Menéndez Márquez (1621)
Captain Juan Bermúdez de Castro (1628)
Don Lorenzo de Villaquirán (1633)
Don Juan de Borja (1637)
Captain don Juan de Salazar
Captain don Luis de Valenzuela Fajardo
Maestre de Campo don Luis Antonio de Guzmán y Toledo (1659)
Maestre de Campo don Gabriel Díaz de la Cuesta (1667)
Maestre de Campo don Miguel García (1674)
Don Fernando Martínez de Fresneda (1679)
Don Gerónimo de Berrío y Mendoza
Captain don Rodrigo Roque de Mañozca
Don Gerónimo José de la Vega y Caviedes, marqués de Nevares (1696)
Don Juan de Miera Ceballos (1702)
Captain don Pedro de Bolaños (1704)
SOURCES: Schaefer, *El Consejo*, II, 548–549; ACC, LC I–VII (1611–1706).
NOTE: The date of entering office is approximate in some cases.

B. BISHOPS OF POPAYÁN, 1601–1714

Dr. Juan de la Roca (1601–1605)
Fray Juan González de Mendoza, O. S. (1609–1618)
Maestro Fray Ambrosio de Vallejo, O. Carm. (1620–1631)
Don Feliciano de la Vega (1632–?)
Dr. don Diego de Montoya y Mendoza (1633–1638)

Don fray Francisco de La Serna, O. S. (1639–1645)
Dr. don Vasco de Contreras y Valverde (1659–1666)
Dr. don Melchor de Liñán y Cisneros (1667, 1669–1671)
Dr. don Christóbal Bernaldo de Quirós (1672–1684)
Don Pedro Díaz de Cienfuegos (1689–1696)
Don fray Mateo de Villafañe, O. Carm. (1701–1714)
SOURCES: Schaefer, *El Consejo*, II, 590–591; Bueno, *Historia*; Buenaventura Ortiz, *Historia*.
NOTE: The dates given are those of a bishop's actual presence in the diocese.

C. DEPUTIES (LUGARTENIENTES) OF POPAYÁN, 1601–1705

Juan de Berganzo
Lorenzo Paz Maldonado
Fernán Díaz de Ribadeneyra
Martín Bueno
Juan de Berganzo
Juan Baca de Ortega
Francisco de Cartagena
Domingo de Aguinaga
Fernando de Mendoza y Silva
Alonso Hurtado del Águila
Don Yñigo de Velasco
Alonso Hurtado del Águila
Gonzalo López Prieto
Don Fernando de Salazar Betancur
Don Bernardino Pérez de Ubillus
Melchor López de Celada
Don Diego Tamaris de Góngora
Don Joseph Hurtado del Águila
Don Diego Ignacio de Aguinaga
Don Francisco de Arboleda
Don Joseph Hurtado
Don Diego Ignacio de Aguinaga
Don Francisco de Hurtado
Don Diego Joseph de Velasco
Don Francisco Hurtado
Don Christóbal de Mosquera
Don Gaspar de Borja y Ezpeleta
SOURCES: ACC, LC I–VII (1611–1706).
NOTE: This list is incomplete because of missing libros capitulares.

D. ENCOMENDEROS AND ENCOMIENDAS OF POPAYÁN, 1607

	Number of Inhabitants
Don Francisco de Belalcázar; Jambaló, Guambía, Yaumbitaró, Pisotará	890
Juan de Ampudia; Cocomito	157
Lorenzo de Paz Maldonado; Mambasabalá, Ambaló, Usenda	416

Juan de Angulo; Totoró	133
and a share in Bamba (together with Melchior Quintero Príncipe)	358
Christóbal de Mosquera; Benchica, Nobirao	117
Diego de Alvarado; Polindará	177
Martín de Larrainzar; Pisabaró	106
Andrés del Campo Salazar; Pichabo, Pisojé	354
Captain Pedro de Velasco y Zúñiga; Puelemsi, Buena Vista	374
San Pedro de Cubaló de los Coconucos	814
Cajibío	not counted
Antonio de Alegría; Jolomito	180
Sebastián Núñez; Calomito	140
Rodrigo de Quadros; Piolomo, Ríoblanco	52
Lope Ortiz de Tabuada; Puelembio, Ninichápulo	89

Doña Catalina de Guzmán Ponce de León ⎤
Pedro Cepero ⎬ share Timbío and Chapa 988
Pedro de Collazos ⎦

Diego Delgado Salazar ⎤ share Piagua and 643
Francisco de Figueroa ⎦ Espandí 323

Crown; Undulalgue	316
Agustín Arias Zambrano; Puracé	468
Diego de Herrera; Santiago de la Cruz	56
Melchior Quintero Príncipe; Ceyna	407
and a share in Bamba	358
Don Felipe de Herrera; Pinguata	304
Juan de Berganzo; Tunia, Los Cerrillos, minas de Jelima	not counted

SOURCE: AGI/AQ 9, visita Armenteros 1607.
NOTE: The figures represent the number of inhabitants (ánimas).

E. ENCOMENDEROS AND ENCOMIENDAS OF POPAYÁN, 1681

Don Diego de Velasco Noguera; San Isidro de los Robles, 1st vida*
  Cubaló, Coconuco, Zaguináez, 1st vida
Don Christóbal de Mosquera Figueroa; Páez, Paniquitá, 1st vida
  Timbío, 1st vida
Don Diego Ignacio de Aguinaga; Piagua, 2d vida
  Calocé, 1st vida
  San Juan, La Ascensión (in Almaguer)
Don Matías Daza; Guambía
  Caqueone (in Almaguer)
Don Pedro de Salazar Betancur; Chapa
  Guacarí (in Buga)
Doña Francisca de Belalcázar y Aragón; Guambía, Jambaló, Páez, 2d vida
Don Nicolás de Gaviría y Gamboa; Ríoblanco, Sotará, 1st vida
Don Yñigo Lucas de Velasco; Puelenje and Cajibío
Don Andrés Cobo; Piagua, 1st vida
Don Agustín Cobo; Tunia, 1st vida
Don Gregorio de Bonilla; Polindará, 1st vida
Don Lucas Gonzalo López del Águila; Pandiguando, 1st vida
Don Francisco Hurtado del Águila; Chapa, 1st vida

Diego Polo de Salazar; Cajete, 1st vida
Doña Juana (Prieto) de Figueroa; Puracé, 2d vida
Doña María Hurtado del Águila; Julumito, 2d vida
Doña Ysabel de Mosquera Figueroa; Totoró, 2d vida
Don Juan Casimiro de Mera; Ambaló, 2d vida
Don Antonio del Campo Salazar; Guanacas, 3rd vida (with indulto)
SOURCE: ACC, Sig. 2221 (1681).
*Encomiendas were granted for two lives (vidas); they could be extended for another life by payment of a fee (indulto). One encomienda might include more than one settlement.

F. VECINOS AND RESIDENTS OF POPAYÁN WITH ENCOMIENDAS ELSEWHERE, 1681

Don José Tiburcio Guerrero; San Sebastián, 1st vida (Almaguer)
Andrés Esteban de Obando; Pancitará, 1st vida (Almaguer)
Don Bernardo Alfonso de Saa; Yumbo, 2d vida (Cali)
Diego de Victoria Salazar; Páez, 2d vida (Caloto)
Don Ambrosio del Campo Salazar; Páez, 1st vida (Caloto)
Don Francisco de Arboleda Salazar; 1st vida in Santa María del Puerto de Barbacoas
Don Agustín Fernández de Belalcázar; Carlosama, 1st vida (in Pasto)
Don Pedro de Salazar Betancur; Guacarí (Buga)
Don Matías Daza; Caqueona (Almaguer)
SOURCE: ACC, Sig. 2221 (1681).

G. MINE OPERATORS OF POPAYÁN, 1684

	Contribution (in patacones)
Don Diego de Velasco Noguera	175
Don Francisco de Arboleda Salazar	177
Children of don Lorenzo del Campo	155
Joseph de Morales Fravega	80
Don Christóbal de Mosquera	62
Don Joseph Hurtado del Águila	60
Don Gregorio de Bonilla	60
La Compañía de Jesús	50
Don Agustín Fernández de Belalcázar	40
Jacinto de Alarcón	40
Don Jacinto de Arboleda Salazar	35
Don Bernardo Alfonso de Saa	30
Convento of Encarnación	26
Don Andrés Cobo de Figueroa	15

SOURCE: AGI, Contaduría 1371, ramo 3, no. 7.

Notes

Abbreviations Used
AGI   Archivo General de Indias, Seville.
AGI/AQ   Section Audiencia de Quito, AGI.
AGI/EC   Section Escribanía de Cámara, AGI.
ACC   Archivo Central del Cauca, Popayán.
ACC, LC   Section Libros Capitulares, ACC.
ACC, PN   Section Protocolos Notariales, ACC.
ACHSC   *Anuario Colombiano de Historia Social y de la Cultura.*
ANE   Archivo Nacional del Ecuador, Quito.
ANE, ACS   Section Corte Suprema de Justicia, ANE.
ACJ   Archivo de la Compañía de Jesús, Colegio de San Gabriel, Quito.
ANC   Archivo Nacional de Colombia, Bogotá.
HAHR   *Hispanic American Historical Review.*

Introduction

1. See the discussion in *Latin American Research Review* 5 (1970): 57–110, in particular Jorge E. Hardoy and Carmen Aranovich, "Urban Scales and Functions in Spanish America towards the Year 1600: First Conclusions," and the commentary by Rolando Mellafe. For an orientation there are articles by Richard M. Morse, in particular "Some Characteristics of Latin American Urban History," *American Historical Review* 67 (1962): 317–338, "A Prolegomenon to Latin American Urban History," *HAHR* 52 (1972): 359–394, and his "Trends and Issues in Latin American Urban Research, 1965–1970," *Latin American Research Review* 6 (1971): 3–52, 19–76.

2. George A. Kubler, "Cities and Culture in the Colonial Period in Latin America," *Diogenes* 47 (1964): 53–62.

3. A work that shows this in depth and breadth is Murdo J. MacLeod, *Spanish Central America: A Socioeconomic History, 1520–1720.*

4. An interpretation of these procedures can be found in John L. Phelan, "Authority and Flexibility in the Spanish Imperial Bureaucracy," *Administrative Science Quarterly* 5 (1960): 47–65. See also Mario Góngora, *El estado en el derecho indiano, Época de fundación 1492–1570,* pp. 289, 307–310, for a view of these procedures in a less political or even Machiavellian light, as permitting the idea of what is right, of law in its equitable dimension (derecho), to subsist in the face of laws (leyes) contrary to it. Góngora also emphasizes how these procedures could counter the arbitrariness of decrees and administrators.

5. The former interpretation has been common in Latin America; see Jaime Eyzaguirre, *Ideario y ruta de la Emancipación chilena,* for an exposition and contrary point of view. The latter interpretation has been common in the United States.

6. A critical assessment of Latin American historiography within the framework of the history of ideas is very much needed; it also should pay attention to its ideological and apologetic dimensions. For an indication of the possibilities see Charles A. Hale, "The Reconstruction of Nineteenth-Century Politics in Spanish America: A Case for the History of Ideas," *Latin American Research Review* 8 (1973): 53–74.

7. Recent work on these matters includes Leon G. Campbell, "A Creole Establishment: Creole Domination of the Audiencia of Lima during the Late Eighteenth Century," *HAHR* 52 (1972): 1–25; Mark A. Burkholder, "From Creole to Peninsular: The Transformation of the Audiencia of Lima," *HAHR* 52 (1972): 395–415; Mark A. Burkholder and D. S. Chandler, "Creole Appointments and the Sale of Audiencia Positions in the Spanish Empire under the Early Bourbons, 1701–1750," *Journal of Latin American Studies* 4 (1972): 187–206; Jacques A. Barbier, "Elite and Cadres in Bourbon Chile," *HAHR* 52 (1972): 416–435; D. A. Brading, "Government and Elite in Late Colonial Mexico," *HAHR* 53 (1973): 389–414; Brian R. Hamnett, *Politics and Trade in Southern Mexico, 1750–1821.*

8. An exposition of these views is Eyzaguirre, *Ideario y ruta.* A more detailed examination is Nestor Meza Villalobos, *La conciencia política chilena durante la Monarquía.*

9. John L. Phelan, *The Kingdom of Quito in the Seventeenth Century: Bureaucratic Politics in the Spanish Empire.*

10. Manuel Giménez Fernández, *Hernán Cortés y su revolución comunera en la Nueva España,* has used this episode to maintain that the spirit of communal and municipal autonomy was transplanted to America at the very moment when it was dying in Castile in the revolt of the Comuneros.

11. The most convincing exposition of these changes set against an emerging colonial urban pattern is in Guillermo Céspedes del Castillo, "La sociedad colonial americana en los siglos XVI y XVII." See also Céspedes, *Latin America: The Early Years.*

12. Lyle N. McAlister, "Social Structure and Social Change in New Spain," *HAHR* 43 (1963): 349.

13. Magnus Mörner, *La corona española y los foráneos en los pueblos de indios de América,* describes the attempts to impose these definitions and their failure.

14. Peter Marzahl, "Creoles and Government: The Cabildo of Popayán," *HAHR* 54 (1974): 636–656. How much this framework encompassed more than the upper levels of Creole society is very much an open question that needs empirical investigation and that should constitute a sequel to this work. Families were clearly a vehicle of horizontal integration between Creoles and immigrants from Spain. To what extent family and household as *oikos* in the older sense facilitated vertical integration has to remain open for the moment. For a consideration of these problems, mainly in their quantitative dimension, see Sherburne F. Cook and Woodrow Borah, "Family and Household in Mexican Enumerations since the Conquest," in *Essays in Population History: Mexico and the Caribbean,* I, 119–200.

15. See, however, Inge Wolff, *Regierung und Verwaltung der kolonial-spanischen Städte in Hochperu 1538–1650*. This useful work stresses the increasing ability of the crown to run—or at least to interfere in—local affairs; corruption is incidental to the process but does not detract much from its effectiveness. Given the importance of Upper Peru to the crown, government must have been more in evidence there than elsewhere, yet the crown could do little to ward off repeated civil disorders, virtual civil wars between Basques and their antagonists, and could not counter the private power of the miners, except in sporadic interventions, as detailed in Guillermo Lohmann Villena, *El Conde de Lemos, virrey del Perú*.

16. John Lynch, *Spain under the Habsburgs*, II, 195.

17. Cf. Mario Góngora, "Urban Social Stratification in Colonial Chile," *HAHR* 55 (1975): 421–448.

18. Families in politics are discussed in Jorge Comadrán Ruiz, "Las tres casas reinantes de Cuyo," *Revista Chilena de Historia y Geografía*, no. 126 (1958): 77–127, and in Mary Lowenthal Felstiner, "Kinship Politics in the Chilean Independence Movement," *HAHR* 56 (1976): 58–80.

19. Peter J. Bakewell, *Silver Mining and Society in Colonial Mexico, Zacatecas 1546–1700*, pp. 82–95. A more general discussion may be found in James Lang, *Conquest and Commerce: Spain and England in the Americas*, pp. 38–45.

20. Jaime Vicens Vives, "Estructura administrativa estatal en los siglos XVI y XVII," pp. 99–141; Dietrich Gerhard, "Amsträger zwischen Krongewalt und Ständen—ein europäisches Problem," pp. 230–247.

21. Works pursuing this question include Stuart B. Schwartz, "Magistracy and Society in Colonial Brazil," *HAHR* 50 (1970): 715–730; Stephanie Blank, "Patrons, Clients and Kin in Seventeenth-Century Caracas: A Methodological Essay in Colonial Spanish American Social History," *HAHR* 54 (1974): 260–283; J. L. Israel, "Mexico and the 'General Crisis' of the Seventeenth Century," *Past & Present* 63 (1974): 33–57. For the eighteenth century, see the works by Barbier and Brading cited earlier and Reinhard Liehr, *Stadtrat und städtische Oberschicht von Puebla am Ende der Kolonialzeit*.

22. Immanuel Wallerstein, *The Modern World-System: Capitalist Agriculture and the Origins of the European World-Economy in the Sixteenth Century*.

23. J. H. Elliott, *The Old World and the New 1492–1650*, pp. 54–78, discusses the merits of the new data and the interpretations based on them.

24. Lynch, *Spain*, II, 194–228, sets out this point for the Indies in general.

25. A good example of work setting out the details of this process is John C. Super, "Querétaro: Society and Economy in Early Provincial Mexico, 1590–1630."

1. Province and Town

1. I have adopted the Colombian convention regarding Belalcázar's name. A short sketch of his life is in James Lockhart, *The Men of Cajamarca: A Social and Biographical Study of the First Conquerors of Peru*; see also Jacinto Jijón y Caamaño, *Sebastián de Benalcázar*. For the other protagonists see Emilio Robledo, *Vida del Mariscal Jorge de Robledo*, and Hermann Trimborn, *Pascual de Andagoya: Ein Mensch erlebt die Conquista*.

2. Pedro de Cieza de León, *La Crónica del Perú* (first printed 1553 in Seville), gives the first comprehensive description of the province, derived from his own experience; he was one of Robledo's men. A postconquest account is Juan de Castellanos, *Elegías de varones ilustres de Indias*, written between 1570 and 1600.

3. See Juan López de Velasco, *Geografía y descripción universal de las Indias*, pp. 406–409, compiled in the 1570s and based on data from the years 1550 to 1570. Also see Antonio Vázquez de Espinosa, *Compendio y descripción de las Indias Occidentales*, pp. 331–336, written circa 1630.

4. For these see Hermann Trimborn, *Señorío y barbarie en el Valle del Cauca*.

5. Two chroniclers, Fray Pedro de Aguado, *Recopilación Historial*, and Fray Pedro Simón, *Noticias historiales de las conquistas de Tierra Firme en las Indias Occidentales*, give descriptions of this extended warfare. For a recent treatment see Manuel Luceña Salmoral, *Nuevo Reino de Granada, Real audiencia y presidentes: Presidentes de capa y espada (1605–1628)*, pp. 127–249.

6. Robert C. West, *Colonial Placer Mining in Colombia*, pp. 7–20. For the Barbacoas campaign, AGI/AQ 16, Governor Lorenzo de Villaquirán to crown, May 30, 1635, and 1636.

7. Juan Friede, "Historia de la antigua ciudad de Cartago."

8. Gustavo Arboleda, *Historia de Cali*, I.

9. Fray Jerónimo de Escobar, "Relación sobre el carácter y costumbres de los Indios de la provincia de Popayán." For Almaguer see AGI/AQ 9, oidor Luis de Quiñones to crown, April 22, 1616.

10. Recent assessments of the history of population for New Granada include Jaime Jaramillo Uribe, "La población indígena de Colombia en el momento de la conquista y sus posteriores transformaciones,"*ACHSC* 2 (1964): 239–284; Hermes Tovar Pinzón, "Estado actual de los estudios de demografía histórica en Colombia, *ACHSC* 5 (1970): 65–140, which offers a critique of the above and other studies; and Juan Friede. *Los Quimbayas bajo la dominación española*, which concentrates on one region.

11. See chapter 2.

12. See chapter 2.

13. Pierre Chaunu, *Les Structures: Structures géographiques*, pp. 1069–1077, gives some figures concerning the movement of ships between Panama and Buenaventura. Fray Jerónimo de Escobar (see note 9) had already stated in the 1580s that the soldiers posted there "hacen vida tristísima" (have a very sad life). See also Gustavo de Arboleda, *Historia de Cali*, I, 127–128, 161, 195–200, for later attempts to open the port and route.

14. AGI/AQ 18, Pedro León de Mera to crown, November 25, 1683.

15. Ibid., 28, treasurer Gerónimo Pérez de Ubillus to crown, April 4, 1615.

16. West, *Colonial Placer Mining*, pp. 112–116.

17. AGI/AQ 32, Relación de las provincias, ciudades y lugares que se contienen y comprehenden en el gobierno de Popayán (1635); ibid., 215 (III), cédula to bishop, February 16, 1688.

18. ANC, Poblaciones del Cauca, II, fols. 904–925.

19. AGI/AQ 29, contador Juan Palacios de Alvarado to crown, April 17, 1616. See also chapter 9.

20. *Colección de Cédulas Reales dirigidas a la audiencia de Quito, 1601–1660*, pp. 221–224.

21. For the audiencia of Quito see John L. Phelan, *The Kingdom of Quito in the Seventeenth Century: Bureaucratic Politics in the Spanish Empire.*

22. AGI, Audiencia de Santa Fé 54, 'Relación de los géneros y miembros de hacienda Real que se administren en las Reales Cajas . . .' (1663).

23. ACC, LC II, fols. 17–20 (1627).

24. See chapter 9.

25. There is no satisfactory history of the town of Popayán. José María Arboleda Llorente was engaged in writing a descriptive history of which one volume has appeared, *Popayán a través del arte y de la historia.* Some of the descriptive data that follow are taken from it, others from scattered evidence in the notarial registers and the libros capitulares that it would be pointless to cite at every instance. A model account of an early seventeenth century town is Vicenta Cortés, "Tunja y sus vecinos," *Revista de Indias* 25 (1965): 155–207.

26. ACC, LC III, fols 156–157 (1663). A modern account is Horst Nachtigall, *Tierradentro.*

27. Kathleen Romoli, "Apuntes sobre los pueblos autóctonos del litoral colombiano del Pacífico en la época de la conquista española," *Revista Colombiana de Antropología* 12 (1963): 259–292.

28. Pedro de Mercado, S. J., *Historia de la provincia del Nuevo Reino y Quito de la Compañía de Jesús,* IV, 7.

29. Jorge Juan and Antonio de Ulloa, *A Voyage to South America,* I, 335–346.

30. The assessment that includes the names of all taxable inhabitants (138 in 1608) is in ACC, Sig. 1380 (1608). José María Arboleda, *Popayán,* pp. 251–288; Santiago Sebastián, *Arquitectura colonial en Popayán y Valle del Cauca,* p. 39.

31. ACC, LC II, fols. 116–117 (1631); ibid., III, fol. 139 (1663); AGI/AQ 215 (III), cédula to governor, April 21, 1679 and cédula to bishop, August 7, 1689; José María Arboleda, *Popayán,* p. 240.

32. ACC, Sigs. 9563 (1605), 8212 (1613). They donated two houses, three town lots, and other objects worth one thousand gold pesos; one-half of the chapel was to serve as pew and exclusive burial place of the founders and their progeny.

33. José María Arboleda, *Popayán,* pp. 263–270. Of the first three nuns to take the veil, two were daughters of Francisco de Mosquera, founder of one of the town's most prominent families (Manuel Antonio Bueno y Quijano, *Historia de la diócesis de Popayán,* p. 105).

34. See chapter 9.

35. AGI/AQ 75, prioress to crown, September 25, 1662, Governor Antonio de Guzmán y Toledo to crown, March 20, 1665. An account of the convent's receipts over the years 1653–1655 seems to corroborate the contention. Many payments were in arrears and were made only irregularly; most were in kind rather than in cash. The convent's mining operations yielded only 427 pesos over two years although twelve slaves were employed in them (ACC, Sig. 1159).

36. ACC, LC V, fols. 6, 14–15 (1698).

37. ACJ III, 215, Governor Juan de Borja to crown, May 10, 1643; ibid., VI, 647, visitation 1692; ibid., VIII, 748, estado temporal 1705; ACC, LC I, fols. 248–251 (1624); ibid., II, fol. 113; ACC, Sig. 1613 (1631). The Jesuits'

establishment in town is chronicled by Juan Manuel Pacheco, S. J., *Los Jesuitas en Colombia*, I, 200–229.

38. José María Arboleda, *Popayán*, p. 208.

39. See chapter 5.

40. ACC, LC IV, fols. 161–162 (1675), 356–357 (1680). See also Antonio Olano, *Popayán en la colonia*, pp. 112–118.

41. AGI/AQ 16, Governor Gabriel Díaz de la Cuesta to crown, August 1, 1669.

42. José María Arboleda, *Popayán*, pp. 243–245.

43. These data are taken from wills, inventories, and sales in the notarial registers and from scattered documentation in the ACC. Pedro de Velasco's will and the inventory of his estate are in ACC, Sig. 8101 (1617).

44. AGI/AQ 16, Governor Francisco Sarmiento de Sotomayor to crown, April 20, 1610.

45. The contracts can be found in Peter Marzahl, "Documentos para la historia social de Popayán en el siglo XVIII,"*ACHSC* 5 (1970): 165–168. The XVIII in the title is a printer's error; it should have read XVII. For the domestic architecture of the period see Carlos Arbeláez Camacho and Santiago Sebastián López, *Las artes en Colombia: La arquitectura colonial*, pp. 449–490; also José Gabriel Navarro, *El arte en la provincia de Quito*, pp. 3–12.

46. ACJ, VI, 647 (visitation of 1692).

47. ACC, Sigs. 9991 (1684), 9747 (1718).

2. Estates, Mines, and Commerce

1. ACC, PN 1619, fols. 18–21; 1620, fols. 110–111. See also José María Arboleda Llorente, *Popayán a través del arte y de la historia*, pp. 94–135, for Paz Maldonado's first marriage.

2. See the inventories in Marzahl, "Documentos," pp. 176–180.

3. ACC, Sig. 1159 (Libro de cuentas 1653–1656); see also note 47, chapter 3.

4. ANE, Popayán #12 (indios Guambía).

5. ACC, PN 1633, fols. 53ff; ibid., 1673, fols. 122–123 (a sugar mill with twelve slaves, part of don Joseph Hurtado's estate); also, ACJ, VIII, 74 (estado temporal 1705). For a summary account of Jesuit rural enterprise see Germán Colmenares, *Las haciendas de los Jesuitas en el Nuevo Reino de Granada*.

6. See chapter 3.

7. AGI/AQ 18, Governor Gabriel Díaz de la Cuesta to crown, April 12, 1669 (with testimony appended).

8. See Juan Friede, *Vida y luchas de don Juan del Valle, primer obispo de Popayán y protector de indios*, pp. 229 ff., which contain a listing of tribute obligations in 1555.

9. ACC, Sig. 9991, fols. 10, 21. For the situation in New Spain see François Chevalier, *La Formation des grands domaines au Mexique: Terre et société aux XVIᵉ–XVIIᵉ siècles*, especially pp. 345–347, and a critique in William B. Taylor, "Landed Society in New Spain: A View from the South," *HAHR* 54 (1974): 387–413.

10. Marzahl, "Documentos," pp. 179–183.

11. For a general treatment of gold mining in New Granada see Robert C. West, *Colonial Placer Mining in Colombia*.

12. ACC, PN, passim.

13. ACC, Sig. 2418 (1690).

14. AGI/EC 839 A, pieza 18 (comisión de cobranza).

15. Inventory in ACC, Sig. 8101 (1617), fol. 41.

16. ACC, PN 1617 and 1619. The proportion of panners to workers of 1:8 to 1:15 does not coincide with the proportion of 1:5 mentioned by Gonzalo Fernández de Oviedo for the Caribbean in the sixteenth century; the difference in workers needed may indicate the relative difficulty in extracting ores and may also account for the low profitability of mining in the area, at least until the deposits of Caloto and the Pacific area began to be exploited. I owe the reference to Mario Góngora, *Encomenderos y estancieros: Estudios acerca de la Constitución social aristocrática de Chile después de la Conquista, 1580–1660*, p. 134.

17. ACC, Sig. 1639 (1631); AGI/EC 921 B, pieza 16, fols. 194 ff. (proceso contra Lupercio Pérez de Ubillus); West, *Colonial Placer Mining*, p. 13.

18. The largest outlay was food for the miners: more than 650 pesos (gold) for maize, 186 pesos for meat, and 82 pesos for salt. Workers' wages amounted to 421 pesos (paid in cloth). The outlay for religious care, paid to the Dominican monastery in town, was 178 pesos. Smaller amounts went for tools and mules and to the notary for drawing up papers; he also collected from each worker at pay time. Finally there was the corregidor's take of 77 pesos and the miner's share of ten percent of the gross, which came to 282 pesos.

19. AGI/EC 839 A, pieza 18; AGI, Contaduría 1371, ramo 3, no. 7, Governor Gerónimo de Berrío to crown, November 30, 1684.

20. ACC, PN 1671, fols. 39–44; ibid., 1633, fols. 229–230; ibid., 1660, fols. 48–66.

21. AGI/EC 839 A, pieza 18.

22. AGI, Contaduría 1493 (Relación de hacienda de Popayán, 1654–1663).

23. See chapter 5.

24. The dowry was 13,500 silver pesos, much of it in cash; this would seem to indicate that Arboleda's net worth at the time must have been over 80,000 silver pesos. See also chapter 9.

25. Juan Manuel Pacheco, S. J., *Los Jesuitas en Colombia*, II, 176–177.

26. See note 20.

27. ACC, Sigs. 949 (1688), 942 (padrón de los dueños de minas 1693); also AGI, Contaduría 1371, ramo 3, no. 7, which lists fourteen miners contributing to a donativo of one thousand silver pesos.

28. AGI/EC 647 A, pieza 2, fols. 533–548.

29. AGI/AQ 185, Bishop Villafañe to crown, May 18, 1709.

30. ACC, Sig. 8715 (1687).

31. AGI/AQ 18, treasurer Pérez de Ubillus to crown, April 28, 1615; ibid., 32, contador Bonilla to crown, June 28, 1634; AGI, Contaduría 1493, Relación de hacienda de Popayán, 1654–1663; AGI, Contaduría 1496–1501, contains the accounts for the period, some of which I have sampled. See also Germán Colmenares, "Problemas de la estructura minera en la Nueva Granada (1550–1700)," *ACHSC* 6–7 (1971–1972): 5–55.

32. AGI/AQ 32, contador Leandro de Bonilla to crown, June 28, 1634.

33. See note 28; *The Cambridge Economic History of Europe*, IV, 384–385, and fig. 5; Peter J. Bakewell, *Silver Mining and Society in Colonial Mexico, Zacatecas 1546–1700*, pp. 215–217.

34. In 1674 there were at least thirty-eight stores in town (ACC, Sig. 1700 [1674]).

35. The accounts of don Ambrosio del Campo Salazar's estate (administered for his heirs by don Diego de Velasco Noguera) give some idea of such investment in trade (ibid., Sig. 8715 [1687]). See other examples of such lending in ACC, PN 1634, fols. 62–65.

36. These observations are derived from a study of the notarial registers of Popayán, some years investigated in comprehensive fashion and others sampled. For merchants in Peru during an earlier period, see James Lockhart, *Spanish Peru, 1532–1560,* pp. 77–95.

37. ACC, PN 1621, fol. 141. A plaintiff had to sue in the defendant's court (N. M. Farriss, *Crown and Clergy in Colonial Mexico, 1759–1821: The Crisis of Ecclesiastical Privilege,* pp. 150–152).

38. A series of such transactions indicates that the net rate of interest charged in such transactions was approximately thirteen percent (ACC, PN 1634, fols. 62–65).

39. See an example of such a partnership in Marzahl, "Documentos," pp. 161–164; see also ACC, PN 1624, fol. 63; and 1629, fol. 9.

40. Evidence concerning Hurtado's operations is in ACC, PN 1616–1635 passim; compañía between Hurtado and Daza in Marzahl, "Documentos," pp. 157–159; Gustavo Arboleda, *Diccionario biográfico y genealógico del antiguo departamento del Cauca,* pp. 170, 217–218; for Hurtado's descendants in Popayán see chapter 6.

41. See chapter 7.

42. See chapter 2.

43. See chapter 6. Victoria's declaration of capital, which gives a good idea of a well-stocked store of the time, is in ACC, PN 1620, fols. 15–22; it shows the extent of imports from Europe but also includes Mexican cloth from Puebla. His will is in ibid., 1660, fols. 48–66. For more detail on Victoria see Peter Marzahl, "Creoles and Government: the Cabildo of Popayán," *HAHR* 54 (1794); 641–642.

44. For Belo see ACC, PN 1629, 1626 passim, and especially 1621, fols. 75–78.

45. Marzahl, "Documentos," pp. 145, 171–176; also ACC, PN 1614, fol. 35, 1617, fol. 34, 1621, fols. 100–103, 1634, fol. 78; ACC, LC II, fol. 199; ACC, Sig. 8719 (1686). In the 1640s Huegonaga was one of the biggest merchants in town, with many customers in Cali as well (Gustavo Arboleda, *Historia de Cali,* I, 202, 222).

3. Spaniards, Indians, and Negroes

1. In the absence of population counts, some evidence about the size of households is derived from wills and inventories. Wills, for instance, also list bequests to domestic servants and slaves, thus providing a minimum range. The alguacil mayor Melchor de Cabrera had one indio and one india de mi servicio, to each of whom he willed a cash sum and clothing. Doña Francisca Manuela de Belalcázar had four indias de mi servicio. Diego Daza and Alonso Hurtado del Águila each had several Pijao slaves in their houses, as did other inhabitants at the time. Merchants may have been the first to have a large number of Negro slaves in their houses, as for instance Lope de Labayen, a merchant and muleteer who had six in the 1620s. In a later generation, don

Joseph Hurtado, a representative of the group of mine and estate owners, had eleven domestic slaves. (ACC, PN 1617, fols. 75–80, 1629, fols. 57–63; ACC, Sigs. 9991 [1684], 8726 [1690]).

2. Tunja had at the same time 440 houses and a Spanish population of 2,300 (Vicenta Cortés, "Tunja y sus vecinos," Revista de Indias 25 [1965]: 196). These figures would appear to mean there were 440 households and perhaps eight persons denominated "Spaniards" per household.

3. AGI/AQ 9, "Relación de la visita de la tierra" by the oidor Diego de Armenteros y Henao. The oidor and visitador Antonio Rodríguez de San Isidro Manrique in 1637 gives a figure of 1,117 tributaries (ibid., 68, "traslado de las ordenanzas de las ciudades de Popayán y Pasto . . . ," fol. 12). By 1658 there appear to have been only 675 tributaries (indios útiles) left (ACC, Sig. 2050 [1671]).

4. AGI/AQ 18, cabildo of Popayán to crown, April 28, 1628; AGI/EC 839 A, pieza 18.

5. See note 17, chapter 1.

6. In 1637, for instance, three mulattoes were confirmed in the possession of rural properties by the visitador Rodríguez de San Isidro Manrique (AGI/AQ 12, "memoria de las composiciones de las tierras y estancias hechas en la gobernación de Popayán" [1639]). In outlying frontier areas, racial distinctions were even less important; most of the founders and first settlers of Santa María del Puerto (Barbacoas) were mulattoes and mestizos, as Governor Villaquirán had reported in 1635. A general study of segregation policy and practice is Magnus Mörner, La Corona española y los foráneos en los pueblos de indios de América.

7. See ANC, Visitas del Cauca, vol. 5, fols. 750–778, for a graphic example. Also see Zamira Díaz de Zuluaga, "Gestación histórica de Palmira," and Jaime Jaramillo Uribe, "Mestizaje y diferenciación social en el Nuevo Reino de Granada en la segunda mitad del siglo XVIII," ACHSC 3 (1965): 26–27.

8. ACC, Sigs. 9566 (1646), 9543 (Cofradía de Nuestra Señora de la Consolación, memoria). Baptismal records begin in 1680 and continue in intermittent fashion through the eighteenth century; they are kept in the Church of San Francisco, Popayán.

9. In an alarde (muster) of 1627, 141 men were counted; 24 were vecinos feudatarios and the remainder were vecinos soldados [ACC, Sig. 8529].

10. Pedro de Aguado, Recopilación historial, II, 560.

11. AGI/EC 921 B, pieza 16, fols. 210–211. See also Germán Colmenares, La provincia de Tunja en el Nuevo Reino de Granada: Ensayo de historia social, 1539–1800, pp. 85–91.

12. AGI/EC 951 B, pieza 6, Real provisión of audiencia of Quito, June 15, 1676. See also chapter 6.

13. ACC, LC IV, fols. 32–43.

14. AGI/AQ 68, "traslado de las ordenanzas" (see note 3 above).

15. Coconuco, one of the more stable encomiendas, counted 460 tributaries in 1555, 817 inhabitants (almas) in 1607, and 88 tributaries in 1667. In 1692 there were 38 tributaries, of a total population of 175 inhabitants (yielding a conversion factor of 1:5.5) (ANE, Popayán #9, "Razón de los encomenderos de Popayán", ACC, Sig. 7904 [1692]). See also note 9 above and Marzahl, "Documentos," pp. 145, 171–178. For an extended discussion of seventeenth-century encomiendas in a comparable setting, see Mario Góngora, Encomen-

deros y estancieros: Estudios acerca de la Constitución social aristocrática de Chile después de la Conquista, 1580–1660, pp. 102–112. See also Doña María Magdalena de Noguera's will in ACC, Sig. 8114 (1638); examples of encomienda extensions are in ibid., Sig. 1954 (1654).

16. In 1650 the family died out in the male line; a surviving daughter married a wealthy encomendero and merchant from Timaná, Captain Bernabé Fernández Rico, whose descendants assumed the name of Fernández de Belalcázar (ACC, Sig. 9991 [1684]).

17. AGI/AQ 29, Joseph Hurtado del Águila to crown, March 31, 1650; ibid., 55, Hurtado to crown, April 4, 1647, September 17, 1652.

18. Ibid., 148, Captain Juan Álvarez de Uria to crown, September 23, 1706.

19. For a more detailed discussion of social mobility in Popayán, see Peter Marzahl, "Creoles and Government: the Cabildo of Popayán," *HAHR* 54 1974): 636–656; see also chapter 6.

20. José María Arboleda Llorente, *Popayán a través del arte y de la historia*, pp. 290–291.

21. See chapter 2.

22. D. A. Brading, *Miners and Merchants in Bourbon Mexico, 1763–1810*, documents this phenomenon for New Spain.

23. ACC, PN 1623, fols. 227–228; 1629, fols. 57–63; see also chapter 8.

24. ACC, PN 1634, fols. 6–8.

25. Ibid., 1620, fols. 65–68, 75–76.

26. See also chapter 8.

27. AGI/AQ 80, cathedral chapter of Popayán to crown, November 21, 1625.

28. Examples of his dealings can be found throughout the notarial registers of the 1610s and 1620s. In 1621, for example, he sold various parcels of land to Diego Delgado. One parcel and one town lot he had acquired from don Francisco Ventura de Belalcázar as executor of Juana Guacheta, in return for thirty-five masses to be said by the beneficiado. Two lots the beneficiado had inherited from Magdalena, india, wife of Juan Mindala (ACC, PN 1621, fols. 154–155). Belalcázar also dealt in cloth bought from Alonso Hurtado del Águila, for which he ceded his stipend; in return, Hurtado was to collect from the encomenderos and the corregidor de naturales (ibid., 1617, fol. 2). He also was sued at various times for debts incurred (ACC, Sigs. 1426 [1617], 2283 [1625]).

29. See chapter 8.

30. The purchase of quantities of cloth by clerics indicates as much. See also chapter 8.

31. AGI/AQ 185, subsidy of clergy 1701.

32. Examples of such patrimonies are in ACC, PN 1617, fol. 5; ACC, Sig. 9668 (1682).

33. See chapter 8.

34. ACC, PN 1615, fols. 144–146, and note 37 below.

35. Marzahl, "Documentos," pp. 144, 147–156.

36. In 1678 he established a capellanía for one of his sons who joined the priesthood (ACC, Sig. 827 [1678]).

37. See the census of Indians settled in town and close to it (AGI/EC 921 B, pieza 16, fols. 141–169).

38. Marzahl, "Documentos," pp. 165–169.

39. The census of 1607 (see note 37) provides the basis for the discussion that follows.

40. In 1701, for instance, the registers record thirty-three sales of slaves, among them one large consignment of twenty. In the same year five cartas de libertad for eight slaves were recorded, all of them either children or female slaves. In one case Faustina Ruiz, esclava mulata, brought suit before the governor for her freedom. An appraisal of her worth was ordered and the price of two hundred silver pesos was set, which she deposited with the depositario general. Her owner thereupon petitioned for release of the sum, promising to grant her freedom. In another case the prioress of the convent of Encarnación purchased the freedom of a six-months-old mulatico, with fifty pesos given her by a person who "tenía amor y voluntad a un mulatico" (loved a little mulatto) (ACC, PN 1701, passim).

41. Ibid., 1626, fols. 38–39.

42. Ibid., 1633, fols. 323 ff.

43. Marzahl, "Documentos," pp. 185–188.

44. ACC, PN.

45. Governor Villaquirán had noted the speedy arrival of slaves from Panama after Barbacoas had been pacified in the 1630s. See note 17, chapter 1.

46. Of don Jacinto de Arboleda's 145 slaves in 1671, 61 were female and 26 were children, i.e., boys under fifteen and girls under twelve years of age (ACC, PN, 1671, fols. 30 ff). A census of the slave population taken in the mining camps of Barbacoas in 1717 revealed a population of 533, with 477 of this total broken down by age and sex; of this latter figure there were 322 males and 155 females; 117 of the total were children (ACC, Sig. 2834 [1717]).

47. Where not otherwise documented these ordinances provide the information for the following discussion. The ordinances of 1607 are in AGI/AQ 9; specific rules governing the urbanized Indian population are also in AGI, EC 921 B, pieza 16. The ordinances of 1638 are in AGI/AQ 68, and the ordinances of 1668 in ACC, Sig. 12651; a major portion of the latter can be found in Antonio Olano, *Popayán en la colonia*, Appendix 1. The ordinances of 1692 are in ACC, LC V, fols. 100–192 (1696). For a comprehensive analysis of the status and situation of the native Indian population in a focal part of the empire, see Charles Gibson, *The Aztecs under Spanish Rule: A History of the Indians of the Valley of Mexico, 1519–1810.*

48. A specific decree and the sentences against a number of encomenderos (Diego Gerónimo Delgado, Juan de Larrainzar in Popayán) by the visitador Rodríguez de San Isidro Manrique substantiate the point (ACC, LC II, fols. 285–286 [1637]). Nomenclature also provides evidence: The "estancia of Coconuco in the pueblo of Cubaló," the "sitio and estancia of San Isidro de los Robles, jurisdiction of the pueblo of Pisojé" (ACC, Sig. 7904 [1692]).

49. The Mosqueras, for example, moved Indians from Páez (Tierradentro) to their encomienda at Timbío, the Gavirías moved them from Guachicono to Sotará and back (ACC, Sig. 8960 [1666]).

50. Of the ninety-four tributaries counted in town in 1607, eleven were absentees; of thirty-eight tributaries counted in Coconuco in 1692, five were absentees (ibid., Sig. 7904, and note 37 above).

51. Examples in ACC, PN 1620, fols. 47–49; ACC, Sig. 1608 (1643); see also Margarita González, *El resguardo en el Nuevo Reino de Granada.*

52. ACC, Sig. 9622 (1677).

53. Ibid., 9361 (1703).

54. For New Granada there is now Germán Colmenares's work, which

affords a comparison; see *La provincia de Tunja* and in particular *Historia económica y social de Colombia, 1537–1719*.

55. The miners were to work from sunrise to sunset, with a noon break; they were not held liable for a production quota. They were supposed to be given tools and a weekly ration of meat, maize, and salt. See also note 8, chapter 2. A general treatment of labor is in Robert C. West, *Colonial Placer Mining in Colombia*, pp. 78–101. The labor ordinances as part of local politics are treated in chapter 5.

56. Workers in farming were to be given two almudes of maize and six pounds of meat weekly, and one-half pound of salt per month. Plows and oxen were to be supplied; cowboys were to get a horse. They were to work only eight hours per day and were not to be whipped or shaven (presumably common punishments). The regular rate for day laborers was one real per day.

57. ACC, PN 1624, fol. 97.

58. AGI/AQ 16, Governor Sarmiento to crown, April 20, 1610; ACC, LC I, fol. 96 (1616).

59. See chapter 5.

60. See chapter 8.

61. In a Real provisión of May 12, 1627, the audiencia of Quito allowed the substitution of cloth for cash (ACC, LC II, fols. 55–57 [1628]).

62. A listing of such abuses is contained in a letter of the oidor Rodríguez de San Isidro Manrique to the crown, April 12, 1639, AGI/AQ 12.

63. See chapter 4.

64. I have not come across any information concerning the internal functioning of native hierarchies or the succession to cacicazgos in Popayán; inferentially, such data may be available, for instance, from lawsuits. Their absence in the archives of Quito—in contrast to the voluminous documentation preserved for areas under the direct jurisdiction of Quito—would seem to show that such matters were handled at the provincial level.

65. See chapter 8.

4. Cabildo Government

1. A general treatment of government in Spanish America is C. H. Haring, *The Spanish Empire in America;* for specific area studies see Ricardo Zorraquín Becú, *La organización política argentina en el período hispánico,* and José Miranda, *Las ideas y las instituciones políticas mexicanas, Primera parte (1521–1820).* The best treatment of its formative stage is Mario Góngora, *El estado en el derecho indiano: Época de fundación, 1492–1570.*

2. Rafael Altamira y Crevea, *Manual de investigación de la historia del derecho indiano,* pp. 70–74. Standard accounts of the municipality in Spanish America are Constantino Bayle, S. J., *Los cabildos seculares en la América española;* and John Preston Moore, *The Cabildo in Peru under the Hapsburgs* and *The Cabildo in Peru under the Bourbons.* For Spain, see Antonio Domínguez Ortíz, *El Antiguo Régimen: Los Reyes Católicos y los Austrias,* pp. 196–209.

3. ACC, LC III, fol. 269 (1664). The capítulos are reprinted in facsimile, with a commentary by Antonio Muro Orejón, in *Anuario de Estudios Americanos* 19 (1962): 699–725.

4. See chapter 5.

5. ACC, LC III, fol. 169 (1664).
6. AGI/EC 1191.
7. ACC, LC I, fol. 245 (1624); ibid., III, fols. 106–110 (1662). See also chapter 8.
8. ACC, LC II, fols. 6, 20; ibid., III, fol. 207; AGI/EC 1191, sentence of Governor Valenzuela y Fajardo.
9. ACC, LC I, fols. 237–241 (1624).
10. Ibid., II, fols. 240–246 (1637).
11. Ibid., I, fol. 23 (1613); ibid., IV, fols. 277–289 (1676).
12. ACC, Sig. 8179.
13. John H. Parry, *The Sale of Public Office in the Spanish Indies under the Hapsburgs.* See also chapter 6.
14. When not otherwise noted, evidence for the following discussion is taken from the Libros Capitulares of Popayán, 1612–1642, 1657–1682, 1696–1699, 1703–1707.
15. ACC, LC VII, fol. 36 (1706).
16. See chapter 8.
17. The conduct of the election conformed in essentials to a uniform pattern. See Bayle, *Los cabildos,* pp. 111–154, and, for procedural similarities in the Portuguese world, C. R. Boxer, *Portuguese Society in the Tropics: The Municipal Councils of Goa, Macao, Bahia and Luanda, 1510–1800,* pp. 5–7.
18. ACC, LC I, fol. 231 (1624).
19. Ibid., II, fols. 1–9 (1627).
20. Ibid., fols. 263–265 (1625), Real provisión of February 28, 1619, obtained by the regidor Antonio Ruiz de Alegría from the audiencia in Quito, presented again in 1623 and entered finally in 1625.
21. AGI/EC 674 B, Governor Antonio de Guzmán y Toledo to cabildo, December 23, 1664. See also chapter 8.
22. ACC, LC II, fols. 137–141 (1632); ibid., I, fols. 84–86 (1616).
23. Two proprietary members and the senior alcalde had been in favor of reception, two other proprietary members and the junior alcalde were against; as the minutes read: "Because of the discord order was lost and the vote of the senior alcalde did not decide the matter" (as it ordinarily should have done) (ibid., I, fols. 152–155 [1619], 163–164, 166 [1620]). See also chapter 6.
24. See chapter 7.
25. ACC, LC I, fols. 67–73 (1615).
26. AGI/AQ 13, Real provisión of audiencia of Santa Fé de Bogotá, February 17, 1661; ACC, LC III, fols. 23–44 (1658), 58–95 (1659).
27. See chapter 9.
28. AGI/AQ 35, sale of alferazgo of Popayán (1598); ibid., 44, confirmation of title, October 27, 1690. A discussion of the duties and functions of this and other offices (the cargos concejiles) is found in Bayle, *Los cabildos.*
29. AGI/EC 1186, sentence of Governor Sarmiento de Sotomayor.
30. ACC, LC I, fols. 135–136, 140–142, 159–162 (1618–1619); ibid., II, fols. 223–225, 248–264 (1636–1637); ibid., IV, fols. 290–291 (1677).
31. Ibid., III, fols. 205–206.
32. Ibid., II, fols. 226–229 (1636); AGI/AQ 35, confirmation of title of Juan Ortíz (1594); AGI/AQ 148, petition for confirmation of don Manuel de Morales Fravega (1703).
33. This is evident, for instance, from the title of Francisco Ruiz de Alegría,

who as regidor was charged with maintaining the quality of the town's supplies (ACC, LC I, fols. 172–174, 223, 234–235 [1623–1624]); AGI/AQ 215 (I), cédula to cabildo, November 14, 1590. Mario Góngora, *Encomenderos y estancieros: Estudios acerca de la Constitución social aristocrática de Chile después de la Conquista, 1580–1660*, p. 79, describes an arrangement whereby the cabildo of Santiago purchased memberships (varas de regidores) from the crown to enable it to continue electing its own members.

34. ACC, LC III, fol. 162 (1664); IV, fols. 156–160 (1673); ACC, Sig. 2390 (1662), ANE, Popayán #40.

35. A cédula of 1619 had directed that all fines imposed locally were to be entered in the local treasury; they were not to be collected by the judge who had imposed them or in his name, as had been the practice (AGI/AQ 215 [II], November 1, 1619). The media anata paid by alcaldes ordinarios was six ducats (ACC, LC II, fol. 188).

36. For these charges and others see the residencias and sentences of governors Bermúdez de Castro, Valenzuela y Fajardo, Guzmán y Toledo, and Díaz de la Cuesta in AGI/EC 1188, 1191, 1192; ACC, LC II, fol. 69 (1629).

37. ACC, Sig. 1499, 304 (1621).

38. Ibid., Sig. 539, 1581 (1626).

39. Ibid., Sig. 106 (1645).

40. Ibid., Sig. 1572 (1625). In this case, as in so many others, nothing of this action on the part of the cabildo transpired in the libros capitulares.

41. Ibid., Sig. 1680 (1635). The rules governing appeals for the province were laid down in a cédula to the governor and judges of the province of October 28, 1575, and are reiterated in *Recopilación de leyes de los reynos de las Indias* (first published in 1681), V, XII, 26.

42. ACC, LC II, fols. 12–15 (1627); ibid., IV, fols. 423–425 (1682).

43. For a general discussion of the office see Francisco Domínguez Company, "El procurador del municipio colonial hispanoamericano," *Revista de Historia de América*, 57–58 (1964): 163–176.

44. ACC, LC I, fol. 78.

45. Good examples of petitions by the procurador can be found in ibid., III, fols. 158–159 (1673), and ibid., IV, fols. 10–12 (1697).

46. See chapter 3.

47. ACC, LC I, fols. 26, 39, 96, 263; ibid., IV, fols. 148, 202–203.

48. Ibid., II, fols. 186–187 (1633). For the indulto, see AGI/EC 647 A, pieza 2, fols. 533–548.

49. ACC, LC II, fols. 95–98 (1630); ibid., III, fols. 12, 44–45 (1659); ibid., IV, fols. 384-385 (1681), 434 (1682); ibid., V, fols. 14–15 (1698).

50. AGI/EC 647 A, pieza 2, fols. 533–548.

51. AGI/AQ 215 (II), cédulas to Governor Díaz de la Cuesta and to treasury officials, August 3, 1669.

52. ACC, LC III, fol. 208 (1668).

53. Ibid., IV, fols. 95–97 (1679); ibid., V, fols. 9–16 (1698).

54. Ibid., IV, fols. 157–160 (1673), 219 (1675); ibid., V, fols. 56–76 (1696). In 1675, for example, the cabildo appropriated the following: eighteen pesos for the chaplain, whose principal duty was to say mass on election day, six pesos to the scribe (escribiente), there being no escribano proper, six pesos to the procurador general for stamped paper, six for the portero (usher), and twenty-five pesos for the mayordomo.

55. ACC, Sig. 260 (1604–1610); ACC, LC II, fols. 137 (1632), 186–187 (1633), 221–222 (1636); ibid. V, fols. 56–76 (1696).

56. Ibid. V, fols. 56–76 (1696).

57. The petition of 1597 is in ibid., IV, fols. 340–344 (1680). See also Moore, *The Cabildo in Peru under the Hapsburgs*, pp. 164–167, and the *Recopilación*, IV, XIII, 4.

58. An example is the assessment of 1608 destined to finish the cathedral's construction (ACC, Sig. 1380 [1608]).

59. ACC, LC IV, fols. 140–146 (1672).

5. Settler Affairs

1. "Informe sobre la población indígena de la gobernación de Popayán. . . . Año de 1592," *ACHSC* I, (1963): 197–208.

2. ACC, LC IV, fols. 340–344 (1680), copy of petition of 1598; AGI/AQ 16, Governor Mendoza y Silva to crown, May 15, 1603; AGI/AQ 215 (II), cédula to treasurer, June 18, 1616.

3. On slave imports in this period see Philip D. Curtin, *The Atlantic Slave Trade: A Census*, pp. 23–30; on the asientos, Rolando Mallafe, *La introducción de la esclavitud negra en Chile. Tráfico y rutas*, pp. 23–26.

4. See chapter 2.

5. See chapter 6.

6. AGI/AQ 1, consultas Council of the Indies, October 9, 1604, February 8, 1620; ACC, LC I, fols. 8–10 (1611), 132–134 (1618); ACC, LC II, fol. 49 (1628).

7. See chapter 3.

8. AGI/AQ 32, contador Leandro de Bonilla to crown, June 28, 1634; ibid., 18, towns of province to crown, August 2, 1635; ACC, LC II, fols. 200–202 (1634).

9. ACC, LC II, fols. 270–274 (1637).

10. Ibid., fol. 291 (1638).

11. AGI/AQ 18, Governor Díaz de la Cuesta to crown, with testimony appended, April 12, 1669.

12. Ibid., Bishop Liñán de Cisneros to crown, April 4, 1669; ibid., audiencia of Quito and oidor Ynclán Valdés to crown, June 15, 1675; ibid., 215 (III), cédula to audiencia, September 17, 1680; ACC, LC IV, fols. 117–119 (1671).

13. ACC, LC I, fols. 144–145 (1618); ibid., II, fols. 61–62.

14. Ibid., II, fols. 151–152 (1632), 190 (1633).

15. AGI/EC, 947 A, pieza 2.

16. ACC, LC IV, fol. 182 (1674), 240 (1675), 400–407 (1681).

17. Ibid., V, fols. 157–168 (1697).

18. For examples see ibid., II, fol. 325 (1641) and ibid., III, fol. 9 (1658).

19. AGI, EC 647 B, pieza 16, autos de los remates de carne (1662). These arguments concerning the auction again are not transcribed in the libros capitulares but rather form part of a residencia.

20. ACC, LC II, fol. 198 (1634); ACC, Sig. 321 (1652).

21. ACC, LC IV, fols. 400–407 (1681); ibid., V, fol. 16 (1699).

22. See note 17 above.

23. ACC, LC V, fols. 128–156 (1697).

24. See note 17 above.

25. ACC, LC V, fols. 226–232 (1697).

26. Ibid., I, fols. 15, 17 (1612), 141 (1618).

27. Ibid., V, fols. 19–20 (1698).

28. Ibid., III, fols. 132–134 (1662).

29. AGI/EC 1187, sentence of Governor Lasso de la Guerra.

30. See chapter 4.

31. AGI/AQ 18, Bishop Liñán de Cisneros to crown, April 4, 1669, Governor Díaz de la Cuesta to crown, April 12, 1669.

32. See Magnus Mörner, *La corona española y los foráneos en los pueblos de indios de América*.

6. Offices and Officeholders

1. See John H. Parry, *The Sale of Public Office in the Spanish Indies under the Hapsburgs*, pp. 28, 44–45, 60–66.

2. AGI/AQ 215 (I), cédula to governor, March 20, 1584; this tome of the province's cedulario contains more cases of this type.

3. Ibid., 9, audiencia to crown, April 16, 1600.

4. The evidence for this paragraph and for much of what follows has been taken from the libros capitulares, especially the record of elections between 1611 and 1707.

5. ACC, Sig. 923 (1650); ACC, LC IV, fols. 287–289 (1676), cédula to audiencia, December 3, 1670.

6. The evidence for these prices paid for office can be found with the title to office entered in the libros capitulares; in addition AGI/AQ 35–43 contain the petitions for confirmation to the Council of the Indies, which yield much scattered information.

7. ACC, LC IV, fols. 290–291 (1677), 296 (1678); ACC, Sig. 2398, cédula to audiencia of November 7, 1678.

8. *Recopilación de leyes de los reynos de las Indias*, VIII, XX, 22, which incorporates decrees of 1615 and 1626; AGI/AQ 215 (II), cédula to audiencia, July 6, 1616.

9. For examples for the dispatch of title to office by governors, see ACC, LC I, fols. 276–277 (1626), and ibid., II, fols. 121–122, 124 (1631). For confirmation by the Council of such a title see petition of January 5, 1636, of Diego Gerónimo Delgado, AGI/AQ 39. At the same time the Council prohibited the dispatch of title to office by the audiencia of Quito, reiterating this prohibition repeatedly (*Colección de Cédulas Reales dirigidas a la audiencia de Quito, 1601–1660*, pp. 234–236, 250–251, 265–266, 287–288).

10. AGI, AQ 215 (II), cédula to governor, March 3, 1661; ibid., (III), cédula to governor, February 16, 1688.

11. Ibid., 40, petition for confirmation, May 21, 1661; ACC, Sigs. 1552 (1648), 314 (1650).

12. *Recopilación*, III, II, 17, 18; ACC, LC II, fols. 157–159 (1633); AGI/AQ 215 (II), cédula to governor, November 17, 1649.

13. The duties of the deputy are specified in his title; for an example see ACC, LC I, fols. 87–88 (1616). For a corregidor's title see ibid., I, fols. 82–83 (1616). See also chapter 3 for his functions. Ricardo Zorraquín Becú, *La organización política argentina en el período hispánico*, pp. 176–178, contains a useful discussion of the office of deputy.

14. Antonio Olano, *Popayán en la colonia: Bosquejo histórico de la gober-*

nación y de la ciudad de Popayán en los siglos XVII y XVIII, Appendix 3, pp. 51–53.

15. ACC, LC I, fol. 189 (1621); ibid., IV, fols. 65–72 (1671).

16. See D. A. Brading, *Miners and Merchants in Bourbon Mexico, 1763–1810*, pp. 104–114, for its presence in New Spain.

17. ACC, LC II, fols. 137–141 (1632).

18. The source of these identifications is the libros capitulares, especially the record of elections and the notarial registers.

19. ACC, Sig. 2211 (1680), probanza de méritos of don Gerónimo de Mera Paz Maldonado; see also chapter 2.

20. ACC, Sig 10757 (1673); his wife's will noted that "he had brought nothing with him" (no había traído bienes).

21. AGI/AQ 2, consulta Council, January 19, 1633; ACC, Sig. 1863 (1684), probanza de méritos of don Pedro de Salazar Betancur; ACC, PN 1670, fols. 54–65, testament of don Fernando.

22. Gustavo Arboleda, *Diccionario biográfico y genealógico del antiguo departamento del Cauca*, demonstrates this in innumerable cases although most of them are from the eighteenth century. See also Peter Marzahl, "Creoles and Government: The Cabildo of Popayán." I note the question-begging character of much of this evidence, which emphasizes successful and prominent people.

23. ACC, LC VII, fol. 36.

24. See chapter 4.

25. ACC, LC I, fol. 233.

26. AGI, AQ 9, petition for confirmation in office of alférez real by Captain Pedro de Velasco, March 7, 1598; ACC, PN 1621, fols. 18–21 (testament of Catalina Moreno de Zúñiga); ACC, PN 1708, fol. 155. See also Marzahl, "Documentos," pp. 143, 179–83, and J. León Helguera, "Coconuco; datos y documentos para la historia de una gran hacienda Caucana, 1827, 1842, y 1876," *ACHSC* 5 (1970): 189–203.

27. ACC, PN 1632, fols. 6–16, testament of Juan de Berganzo; AGI/EC 921 C, pieza 31, memoria y razón de los bienes raíces y muebles que tiene Juan de Berganzo (1626).

28. ACC, PN 1647, fols. 109–114, testament of Juan de Angulo.

29. Examples of their dealings are found throughout the notarial registers between the 1610s and the 1630s. During many of these years, for example, they exchanged mutual powers of attorney (poderes). Francisco de Anaya's testament is in ibid., 1629, fols. 158–160.

30. The brothers Simón and Pedro Muñoz were among his main creditors, to whom he had mortgaged his herds, his slaves, the gold to be fetched by the miners of his encomienda, and the office of alguacil mayor (ibid., 1632, fol. 58).

31. Ibid., 1626, fol. 47; ACC, LC I, fol. 201 (1621).

32. AGI/AQ 52, petition for confirmation of Lorenzo de Anaya, September 22, 1632; ACC, LC I, fols. 152–168 (1619).

33. ACC, PN 1617, fols. 75–80.

34. ACC, Sig. 4; ibid., Sig. 2037.

35. ACC, PN 1620, fols. 13–27, declaration of capital and dowry received; ibid., 1660, fols. 48–66, testament; Gustavo Arboleda, *Diccionario*, p. 170. See also chapter 4.

36. AGI/AQ 78, Bishop Ambrosio de Vallejo to crown, March 22, 1631. It is possible that Rodríguez Migolla obtained the regimiento as part of his wife's dowry; see ACC, PN 1623, fol. 165.

37. ACC, PN 1627, fols. 11–14, declaration of capital, dowry; ibid., 1629, fol. 71, daughter's dowry; AGI/EC 1187, 1188, sentences of governors Lasso de la Guerra and Menéndez Márquez. Although his being a native of Spain is not proved, it seems reasonably certain; he may have begun as an escribano, since the notarial registers of 1604 list a person by that name as escribano público.

38. See chapter 4.

39. See chapter 3.

40. ACC, LC IV, fols. 72–88 (1671).

41. ACC, Sig. 8715 (1685); see also chapter 7.

42. AGI/AQ 33, información de nobleza, servicios, etc., of doña Gerónima de Velasco Noguera; ibid., 4, consultas Council, June 18, July 4, 1680.

43. Ibid., 56, petition for confirmation of encomienda, June 10, 1657.

44. See chapter 2.

45. See chapter 2.

46. See chapters 4 and 8.

47. AGI/AQ 160, Governor Nevares to crown, September 25, 1701.

48. See chapter 7.

49. AGI/AQ 148, petition for confirmation of regimientos of don Christóbal de Mosquera et al., May 7, 1701.

50. ANE, Popayán #34 (Vecinos de Popayán).

51. AGI/AQ 2, consulta Council, April 4, 1631. See also chapter 7, and Gustavo Arboleda, *Historia de Cali*, I, 168, 184.

52. AGI/AQ 1, consulta Council, June 5, 1613; ACC, Sig. 8282 (1707), testament don Bernardino Pérez de Ubillus; ACC, Sig. 8477 (1716), testament don Sebastián Torijano.

53. AGI/AQ 2, consulta Council, May 2, 1631; ACC, PN 1633, fols. 326–329, dowry.

54. See chapter 4.

55. AGI/AQ 7, fiscal to Council, July 14, 1687; Gustavo Arboleda, *Diccionario*, pp. 218–219.

7. Governorship and Treasury

1. A succinct treatment of the governorship in its formal outline can be found in Ricardo Zorraquín Becú, *La organización política argentina en el período hispánico*, pp. 143–176, which to an extent summarizes the *Recopilación de leyes de los reynos de las Indias*, V, II; for Castile see B. González Alonso, *El corregidor castellano*.

2. Richard Konetzke, ed., *Colección de documentos para la historia de la formación social de Hispano-América, 1493–1810*, I, 675.

3. See note 7.

4. Some information on the governors is found in the consultas of the Council of the Indies concerning their appointment, but for the period after 1630 there are no such data.

5. See note 20, Introduction.

6. AGI/EC 1188, sentence of Governor Bermúdez de Castro.

7. AGI/AQ 29, Juan de Espinosa, escribano mayor de gobernación to crown, n.d. (1619?).

8. See chapter 8.

9. Earlier in the century there had been one or, at most, two fiadores. For Governor García there were ten, all of them local merchants, some prominent and others not (ACC, LC IV, fols. 172–176 [1674]). One may presume that such a change had to do with the greater risk involved, which had to be spread, or with a stronger involvement on the part of governors with the mercantile community.

10. AGI/AQ 1, consulta Council, April 4, 1626.

11. Ibid., 215 (II), cédula to audiencia, December 12, 1619; ibid., 29, Governor Lasso de la Guerra to crown, April 30, 1620.

12. Ibid., 16, Governor Bermúdez de Castro to crown, April 16, 1629, March 30, 1630, March 1, 1631, May 25, 1632.

13. Ibid., memorial de las cosas de guerra, gobierno y justicia (1630).

14. AGI/EC 1188, sentence of Governor Bermúdez de Castro.

15. AGI/AQ 78, Bishop Ambrosio Vallejo to crown, March 22, 1631.

16. See chapter 4.

17. AGI/AQ 16, Governor Bermúdez de Castro to crown, April 15, 1630.

18. See note 10.

19. The sentences of their residencias are in AGI/EC 1186, 1187, 1191.

20. Ibid., 651 C, pieza 1, Counsel (parecer) of fiscal, fols. 19–33. See also chapter 8.

21. See chapter 8.

22. Some details can be found in Ernst Schaefer, El Consejo Real y Supremo de las Indias, II, 549. See also John H. Parry, The Sale of Public Office in the Spanish Indies under the Hapsburgs, pp. 53–55, and Luis Navarro García, Don José de Gálvez y la comandancia general de las provincias internas del norte de Nueva España, pp. 48–56, which documents the practice for the governorships of northern New Spain in the last decades of the century.

23. AGI/AQ 5, decreto, June 1, 1677; ibid., 7, don Gerónimo de Berrío y Mendoza to crown, November 30, 1682.

24. Ibid., 5, decreto, May 29, 1674.

25. See Schaefer, Consejo Real, and AGI/AQ 5, decretos of April 18, 1692, February 5, 1695.

26. AGI/AQ 5, decretos of May 3, December 24, 1686.

27. AGI/EC 654 B, pieza 20, Licenciado Pedrosa to president of audiencia of New Granada, August 30, 1705.

28. Germán Colmenares, Historia económica y social de Colombia, 1537–1719, p. 235.

29. ACC, Sigs. 8354, 8359, 8170, 8364. See also the Real provisión of the audiencia of Santa Fé, December 14, 1699, to the fiscal Sarmiento y Huesterlin, instructing him to investigate the frauds and evasions of the quinto in the Chocó and to establish a subsidiary treasury there (AGI/EC 652 A, pieza 1).

30. ACC, Sig. 762, fol. 52.

31. See chapter 6.

32. Governor Roque de Mañozca, for example, was charged with having appointed a mine owner instead of the alcalde ordinario in line (see note 20 above).

33. Ismael Sánchez Bella, La organización financiera de las Indias, describes

financial administration in the early stages of settlement, but his outline is valid until the reorganization of the eighteenth century.

34. ACC, Sig. 2259 (1687).

35. For such inspections see AGI/EC 839 A, pieza 18; AGI, Contaduría 1371, ramo 3, no. 7.

36. ACC, Sig. 8755. In theory it was advantageous to have the miners pay the tax, but when an attempt was made to have them pay instead of the merchants—by introducing discriminatory rates, with the merchants paying twenty percent instead of the miners' five percent—the results were counterproductive. Collections dropped precipitously and the attempt was quickly abandoned.

37. AGI, Santa Fé 293, president of audiencia of Santa Fé to crown, January 8, 1704.

38. The principal secondary source for this "war" is the account of Jaime Arroyo, "La guerra de los Tripitenorios y Pambazos"; it seems generally reliable as concerns the outline of events. The clearest exposition of developments is found in a long letter of the audiencia of Lima to the crown, February 16, 1707, AGI/AQ 128. Other letters can be found in AGI/AQ 142 and 160. A transcript of the Marquis of Nevares's proceedings against the contador García Hurtado is in pieza 10, AGI/AC 654 A. The main obstacle to a fuller reconstruction of this episode is the absence of local records, in particular the libros capitulares between 1700 and 1703, and of relevant materials in the archives of Quito.

39. For examples of the intendants reorganizing the cabildos for purposes of government in a later period, see John Lynch, "Intendants and Cabildos in the Viceroyalty of La Plata, 1782–1810," *HAHR* 35 (1955): 337–362, and John Fisher, "The Intendant System and the Cabildos of Peru, 1784–1810," *HAHR* 49 (1969): 430–453.

8. Imperial Control

1. See John H. Parry, *The Spanish Theory of Empire in the Sixteenth Century* and *The Spanish Seaborne Empire*.

2. For the formation of these lawyers see Richard L. Kagan, *Students and Society in Early Modern Spain*, pp. 77–105.

3. For a general treatment of the residencia see José María Mariluz Urquijo, *Ensayo sobre los juicios de residencia indianos*, and R. S. Chamberlain, "The Corregidor in Castile in the Sixteenth Century and the Residencia as applied to the Corregidor," *HAHR* 23 (1943): 222–257. See also C. H. Haring, *The Spanish Empire in America*, pp. 138–146. For the antecedents, see Luis García de Valdeavellano, "Las 'Partidas' y los orígenes medievales del juicio de residencia," *Boletín de la Real Academia de Historia* 153 (1963): 205–246.

4. Haring, *The Spanish Empire*, p. 147, maintains the distinction as concerns the secret proceeding, but see also Guillermo Lohmann Villena, *El corregidor de Indios en el Perú bajo los Austrias*, pp. 470–485, and Ricardo Zorraquín Becú, *La organización judicial argentina en el período hispánico*, pp. 186–188. John L. Phelan, *The Kingdom of Quito in the Seventeenth Century: Bureaucratic Politics in the Spanish Empire*, analyzes a particular visita. His emphasis on the audiencia complements the local perspective of this book. For the importance of publicity see Mario Góngora, *El estado en el derecho indiano: Época de fundación, 1492–1570*, pp. 226–232.

5. ACC, LC I, fols. 194–197 (1621).

6. *Recopilación de leyes de los reynos de las Indias*, V, XV, 48, contains the specific legislation for the province.

7. ACC, LC IV, fols. 157–168 (1697).

8. ACC, Sigs. 1549, 1823, 1874 (1714). See also José María de la Peña y Cámara, *A List of Spanish Residencias in the Archives of the Indies, 1516–1775*. Visitas de la tierra were another matter. In his visitation of 1607, the oidor and visitador Armenteros y Henao noted that no visita had been made in the region in the last thirty-seven years, since the province was a land "rough and broken in the extreme, diseased, expensive, and without supplies." He also noted that 200,000 maravedis (about 500 pesos) as the assigned compensation did not make it worthwhile for the oidores to come, even if there were enough of them in Quito. The scheduling of these visitations involved in practice an element of discretion in contrast to residencias (AGI/AQ 9, Armenteros y Henao to crown, March 3, 1607).

9. AGI/EC 647 A, B, 648 A, B, C furnish the evidence for the discussion that follows.

10. AGI/AQ 13, Governor Guzmán y Toledo to crown, March 16, 1669; ANE, vol. 5, no. 248, audiencia of Quito to crown, April 12, 1669.

11. AGI/EC 647 A, pieza 2, fols. 533–548.

12. The sentence is in ibid., 1191.

13. See also chapter 5.

14. ACC, Sigs. 1709, 571, 2084.

15. AGI/AQ 29, Governor Lasso de la Guerra to crown, April 20, 1618.

16. AGI/EC 647 A, pieza 1.

17. Early in the century the interval between the residencia and the final collection of fines was short—five years or less! Later on, thirteen, fifteen, or more years passed before final collection; see ACC, LC II, fols. 162–166 (1633), and ACC, Sigs. 1876 and 452 for examples.

18. ACC, LC IV, fol. 263 (1675).

19. AGI/EC 963, sentence confirmed in Council, March 1, 1687.

20. Ibid., 651 B, former governor Miguel García to crown, August 2, 1685.

21. ACC, Sig. 7300; see also chapter 7.

22. The fiscal's investigatory enterprises fill six legajos in AGI/EC 652 A, B, C, 653 A, B, C. Details concerning the investigation are in 652 C, 653 A and B; the sentence of February 4, 1726, is in AGI/EC 1194.

23. ACC, LC V, fols. 9–12, 23–26, 29–42 (1699).

24. ANE, Popayán No. 15, expediente don Bartolomé de Estupiñán.

25. See note 23 above.

26. AGI/EC 1194, sentence of February 2, 1726.

27. ACC, Sigs. 1894 and 596.

28. Lohmann Villena, *El corregidor de Indios*, p. 494.

29. See chapter 7, note 39.

9. Church and Settlers

1. General works on the Church in Spanish America include Antonio Ybot León, *La iglesia y los eclesiásticos españoles en la empresa de Indias;* Rafael Gómez Hoyos. *La iglesia en América en las leyes de Indias;* Enrique Dussel, *Les évêques hispanoaméricains: Défenseurs et évangélisateurs de l'Indien,*

1504–1620. A regional history of South America is Antonio de Egaña, S. J., *Historia de la iglesia en la América española: Desde el Descubrimiento hasta comienzos del siglo XIX. Hemisferio sur.*

2. ACC, LC III, fol. 253 (1675).

3. The *constituciones synodales* are printed in Javier Piedrahita Echeverri, *Historia eclesiástica de Antioquia,* pp. 101–189.

4. See Manuel Antonio Bueno y Quijano, *Historia de la diócesis de Popayán,* pp. 193–198, for a somewhat incomplete listing of the cathedral chapter's membership.

5. AGI/AQ 18, cabildo to crown, April 4, 1677.

6. ACC, Sig. 9536 (1719); also Bueno, *Historia,* p. 17.

7. Juan Manuel Pacheco, *Los Jesuitas en Colombia,* I, 360–370.

8. AGI/AQ 185, Bishop Villafañe to crown, April 6, 1706.

9. Piedrahita, *Historia eclesiástica.*

10. Mario Germán Romero, *Fray Juan de los Barrios y la evangelización del Nuevo Reino de Granada,* p. 286. This book contains an extended discussion of synodal legislation in New Granada and includes comparisons with other regions.

11. Juan Friede, *Vida y luchas de don Juan del Valle, primer obispo de Popayán y protector de indios,* pp. 61–78.

12. Ibid., pp. 139–147.

13. To give a few examples: the sale of cheap liquor (guarapo) had been forbidden to Spaniards by the Church. But the prohibition, so the towns of the region argued, had only led to the Indians manufacturing and selling it themselves, under no supervision at all. Tremendous excesses of drunkenness were the consequence. Hence Spaniards were again allowed to sell guarapo, as long as they added no additive stimulants. The chewing of coca was also prohibited. Priests were not supposed to take snuff or to smoke, at least not before mass, because of the "indecency, revulsion, and bad smell" these habits caused (Piedrahita, *Historia eclesiástica,* pp. 76, 79, 84).

14. Ibid., pp. 170–179.

15. See the listing of nominees in Ernst Schaefer, *El Consejo Real y Supremo de las Indias,* II, 590–591.

16. An instructive comparison can be made with Juan del Valle's case as discussed in Juan Friede's study of this bishop.

17. Much of the above, and some of what follows, is taken from Juan Manuel Pacheco, S. J., "Fray Juan González de Mendoza, obispo de Popayán," *Boletín de Historia y Antigüedades,* April–June 1966, pp. 301–313, and from José Toribio Medina, *Biblioteca hispanoaméricana, 1493–1810,* I, 549 ff.

18. AGI/AQ 9, audiencia to crown, March 22, 1611.

19. Witnesses favorable to the bishop's cause assert this in "información hecha del Licenciado Zorrilla sobre su buen proceder" (ibid., 78).

20. Ibid., 18, cabildo to crown, May 18, 1610.

21. Ibid., 9, audiencia to crown, March 22, 1611; ibid., 28, deputy Fernán Díaz de Ribadeneyra to crown, n.d. (1611); ACC, LC I, fols. 4–5 (1611).

22. AGI/AQ 29, dean to crown, May 16, 1609.

23. Ibid., 215 (II), cédula, August 28, 1610.

24. Ibid., 19, Licenciado Diego de Zorrilla to crown, November 5, 1612.

25. Ibid., contador to crown, March 31, 1611; ibid., 29, contador to crown, April 17, 1616; ibid., 9, audiencia to crown, May 8, 1611.

26. Ibid., President Juan Fernández de Recalde to crown, March 25, 1612; ibid., fiscal Sancho de Múgica to crown, April 19, 1613.

27. Ibid., 19, Licenciado Diego de Zorrilla to crown, August 8, 1612.

28. Ibid., 9, audiencia to crown, April 4, 1613.

29. Ibid., 78, Bishop Juan González de Mendoza to crown, April 25, 1613.

30. See note 28 above.

31. AGI/AQ 9, Licenciado Diego de Zorrilla to crown, April 20, 1613.

32. See note 19 above.

33. AGI/AQ 78, Bishop Juan González de Mendoza to crown, April 25, 1615; ibid., 10, audiencia to crown, April 29, 1615; ACC, LC I, fols. 41–42, Real provisión of audiencia of Quito, October 5, 1614.

34. ACC, LC I, fol. 43 (1614).

35. AGI/AQ 29, contador to crown, April 17, 1616.

36. Ibid., 10, audiencia to crown, April 29, 1615; ACC, LC I, fol. 51 (1615).

37. AGI/AQ 29, Licenciado Fernando de Betancor y Barreto to crown, Quito, April 18, 1616; see also Juan Flórez de Ocáriz, *Genealogías del Nuevo Reino de Granada*, II, 24.

38. ACC, LC I, fols. 51–52 (1615).

39. AGI/AQ 10, fiscal Sancho de Múgica to crown, n.d. (1615).

40. Ibid., 29, Governor Lasso de la Guerra to crown, April 15, 1616.

41. Ibid., 8, cabildo de Popayán to crown, March 20, 1617; cabildo of Cali to crown, April 8, 1617; ibid., 29, Governor Lasso de la Guerra to crown, April 8, 1617. These dates certainly give the appearance of a concerted effort.

42. ACC, LC I, fols. 106–107 (1617).

43. AGI/AQ 215 (II), cédula, April 16, 1618.

44. ACC, LC I, fol. 137, Real provisión of audiencia of Quito, March 8, 1618.

45. Ibid., IV, fols. 253–256 (1675).

46. AGI/AQ 215 (III), cédula to bishop, March 13, 1675.

47. Ibid., 3, consulta Council, February 10, 1672; ibid., 52, cathedral chapter of Popayán to crown, July 2, 1675; ACC, LC IV, fols. 166–168 (1674).

48. ACC, LC IV, fols. 233–240.

49. ANE, ACS, autos seguidos por el cabildo de Popayán con don Gerónimo de Berrío sobre residencia, año 1696.

50. Quoted in Pacheco, "Fray Juan González de Mendoza," pp. 205–206.

51. Santiago Sebastián, *Arquitectura colonial en Popayán y Valle del Cauca*, p. 43.

52. Such inventories abound in the ACC; don Francisco Torijano, a merchant, had thirty-seven devotional paintings in his possession, doña Leonor de Velasco had fifty-seven paintings in her town house, forty-eight of them framed (Sigs. 10652 [1690], 8717 [1701]). Other examples are in Sigs. 8101 (1617) and 8321 (1668).

53. These rules concerning matrimony are laid down in the constituciones synodales (Piedrahita, *Historia eclesiástica*, pp. 55–61, 131–139). One should note that marriage, as an institution with precise juridical consequences within the purview of the Church, was established fully only at the Council of Trent in 1563.

54. See chapter 3.

55. See note 60, below.

56. ACC, PN 1629, fols. 57–63; see also chapter 3.

57. See note 47, chapter 3.

58. ACC, Sigs. 2905 (1719), 2917 (1720).

59. Listings of tithe farmers are in ACC, Sigs. 1423 (1697), 962 (1714).

60. AGI/AQ 80, cathedral chapter to crown, November 21, 1625.

61. ACC, LC I, fols. 249–251 (1624), ibid., II, fols. 206–211 (1635).

62. See chapter 1.

63. ACC, Sig. 1116 1689).

64. See chapter 3. For a general discussion of this phenomenon in its European context, see Jacques Heers, *Occidente durante los siglos XIV y XV: Aspectos económicos y sociales*, pp. 282–293.

65. This listing of the subsidy can be found in AGI/AQ 185.

66. ACJ, VIII, 748 (1705).

67. ACC, Sigs. 9569, 9565, 9353, 9154, 9327.

68. José María Ots Capdequí, *España en América: El régimen de tierras en la época colonial*, pp. 42–49, discusses the legal aspects of censos and capellanías and points out their deformation in America, where cattle and slaves served as security, in opposition to sound precedent. See also Michael P. Costeloe, *Church Wealth in Mexico: A Study of the "Juzgado de Capellanías" in the Archbishopric of Mexico, 1800–1856.*

69. ACC, PN 1671, fols. 30ff. See also chapter 2.

70. AGI/AQ 185, Bishop Villafañe to crown, June 19, 1709.

Glossary

Adelantado: title of leader of conquering expedition
Alcabala: sales tax
Alcalde ordinario: town magistrate
Alcalde de la hermandad: magistrate in charge of the countryside
Alferazgo: post of alférez real
Alférez: ensign
Alférez real: senior regidor, municipal standard-bearer
Alguacil mayor: sheriff
Almud: dry measure, ⅟₁₂ of a fanega
Arroba: weight, ca. 25 lbs.
Asiento: contract, in particular for transatlantic delivery of slaves
Audiencia: appeals tribunal of professional judges

Bachiller: lowest academic degree, below maestro (master) and doctor
Benemérito: descendant of conquerors and first settlers

Cabildo: town council
Cabildo abierto: assembly of local notables
Caja real: provincial treasury
Capellanía: private ecclesiastical benefice, usually an endowment of masses secured by a censo
Cédula real: royal decree
Censo: mortgage or annuity
Cofradía: sodality, lay brotherhood supporting ecclesiastical functions
Composición: payment to clear title, usually to land
Contador: accountant, comptroller
Corregidor de naturales: district magistrate and judge set over Indian settlements

Depositario general: public trustee
Diezmo: tithe
Diputado: person delegated to perform a specific task
Disimulación: conscious toleration of illegalities
Doctrina: Indian parish
Doctrinero: priest ministering to Indians

Ejido: community lands
Encomienda: crown grant of Indian tribute and (initially) labor, but without jurisdiction
Encomendero: holder of an encomienda

197

Escribano: notary
Escribiente: scribe
Estancia: variable grant of land
Estante: temporary resident

Fanega: dry weight, ca. 1.5 bushels; also a measure of land planted
 (fanega de sembradura), ca. 3.5 acres
Fiel ejecutor: market inspector
Fiscal: crown attorney; prosecutor in an audiencia

Gracia: grant, gift

Habitante: inhabitant

Indulto: pardon; exception through payment of a fine

Juez de cobranza: official with power to collect taxes, fees, fines, etc.
Juez receptor: official taking depositions
Juez togado: appeals judge, oidor
Juez visitador: official on tour of inspection
Junta de hacienda: finance committee
Justicia mayor: royal judge

Letrado: lawyer, holder of a law degree

Mandón: overseer
Maravedi: money of account, 34 to one real
Mayordomo: steward, administrator
Media anata: tax, ½ of first annual income of office
Ministro: official
Mitayo: conscript laborer
Mitimaes: transplanted Indian settlers, usually of Peruvian origin
Morador: permanent inhabitant, settled citizen

Oidor: appeals judge, member of an audiencia
Oro común: currency unit worth 300 maravedíes
Ordenanza: ordinance

Parcialidad: group, section
Patacón: silver peso
Peso: silver coin of 8 reales or 272 maravedis; the gold peso of 450
 maravedis served largely as a unit of account
Pesquisa: investigation
Procurador general: legal representative
Procurador de número: solicitor, a post one step below that of notary
Provisor: cleric exercising a bishop's ordinary judicial authority

Quinto: fifth; mining tax

Real: silver coin; 8 reales made one peso
Real provisión: decree emanating from an audiencia

Regidor: town councillor
Regimiento: post of regidor
Repartimiento: rotating assignment of compulsory Indian labor
Residencia: administrative and judicial inquest into an official's performance
Residente: temporary resident

Servicio personal: labor provided by natives, without official assignment or
    contract

Teniente: deputy
Tesorero: treasurer
Tribunal de cuentas: court of audit
Tributarios: natives required to pay tribute

Vara: linear measure, 33 inches
Vecino: full citizen of a town
Vecino feudatorio: town citizen holding an encomienda
Vecino morador: simple town citizen
Vecino patricio: "noble" town citizen
Visita: inspection

Yanacona: Indian of Peruvian origin, unattached to an Indian community
    (ayllu), whose status originally was similar to that of a serf

Bibliography

Note on Sources

The evidence for this work is essentially derived from two repositories, the Archivo Central del Cauca in Popayán (ACC) and the Archivo General de Indias in Seville (AGI). The archive in Popayán provided the core of the evidence: the minutes of the cabildo (libros capitulares) and the notarial registers. Unfortunately the libros are incomplete for the period under investigation. The minute books preserved cover only the years 1611–1642, 1657–1682, and 1696–1699. From 1703 on, there is a virtually complete run until 1810. Besides the minutes proper the libros fairly often contain decrees of the governors, the audiencia of Quito, and the Council of the Indies. By no means all communications, orders, and letters were included; cédulas reales, in particular, and the cabildo's correspondence, appear only rarely. Judged by the published records of other cabildos, such as those of Quito or Caracas, the libros of Popayán are fairly limited in the types of documentation they include.

Another series of great importance to the investigation was the notarial registers of Popayán (protocolos notariales). At the time of my investigation they were still located in the Notaría Primera de Popayán, hidden under layers of dust. Today they are easily accessible in the Archivo Central. The registers begin in the last decade of the sixteenth century; in the seventeenth century fifteen years are missing. Investigation was made difficult by the partial absence of the notaries' indices and the generally poorly preserved condition of the registers for the years between 1635 and 1690. I checked the registers between 1614 and 1633, 1671 and 1679, 1696 and 1709 in fairly comprehensive fashion, made a spot check of every item in 1621 and 1701, and made a few checks of other years. The selection of years was governed by the relative ease of consultation. The variety and range of information that can be gleaned from the registers decrease in the course of the century. Labor contracts and records of wage payments, for instance, cease to be included in later years, and so does graphic description.

Much useful information was derived from other holdings of the Archivo Central, whose consultation was facilitated by its excellent catalogue and a series of indices. The organization of the archive and the categories used do not follow the provenience principle; to this extent the reconstruction of the administrative and institutional history of the period was made difficult. Also, records for the seventeenth century do not compare in quantity or quality with those of the following century.

Quite a few ecclesiastical records can be found in the Archivo Central, mostly pertaining to religious orders. Their bulk, however, is in the Archivo

201

Arzobispal and the chapter archive. The latter is not accessible to the public, while the holdings of the former have only begun to be catalogued. Once that has been done, a clearer appreciation of the social and political role of the Church than that offered in this book may be possible. At the moment, only furtive forays are possible, but they allow one to gauge the possibilities of investigation offered by this archive, especially if used in conjunction with the Archivo Central.

Evidence from the Archivo General de Indias in Seville in many cases complemented that collected in Popayán. Yet the density of documentation for the seventeenth century leaves much to be desired. Correspondence in particular was sparse and decreased still more after the 1630s. For nearly a generation, between the 1630s and the 1660s, communications from the governors practically do not exist, and, since there are no libros capitulares for this period either, there is a pronounced lacuna in this book's documentation, if perhaps not its argument. One may surmise that Popayán was one of the blank spots on the map of the Indies as far as the Council of the Indies was concerned. The most useful section was Escribanía de Cámara, with evidence pertaining to residencias and lawsuits. Contaduría provided some clues to the local situation, but its global figures provide a very uncertain guide to economic matters, in particular the curve of gold production. A critical treatment of gold production in relation to treasury intake and the region's economy would involve three separate operations. First, the accounts preserved in Contaduría would have to be checked; then these would have to be collated with the summary accounts sent by particular cajas to the Tribunales of Account in Bogotá and Lima; and, ultimately, the ledgers of a caja would at least have to be sampled, in order to yield information about methods of collection and the question of who dealt in gold. The accounts of the smelter (fundición) can provide additional information. The second operation involves the dealings of the merchants, and the third, the conditions of production, in particular the size of the labor force. Given the magnitude of this task, I abstained. William F. Sharp's forthcoming work may shed light on these questions.

Other archives and collections used and not specified below include the Archivo Nacional de Quito (in the Casa de la Cultura), where little on Popayán was found, and the former archive of the Corte Suprema de Justicia, which now forms part of the Archivo Nacional and whose holdings are largely housed in the attic of the Casa de la Cultura. At least seventy bundles of documents pertain to areas now belonging to Colombia. Today these materials have been put in some semblance of order, the documents dealing with the province of Popayán have been set aside, and a valuable summary catalogue of the whole archive by Juan Freile Granizo exists and may soon appear in print. Two other collections of interest in Quito were the Archivo de la Compañía de Jesús in the Colegio de San Gabriel (now housed in Cotocollao) and the Vacas Galindo collection in the Dominican monastery. This collection, which contains mainly transcripts from the Archive of the Indies, is under the care of Padre José María Vargas, who has published a summary description of its holdings. The Archivo Nacional de Colombia proved disappointing for the purposes of this book. Its holdings coincide with the limits of the audiencia of Santa Fé and include materials on the southern part of the province of Popayán only for the eighteenth century, after the viceroyalty of New Granada was established.

Little can be said about early materials in print or contemporary sources for this study, since so few exist for the period in question. Some useful information was gleaned from the *constituciones synodales* published by Javier Piedrahita Echeverri, Pbro. Also useful were the works of don José María Arboleda Llorente and Padre Juan Manuel Pacheco.

The list of publications included in the bibliography is selective; it includes all works cited and other items deemed useful. Two abbreviations are used: *HAHR* for *Hispanic American Historical Review* and *ACHSC* for *Anuario Colombiano de Historia Social y de la Cultura*.

ARCHIVAL SOURCES

Archivo Central del Cauca, Popayán (ACC)
  Libros capitulares (LC)
  Protocolos notariales (PN)
  General collections
Archivo General de Indias, Seville (AGI)
  Contaduría: 1371, 1377, 1491–1500.
  Escribanía de Cámara: 646–654, 657, 839, 920, 921, 924, 926, 963, 1185, 1192, 1194.
  Audiencia de Quito: 1–5, 7–16, 18–19, 29–45, 51, 55–56, 67–68, 75, 78–80, 91, 102, 106, 107, 126, 128, 137, 139, 140, 142, 156, 160, 185, 215.
  Audiencia de Santa Fé: 18–36, 52–55, 286, 293, 310.

BIBLIOGRAPHICAL AIDS AND GUIDES

Altamira y Crevea, Rafael. *Manual de investigación de la historia del derecho indiano.* Mexico City, 1948.
Arboleda, Gustavo. *Diccionario biográfico y genealógico del antiguo departamento del Cauca.* 2d. ed. Bogotá, 1962.
Arboleda Llorente, José María. "Organización del Archivo Central del Cauca." *Boletín Comité de Archivos* (Havana) 1 (1958): 65–85.
Cortés, Vicenta. "La sección de la colonia del Archivo Nacional de Colombia." *Studium* (Bogotá) 2, no. 6 (October–December 1958): 183–218.
Freile Granizo, Juan. "Guía del Archivo Nacional de Historia del Ecuador." ms. Quito, 1972.
Medina, José Toribio, *Biblioteca hispanoamericana, 1493–1810.* Facsimile ed. 7 vols. Santiago de Chile, 1958.
Morse, Richard M. "Trends and Issues in Latin American Urban Research, 1965–1970." *Latin American Research Review* 6, no. 1 (1971): 3–52; 6, no. 2 (1971): 19–76.
Peña y Cámara, José María de la. *A List of Spanish Residencias in the Archives of the Indies, 1516–1775.* Washington, D.C., 1955.
———. *Archivo General de Indias: Guía del visitante.* Madrid, 1958.
Romero Arteta, J. R. "El índice del Archivo de la Antigua Provincia de Quito de la Compañía de Jesús." *Boletín del Archivo Nacional de Historia, Quito* 12 (August 1963): 60–110.
Vargas, José María, O. P. *Misiones Ecuatorianas en Archivos Europeos.* Mexico City, 1956.
Vogel, Christian, "Los Archivos." *El Comercio* (Quito), 8, 15, 22, 29, August 1965.

PRINTED DOCUMENTS AND EARLY WORKS

Aguado, Pedro de. *Recopilación historial.* 4 vols. Bogotá, 1956–1957.

Castellanos, Juan de. *Elegías de varones ilustres de Indias.* 4 vols. Bogotá, 1955.

Cieza de León, Pedro de. *La crónica del Perú.* In Enrique de Vedia, ed., *Historiadores primitivos de Indias.* 2 vols. Madrid, 1946–1947.

Colección de Cédulas Reales dirigidas a la audiencia de Quito, 1601–1660. 2 vols. Quito, 1935–1946.

Colmenares, Germán; M. de Melo; and D. Fajardo, comps. *Fuentes coloniales para la historia del trabajo en Colombia.* Bogotá, 1968.

Escobar, Fray Jerónimo de. "Descripción de la Gobernación de Popayán" and "Relación sobre el carácter y costumbres de los indios de la Provincia de Popayán." In Jacinto Jijón y Caamaño, *Sebastian de Benalcázar,* II, Appendix 6. 3 vols. Quito, 1936–1949.

Flórez de Ocáriz, Juan. *Genealogías del Nuevo Reino de Granada.* 3 vols. Bogotá, 1943-1955.

Hamilton, J. P. *Travels through the Interior Provinces of Colombia.* 2 vols. London, 1827.

Helguera, J. León. "Coconuco: Datos y documentos para la historia de una gran hacienda Caucana, 1827, 1842, y 1876." *ACHSC* 5 (1970): 189–203.

"Informe sobre la población indígena de la gobernación de Popayán. . . . Año de 1592." *ACHSC* 1 (1963): 197–208.

Jiménez de la Espada, Marcos. *Relaciones Geográficas de Indias.* 3 vols. Madrid, 1965.

Juan, Jorge, and Antonio de Ulloa. *A Voyage to South America.* 2 vols. London, 1807.

Konetzke, Richard, ed. *Colección de documentos para la historia de la formación social de Hispano-América, 1493–1810.* 3 vols. Madrid, 1953–1962.

López de Velasco, Juan. *Geografía y descripción universal de las Indias recopilada por el cosmógrafo-cronista, Juan López de Velasco, desde el año de 1571 al de 1574.* Edited by Justo Zaragoza, Madrid, 1894.

Marzahl, Peter. "Documentos para la historia social de Popayán en el siglo XVIII [XVII]." *ACHSC* 5 (1970): 143–188.

Mercado, Pedro de, S. J. *Historia de la provincia del Nuevo Reino y Quito de la Compañía de Jesús.* 4 vols. Bogotá, 1957.

Muro Orejón, Antonio. "Los capítulos de corregidores de 1500." *Anuario de Estudios Americanos* 19 (1962): 699–724.

Recopilación de leyes de los reynos de las Indias. 3 vols. Madrid, 1943.

Simón, Pedro. *Noticias historiales de las conquistas de Tierra Firme en las Indias Occidentales.* 9 vols. Bogotá, 1953.

Vázquez de Espinosa, Antonio. *Compendio y descripción de las Indias Occidentales.* Washington, D.C., 1948.

Zamora, Alonso de. *Historia de la provincia de San Antonio del Nuevo Reino de Granada.* 2d. ed. Bogotá, 1945.

CONTEMPORARY WORKS

Alemparte, Julio. *El cabildo en Chile colonial: Orígenes municipales de las repúblicas hispanoamericanas.* Santiago, 1966.

Arbeláez Camacho, Carlos, and Santiago Sebastián López. *Las artes en Colombia: La arquitectura colonial.* Bogotá, 1967.

Arboleda, Gustavo. *Historia de Cali.* 3 vols. Cali, 1956.

Arboleda Llorente, José María. *El indio en la colonia.* Bogotá, 1948.

——. *Popayán a través del arte y de la historia.* vol. 1. Popayán, 1966.

Arroyo, Jaime. *Historia de la gobernación de Popayán seguida de la crono-logía de la gobernación durante la dominación española.* Bogotá, 1906.

——. "La guerra de los Tripitenorios y Pambazos." In Antonio Olano, *Popayán en la colonia: bosquejo histórico de la gobernación de la ciudad de Popayán en los siglos XVII y XVIII,* Appendix 2. Popayán, 1910.

Arroyo, Miguel Antonio. "De como fué poblado el territorio del Cauca." *Revista Universidad del Cauca* 23 (March 1957): 19–44.

Bakewell, Peter J. *Silver Mining and Society in Colonial Mexico: Zacatecas, 1546–1700.* Cambridge, 1971.

Barbier, Jacques A. "Elite and Cadres in Bourbon Chile." *HAHR* 52 (1972): 416–435.

Bayle, Constantino, S. J. *Los cabildos seculares en la América española.* Madrid, 1952.

Bennassar, Bartolomé. *Valladolid au siècle d'or.* Paris, 1967.

Blank, Stephanie. "Patrons, Clients and Kin in Seventeenth-Century Caracas: A Methodological Essay in Colonial Spanish American Social History." *HAHR* 54 (1974): 260–283.

Borah, Woodrow. "La influencia cultural europea en la creación de los centros urbanos hispanoamericanos." In Alejandra Moreno Toscano et al., *Ensayos sobre el desarrollo urbano de México,* pp. 66–94. Mexico City, 1974.

——. "Representative Institutions in the Spanish Empire: The New World ." *The Americas* 12 (1956): 246–257.

Boxer, C. R. *Portuguese Society in the Tropics: The Municipal Councils of Goa, Macao, Bahia and Luanda, 1510–1800.* Madison, 1965.

Brading, D. A. "Government and Elite in Late Colonial Mexico." *HAHR* 53 (1973): 389–414.

——. *Miners and Merchants in Bourbon Mexico, 1763–1810.* Cambridge, England, 1971.

Bueno y Quijano, Manuel Antonio. *Historia de la diócesis de Popayán.* Bogotá, 1945.

Burkholder, Mark A. "From Creole to Peninsular: The Transformation of the Audiencia of Lima." *HAHR* 52 (1972): 395–415.

——, and D. S. Chandler. "Creole Appointments and the Sale of Audiencia Positions in the Spanish Empire under the Early Bourbons, 1701–1750. *Journal of Latin American Studies* 4 (1972): 187–206.

Campbell, Leon G. "A Creole Establishment: Creole Domination of the Audiencia of Lima during the Late Eighteenth Century." *HAHR* 52 (1972): 1–25.

Carmen Carlé, María del. *Del concejo medieval castellano-leonés.* Buenos Aires, 1968.

Castillero Calvo, Alfredo. *Estructuras sociales y económicas de Veragua desde sus orígenes históricos: Siglos XVI y XVII.* Panama City, 1967.

Céspedes del Castillo, Guillermo. "La sociedad colonial americana en los siglos XVI y XVII." In *Historia de España y de América,* edited by Jaime Vicens Vives, III, 388–578. Barcelona, 1961.

——. *Latin America: The Early Years.* New York, 1974.

Chamberlain, R. S. "The Corregidor in Castile in the Sixteenth Century and the Residencia as Applied to the Corregidor." *HAHR* 23 (1943): 222–257.

Chaunu, Pierre. *Les Structures: Structures géographiques.* In Pierre and Huguette Chaunu, *Séville et l'Atlantique, 1504–1650: Structures et conjoncture de l'Atlantique espagnol et hispano-américain (1504–1650),* VIII, part 2, p. 2. Paris, 1959.

Chevalier, François. *La formation des grands domaines au Mexique: Terre et société aux XVIᵉ–XVIIᵉ siècles.* Paris, 1952.

Chinchilla Aguilar, Ernesto. *El ayuntamiento colonial de la ciudad de Guatemala.* Guatemala City, 1961.

Colmenares, Germán. *Historia económica y social de Colombia, 1537–1719.* Bogotá, 1973.

———. *La provincia de Tunja en el Nuevo Reino de Granada: Ensayo de historia social, 1539–1800.* Bogotá, 1970.

———. *Las haciendas de los Jesuitas en el Nuevo Reino de Granada.* Bogotá, 1969.

———. "Problemas de la estructura minera en la Nueva Granada (1550–1700)." *ACHSC* 6–7 (1971–1972): 5–55.

Comadrán Ruiz, Jorge. "Las tres casas reinantes de Cuyo." *Revista Chilena de Historia y Geografía* 126 (1958): 77–127.

Cook, Sherburne F., and Woodrow Borah. *Essays in Population History: Mexico and the Caribbean.* Vol. 1. Berkeley, 1971.

Cortés, Vicenta. "Tunja y sus vecinos." *Revista de Indias* 25 (1965): 155–207.

Costeloe, Michael P. *Church Wealth in Mexico: A Study of the "Juzgado de Capellanías" in the Archbishopric of Mexico, 1800–1856.* Cambridge, England, 1967.

Curtin, Philip D. *The Atlantic Slave Trade: A Census.* Madison, 1969.

Díaz de Zuluaga, Zamira. "Gestación histórica de Palmira." Licentiate thesis, Universidad del Valle, Cali, 1969.

Domínguez Company, Francisco. "El procurador del municipio colonial hispanoamericano." *Revista de Historia de América* 57–58 (1964): 163–176.

Domínguez Ortiz, Antonio. *El Antiguo Régimen: Los Reyes Católicos y los Austrias.* Madrid, 1973.

———. *La sociedad española en el siglo XVII.* 2 vols. Madrid, 1963–1970.

———. *Orto y ocaso de Sevilla.* Seville, 1946.

Dussel, Enrique. *Les évêques hispanoaméricains: Défenseurs et évangélisateurs de l'Indien, 1504–1620.* Veröffentlichungen des Instituts für europäische Geschichte Mainz, 58. Wiesbaden, 1970.

Egaña, Antonio de, S. J. *Historia de la iglesia en la América española: Desde el Descubrimiento hasta comienzos del siglo XIX. Hemisferio sur.* Madrid, 1966.

Elliott, J. H. *The Old World and the New, 1492–1650.* Cambridge, England, 1970.

Eyzaguirre, Jaime. *Ideario y ruta de la Emancipación chilena.* Santiago de Chile, 1957.

Farriss, N. M. *Crown and Clergy in Colonial Mexico, 1759–1821: The Crisis of Ecclesiastical Privilege.* London, 1968.

Felstiner, Mary Lowenthal. "Kinship Politics in the Chilean Independence Movement." *HAHR* 56 (1976): 58–80.

Fisher, John. "The Intendant System and the Cabildos of Peru, 1784–1810." *HAHR* 49 (1969): 430–453.

Friede, Juan. "Historia de la antigua ciudad de Cartago." In Luis Duque Gómez et al., *Historia de Pereira,* pp. 176–341. Pereira, Colombia, 1963.

———. *El indio en lucha por la tierra*. Bogotá, 1944.

———. *Los Quimbayas bajo la dominación española: Estudio documental, 1539–1810*. Bogotá, 1963.

———. *Vida y luchas de don Juan del Valle, primer obispo de Popayán y protector de indios*. Popayán, 1961.

García de Valdeavellano, Luis. "Las 'Partidas' y los orígenes medievales del juicio de residencia." *Boletín de la Real Academia de Historia* 153 (1963): 205–246.

Gerhard, Dietrich. "Amtsträger zwischen Krongewalt und Ständen—ein europäisches Problem." In *Alteuropa und die moderne Gesellschaft: Festschrift für Otto Brunner*. Göttingen, 1963.

Gibson, Charles. *The Aztecs under Spanish Rule: A History of the Indians of the Valley of Mexico, 1519–1810*. Stanford, 1964.

———. *Spain in America*. New York, 1966.

Giménez Fernández, Manuel. *Hernán Cortés y su revolución comunera en la Nueva España*. Seville, 1948.

Gómez Hoyos, Rafael. *La iglesia en América en las leyes de Indias*. Madrid, 1961.

Góngora, Mario. *El estado en el derecho indiano: Época de fundación, 1492–1570*. Santiago de Chile, 1951.

———. *Encomenderos y estancieros: Estudios acerca de la Constitución social aristocrática de Chile después de la Conquista, 1580–1660*. Santiago de Chile, 1970.

———. "Urban Social Stratification in Colonial Chile." *HAHR* 55 (1975): 421–448.

González, Luis. *Invitación a la microhistoria*. Mexico City, 1973.

González, Margarita. *El resguardo en el Nuevo Reino de Granada*. Bogotá, 1970.

González Alonso, B. *El corregidor castellano*. Madrid, 1970.

Hale, Charles A. "The Reconstruction of Nineteenth-Century Politics in Spanish America: A Case for the History of Ideas." *Latin American Research Review* 8 (1973): 53–74.

Hamnett, Brian R. *Politics and Trade in Southern Mexico, 1750–1821*. Cambridge, England, 1971.

Hardoy, Jorge E., and Carmen Aranovich. "Urban Scales and Functions in Spanish America towards the Year 1600: First Conclusions." *Latin American Research Review* 5 (1970): 57–91.

Haring, C. H. *The Spanish Empire in America*. Paperback ed. New York, 1963.

Heers, Jacques. *Occidente durante los siglos XIV y XV: Aspectos económicos y sociales*. Barcelona, 1968.

Israel, J. L. "Mexico and the 'General Crisis' of the Seventeenth Century." *Past & Present* 63 (1974): 33–57.

Jaramillo Uribe, Jaime. "Algunos aspectos de la personalidad histórica de Colombia." *UN: Revista de la Universidad Nacional de Colombia*, December 1970, pp. 57–75.

———. "Esclavos y señores en la sociedad colombiana del siglo XVIII." *ACHSC* 1 (1963): 3–57.

———. "La población indígena de Colombia en el momento de la conquista y sus transformaciones posteriores." *ACHSC* 2 (1964): 239–293.

———. "Mestizaje y diferenciación social en el Nuevo Reino de Granada en la segunda mitad del siglo XVIII." *ACSHC* 3 (1965): 21–48.

Jijón y Caamaño, Jacinto. *Sebastián de Benalcázar.* 3 vols. Quito, 1936, 1938, 1949.

Kagan, Richard L. *Students and Society in Early Modern Spain.* Baltimore, 1974.

Kubler, George. "Cities and Culture in the Colonial Period in Latin America." *Diogenes* 47 (1964): 53–62.

Lang, James. *Conquest and Commerce: Spain and England in the Americas.* New York, 1975.

Liehr, Reinhard. *Stadtrat and städtische Oberschicht von Puebla am Ende der Kolonialzeit.* Wiesbaden, 1971.

Lockhart, James. "Encomienda and Hacienda: The Evolution of the Great Estate in the Spanish Indies." *HAHR* 49 (1969): 411–429.

———. *The Men of Cajamarca: A Social and Biographical Study of the First Conquerors of Peru.* Austin, 1972.

———. *Spanish Peru, 1532–1560: A Colonial Society.* Madison, 1968.

Lohmann Villena, Guillermo. *El Conde de Lemos, virrey del Perú.* Seville, 1946.

———. *El corregidor de Indios en el Perú bajo los Austrias.* Madrid, 1957.

———. "El corregidor de Lima." *Anuario de Estudios Americanos* 9 (1952): 131–171.

López Toro, Alvaro. *Migración y cambio social en Antioquia durante el siglo diez y nueve.* Bogotá, 1970.

Lucena Salmoral, Manuel. *Nuevo Reino de Granada, Real audiencia y presidentes: Presidentes de capa y espada (1605–1628).* Bogotá, 1965.

———. *Nuevo Reino de Granada, Real Audiencia y presidentes: Presidentes de capa y espada (1628–1654).* Bogotá, 1967.

Lynch, John. "Intendants and Cabildos in the Viceroyalty of La Plata, 1782–1810." *HAHR* 35 (1955): 337–362.

———. *Spain under the Hapsburgs.* 2 vols. Oxford, 1964–1969.

McAlister, Lyle N. "Social Structure and Social Change in New Spain." *HAHR* 43 (1963): 349–370.

MacLeod, Murdo J. *Spanish Central America: A Socioeconomic History, 1520–1720.* Berkeley, 1973.

Mariluz Urquijo, José María. *Ensayo sobre los juicios de residencia indianos.* Seville, 1952.

Marzahl, Peter. "Creoles and Government: The Cabildo of Popayán." *HAHR* 54 (1974): 636–656.

Mellafe, Rolando. "Commentary." *Latin American Research Review* 5 (1970): 93–100.

———. *La introducción de la esclavitud negra en Chile: Tráfico y rutas.* Santiago de Chile, 1959.

Meza Villalobos, Nestor. *La conciencia política chilena durante la Monarquía.* Santiago de Chile, 1958.

Miranda, José. *Las ideas y las instituciones políticas mexicanas, primera parte (1521–1820).* Mexico City, 1952.

Moore, John Preston. *The Cabildo in Peru under the Bourbons: A Study in the Decline and Resurgence of Local Government in the Audiencia of Lima, 1700–1824.* Durham, N.C., 1966.

——. *The Cabildo in Peru under the Hapsburgs: A Study in the Origins and Powers of the Town Council in the Viceroyalty of Peru, 1530–1700.* Durham, N.C., 1954.

Mörner, Magnus. *La corona española y los foráneos en los pueblos de indios de América.* Stockholm, 1970.

Morse, Richard M. "A Prolegomenon to Latin American Urban History." *HAHR* 52 (1972): 359–394.

——. "Some Characteristics of Latin American Urban History." *American Historical Review* 67 (1962): 317–338.

Muro Orejón, Antonio. "El ayuntamiento de Sevilla, modelo de los municipios americanos." *Anales de la Universidad Hispalense* (Seville) 21 (1960): 69–85.

Nachtigall, Horst. *Tierradentro.* Zürich, 1955.

Navarro, José Gabriel. *El arte en la provincia de Quito.* Mexico City, 1960.

Navarro García, Luis. *Don José de Gálvez y la comandancia general de las provincias internas del norte de Nueva España.* Seville, 1964.

Olano, Antonio. *Popayán en la colonia: Bosquejo histórico de la gobernación y de la ciudad de Popayán en los siglos XVII y XVIII.* Popayán, 1910.

Ots Capdequí, José María. *El Estado Español en las Indias.* 3d ed. Mexico City, 1957.

——. *España en América: El régimen de tierras en la época colonial.* Mexico City, 1959.

Pacheco, Juan Manuel, S. J. "Fray Agustín de la Coruña, O.S.A. Obispo de Popayán (1564–1589)." *Revista Javeriana* (Bogotá) 45 (1956): 124–134, 158–167.

——. "Fray Juan González de Mendoza, obispo de Popayán." *Boletín de Historia y Antigüedades,* April–June 1966, pp. 301–318.

——. *Los Jesuitas en Colombia.* 2 vols. Bogotá, 1959–1962.

Parry, John H. *The Sale of Public Office in the Spanish Indies under the Hapsburgs.* Berkeley, 1953.

——. *The Spanish Seaborne Empire.* New York, 1966.

——. *The Spanish Theory of Empire in the Sixteenth Century.* Cambridge, England, 1940.

Parsons, James J. *Antioqueño Colonization in Western Colombia.* Berkeley, 1949.

Phelan, John L. "Authority and Flexibility in the Spanish Imperial Bureaucracy." *Administrative Science Quarterly* 5 (1960): 47–65.

——. *The Kingdom of Quito in the Seventeenth Century: Bureaucratic Politics in the Spanish Empire.* Madison, 1967.

Piedrahita Echeverri, Javier. *Historia eclesiástica de Antioquia.* Medellín, 1973.

Pierson, W. W. "Some Reflections on the Cabildo as an Institution." *HAHR* 5 (1922): 573–596.

Pike, Frederick B. "Algunos aspectos de la ejecución de las leyes municipales en la América española durante la época de los Austrias." *Revista de Indias* 18 (1958): 201–223.

——. "Aspects of Cabildo Economic Regulations in Spanish America under the Hapsburgs." *Inter-American Economic Affairs* 13 (1960): 67–86.

——. "The Municipality and the System of Checks and Balances in the Spanish American Colonial System." *The Americas* 15 (1958): 139–158.

Restrepo Sáenz, José María. *Biografías de los mandatarios y ministros de la Real Audiencia, 1671–1819.* Bogotá, 1952.

Rich, E. E., and C. H. Wilson, eds. *The Cambridge Economic History of Europe*. Vol. 3. London, 1967.

Robledo, Emilio, *Vida del Mariscal Jorge de Robledo*. Bogotá, 1945.

Romero, Mario Germán. *Fray Juan de los Barrios y la evangelización del Nuevo Reino de Granada*. Bogotá, 1960.

Romoli, Kathleen. "Apuntes sobre los pueblos autóctonos del litoral colombiano del Pacífico en la época de la conquista española." *Revista Colombiana de Antropología* 12 (1963): 259–292.

———. "El descubrimiento y la primera fundación de Buenaventura." *Boletín de Historia y Antigüedades* 49 (1962): 113–123.

———. "El suroeste del Cauca y sus indios al tiempo de la conquista española, según documentos contemporáneos del distrito de Almaguer." *Revista Colombiana de Antropología* 11 (1962): 239–300.

Ruano, Eloy Benito. *Toledo en el siglo XV: Vida política*. Madrid, 1961.

Russell-Wood, A. J. R. *Fidalgos and Philanthropists: The Santa Casa da Misericordia of Bahia, 1550–1755*. Berkeley, 1968.

Safford, Frank. "Social Aspects of Politics in Nineteenth-Century Spanish America: New Granada, 1825–1850." *Journal of Social History* 5 (1972): 344–370.

Sánchez Bella, Ismael. *La organización financiera de las Indias*. Seville, 1968.

Schaefer, Ernst. *El Consejo Real y Supremo de las Indias*. 2 vols. Seville, 1935–1947.

Schwartz, Stuart B. "Magistracy and Society in Colonial Brazil." *HAHR* 50 (1970): 715–730.

Sebastián, Santiago. *Arquitectura colonial en Popayán y Valle del Cauca*. Cali, 1965.

Stanislawski, Dan. "Early Spanish Town Planning in the New World." *Geographical Review* 37 (1947): 94–105.

Super, John C. "Querétaro: Society and Economy in Early Provincial Mexico, 1590–1630." Ph.D. dissertation, University of California, Los Angeles, 1973.

Tapia, Francisco Javier. *El cabildo abierto colonial: Un estudio de la naturaleza y desarrollo del cabildo abierto durante los tres siglos de la administración colonial española en América*. Madrid, 1966.

Taylor, William B. "Landed Society in New Spain: A View from the South." *HAHR* 54 (1974): 387–413.

Tovar Pinzón, Hermes. "Estado actual de los estudios de demografía histórica en Colombia." *ACHSC* 5 (1970): 65–140.

Trimborn, Hermann. *Pascual de Andagoya: Ein Mensch erlebt die Conquista*. Hamburg, 1954.

———. *Señorío y barbarie en el Valle del Cauca*. Madrid, 1949.

Valdeavellano, Luis García de. *Curso de historia de las instituciones españolas: De los orígenes al final de la Edad Media*. Madrid, 1968.

Vargas, José María, O. P. *Don Hernando de Santillán y la fundación de la Real Audiencia de Quito*. Quito, 1963.

———. *Historia de la iglesia en el Ecuador durante el Patronato español*. Quito, 1962.

Vargas Saez, Pedro. *Historia del Real Colegio Seminario de S. Francisco de Asís de Popayán*. Bogotá, 1945.

Vicens Vives, Jaime. "Estructura administrativa estatal en los siglos XVI y

XVII." In *Coyuntura económica y Reformismo burgués y otros estudios de historia de España.* Barcelona, 1968.

Wallerstein, Immanuel. *The Modern World-System: Capitalist Agriculture and the Origins of the European World-Economy in the Sixteenth Century.* New York, 1974.

West, Robert C. *Colonial Placer Mining in Colombia.* Baton Rouge, 1952.

Whiteford, Andrew H. *Two Cities of Latin America: A Comparative Description of Social Change.* Paperback ed. Garden City, N.J., 1964.

Wolff, Inge. *Regierung und Verwaltung der kolonialspanischen Städte in Hochperu, 1538–1650.* Cologne, 1970.

Ybot León, Antonio. *La iglesia y los eclesiásticos españoles en la empresa de Indias.* 2 vols. Barcelona, 1954–1963.

Zorraquín Becú, Ricardo. *La organización judicial argentina en el período hispánico.* Buenos Aires, 1952.

———. *La organización política argentina en el período hispánico.* Buenos Aires, 1960.

Index